# A2 Drama Study Guide

*Edexcel*

## Max Harvey
### and
## Andrew Psirides

**R·**

## Rhinegold Education

239–241 Shaftesbury Avenue
London WC2H 8TF
Telephone: 020 7333 1720
Fax: 020 7333 1765

www.rhinegold.co.uk

**Drama Study Guides**

AS Drama Study Guide (Edexcel)

AS and A2 Drama Study Guide (AQA)

**Music Study Guides**

GCSE, AS and A2 Music Study Guides (AQA, Edexcel and OCR)

GCSE, AS and A2 Music Listening Tests (AQA, Edexcel and OCR)

GCSE Music Study Guide (WJEC)

GCSE Music Listening Tests (WJEC)

AS/A2 Music Technology Study Guide (Edexcel)

AS/A2 Music Technology Listening Test (Edexcel)

Revision Guides for GCSE (AQA, Edexcel and OCR), AS and A2 Music (AQA and Edexcel)

**Also available from Rhinegold Education**

Key Stage 3 Elements

Key Stage 3 Listening Tests: Book 1 and Book 2

AS and A2 Music Harmony Workbooks

GCSE and AS Music Composition Workbooks

GCSE and AS Music Literacy Workbooks

Baroque Music in Focus, Romanticism in Focus, Modernism in Focus,

*Batman* in Focus, *Goldfinger* in Focus, *Immaculate Collection* in Focus, *Who's Next* in Focus,

Film Music in Focus, Musicals in Focus

Rhinegold Publishing also publishes Choir & Organ, Classical Music, Classroom Music, Early Music Today, International Piano, Music Teacher, Opera Now, Piano, The Singer, Teaching Drama, British and International Music Yearbook, British Performing Arts Yearbook, British Music Education Yearbook, Rhinegold Dictionary of Music in Sound.

First published 2009 in Great Britain by

Rhinegold Publishing Limited

239–241 Shaftesbury Avenue

London WC2H 8TF

Telephone: 020 7333 1720

Fax: 020 7333 1765

www.rhinegold.co.uk

You should always check the current requirements of the examination, since these may change. Copies of the Edexcel specification may be obtained from Edexcel Publications, Adamsway, Mansfield, Notts, NG18 4FN.

Telephone: 01623 467 467, Fax: 01623 450 481, Email: publications@linneydirect.com

See also the Edexcel website at www.edexcel.com

**Edexcel A2 Drama Study Guide**

British Library Cataloguing in Publication Data.

*A catalogue record for this book is available from the British Library.*

ISBN 978-1-906178-81-9

Printed in Great Britain by Headley Brothers Ltd

# Contents

## The authors

Max Harvey was head of drama at Wellsway School for nine years before becoming director of the sixth form. He has been responsible for establishing drama within the school's curriculum and developing schemes of work and assessment structures for all key stages. He studied drama at Exeter University before completing his teacher training at Bretton Hall. Max has worked in an advisory capacity for the education department of the Theatre Royal, Bath and is on the board of directors. More recently, he has contributed to books on the role of citizenship within the school curriculum and has acted as a consultant for *Teaching Drama* magazine.

Andrew Psirides has been teaching drama for 14 years. He trained at Royal Holloway College, London, where he specialised in playwriting, before taking his PGCE at Warwick University where he worked with Jonothan Neelands. Andrew has worked in Luton and Thailand and is currently head of performing and visual arts at Wellsway School in Keynsham, where he has produced exemplar material and student workshops for the Edexcel examination board's new specification. He also contributes regularly to *Teaching Drama* magazine.

## Acknowledgements

In the writing of a guide such as this many people have contributed. The authors would like to acknowledge the input of Nigel Williams, who kindly agreed for a section of his material from *A Student's Guide to Drama and Theatre Studies for the Edexcel Specification* to be repeated in this book. The section appears in the Exploration of Dramatic Performance chapter, subtitled 'Where do I start', beginning on page 11, and finishing at the top of page 18. The author and publishers are grateful to the following people for their specific advice, support and expert contributions: Nicola Harvey, Jackie Psirides, Lucien Jenkins, Sarah Jones, Claudine Nightingale, Ben Robbins and A-level Theatre Studies students at Wellsway school. More recently, the growth in use of the internet has made an unparalleled amount of exciting information and challenging opinion widely available. Although every attempt has been made to acknowledge both the primary and secondary sources drawn upon, it is impossible to do justice to the full range of material that has shaped the creation of this book. The authors would therefore like to apologise if anyone's work has not been properly acknowledged. They would be happy to hear from authors or publishers so that any such errors or omissions may be rectified in future editions.

## Credit notices

Extracts from *Lysistrata – the sex strike* by Germaine Greer and Phil Wilmott (2000), reproduced by kind permission of Aurora Metro Press.

Extracts from *Woyzeck* by Georg Büchner, translated by J. Mackendrick (1979) and *Antigone* by Sophocles, translated by Don Taylor (1986), reproduced by kind permission of Methuen Drama, an imprint of A & C Black Publishers Ltd.

Extracts from *When Then is Now: Three Greek Tragedies* by Brendan Kennelly (2006), reproduced by kind permission of Bloodaxe Books.

Extract from *Woyzeck* by Georg Büchner, from *Complete Plays and Prose* by Georg Büchner, translated by Carl Richard Mueller (1963), reproduced by kind permission of Farrar, Straus and Giroux.

Extracts from *Lysistrata and Other Plays* by Aristophanes, translated with an introduction by Alan H. Sommerstein (1973, revised edition 2002), reproduced by kind permission of Penguin Classics.

Extracts from *Medea and Other Plays* by Euripides, translated with an introduction by Philip Vellacott (1963), reproduced by kind permission of Penguin Classics.

Extracts from *Lysistrata*, translated by Patric Dickinson (1996), reproduced by kind permission of Nick Hern Books Ltd.

Extract from *The Lion & the Unicorn* by George Orwell (Copyright © George Orwell) reprinted by permission of Bill Hamilton as the Literary Executor of the Estate of the Late Sonia Brownell Orwell and Secker & Warburg Ltd.

# Introduction

The A2 Drama and Theatre Studies course is designed to extend and engage you and build on the knowledge, variety and practical insights that you have gained from the AS course. By now you will have been drawn to a particular area of drama, be it as an actor, director or designer, and your confidence in being able to explore dramatic opportunities and seek alternative interpretations will have grown. You may have been exposed to a broad range of styles, practitioners and genres and may have seen live theatre in many forms. You now know what you like and don't like, what inspires you and what bores you. The A2 course gives you the opportunity to apply your ideas and attitudes taken from these multiple influences and apply them practically to your own original work. Furthermore, the experiences gained in the AS units can now be applied to theatre texts from a directorial and contextual point of view. You will be able to use the language of drama to critically analyse and evaluate plays in performance. You will also gain an understanding of how the plays might have been received in their original conditions and what relevance they now have to you as an active audience member in the 21st century.

This guide supports students of Edexcel A2 Drama and Theatre Studies. It is intended to be used alongside the work that you and your teachers do and should not be seen to be a substitute for it. The guide will outline the specific requirements of each unit, giving practical examples, examination guidance and suggestions for practical approaches to texts, which after all is the key to any study of drama. Although specific plays are identified here, the skills used should be applicable to any text, genre or period. This cross-referencing should be something that is central to your personal research throughout the course.

The emphasis is very much on your personal response and your willingness to take ownership of the work that you produce. Exploration of alternatives is the key to success. Be brave, trust yourself and don't be frightened to fail. Much of the work that you will do particularly in Unit 3 will involve group work. There needs to be an atmosphere of openness and honesty within the ensemble and a strong awareness of the needs of others. Don't forget that you are all working towards the same goal of a successful and original piece of theatre. A strong group means a strong final piece. Use each other's strengths and listen to each other's viewpoints. Use the practical exercises in this guide as a starting point for exploration and always maintain the sense of the ensemble. Group work combined with thorough preparation, wider reading and the willingness to explore new ideas, will provide you with an excellent grounding for success on the A2 course.

**Where are you now?**

**What skills do you need?**

## The A2 Modules

### Unit 3: Exploration of Dramatic Performance (40% of total A2 marks)

This unit is internally assessed by your teacher and focuses on the creation of an original piece of theatre lasting between 15 and 30 minutes depending on group size. Each student chooses a particular skill on which to be assessed – as a performer, director or designer. You will be assessed on the whole process of creating drama from initial ideas through rehearsal to performance to a specified audience. This will be evidenced by the recording of the final performance and the completion of a Supporting Written Evidence document by each student.

Your teachers may provide you with a range of stimulus material based on a given theme or a published play. This could be in many different forms:

- Poetry

- Film

- Documentary

- Blogs

- Fiction

- Non-fiction

- Practitioners and performances that you may have encountered at AS.

This material is designed to produce a spark of inspiration within the group, something that will give you an initial idea to produce a piece of drama that may be a story you want to tell, an issue you want to raise, or an injustice you want to expose. The structure and style of your piece will then grow out of these initial ideas using as many influences as suits your piece.

You will be assessed by your teachers continuously throughout the devising process with the focus on the following areas: research and exploration; development and structure; performance and evaluation. At all times you should be aiming to be an active and committed member of the group, able to shape the ideas of others as well as making valuable contributions of your own.

> This document should not exceed 3,500 words.

The Supporting Written Evidence document will trace the journey of your work in an honest and constructive way linked to six guiding questions that the exam board gives. The questions, which will be covered more specifically in the following section, are designed to guide you in response, not provide a rigid structure.

This guide intends to provide you with examples of how to approach the unit as a group, how to divide responsibilities, how to generate and develop ideas and how to structure your piece using a range of practical exercises.

## Unit 4: Theatre in Context (60% of total A2 mark)

This unit is externally assessed through a two-and-a-half hour written examination.

The unit is split into two parts. Sections A and B deal with the study of a set text chosen by your teacher and need to be approached by you as if you were the director preparing a group of actors for performance. The play will be approached through practical workshop activities, with the focus in this section being on how the rehearsal process is used to develop and shape ideas. Section A will focus on a specific extract from the play which will be published in the examination, whereas Section B will refer to an overall interpretation of the whole play with you as director. Your teacher will choose a play from one of three periods of theatrical development as outlined:

* Aristophanes – *Lysistrata* (covering 525BCE – 65CE)

  **Or**

* Christopher Marlowe – *Dr Faustus* (covering 1564–1720)

  **Or**

* George Büchner – *Woyzeck* (covering 1828–1914)

Approaches to all three of these texts will be covered in the guide with practical activities, study of key scenes and examination techniques.

In the second part of the unit – Section C – you will be asked to study and research the original performance conditions of one play performed in one of the three time periods that is not the same as the play chosen for Sections A and B. You will be required to see a live production of the chosen play, compare it to its original conditions and explore how the production you have seen has been interpreted to suit a modern audience. You will need to think about and research such areas as the physical performance space, the audience, performance style, influence of design elements and the relevance of the piece to the audience of the time.

A range of contrasting plays will be chosen for coverage in this guide to give the best opportunities for points of comparison, while drawing out themes and issues that are relevant to you as a member of a modern audience.

You are allowed to take the following into the examination:

* An annotated copy of the set text for Sections A and B with workshop ideas for key sections and overall interpretation.

* Research notes on the live production and comparison to original conditions.

**Tip**

Remember the focus for both sections is on the play in performance and all writing must be approached from a practical perspective.

# Exploration of Dramatic Performance

## What do I have to do?

There is a deliberate structural change in most A levels after the first year of study. Initially, the focus is on the exploration of key concepts, with the teacher leading the student through the subject content. However, during the A2 elements, there is a greater focus on independence, where individuals are expected to consolidate their early learning and use it as a springboard for more independent thought.

This unit is both exciting and challenging, as it expects students to draw on of all their theatrical knowledge and experience while giving them the freedom to apply what they have learnt. If you are to be successful, you will need to take risks. You will need to lead by example and trust the value of practical experimentation. Those students who like to discuss in detail before doing anything may have difficulty with this element of the course.

**Theme or script**

Your response in this unit will be based on stimulus material provided by your teacher. As you begin the course you may wish to offer suggestions on the work you wish to explore. During the AS course, you may have come across a certain theme, image, piece of music or text which has set your creative juices flowing. Before beginning work on the piece itself, your teacher may lead you through a series of workshops to explore a theme or style in greater detail. You may also look at how other theatre groups explore the devising process and be expected to experiment with their approach.

Regular discussions will be at the heart of this work. As a group you will naturally evaluate the ideas you create but your teacher will also want to discuss them with you. It is their responsibility to facilitate rather than lead the process. However, they will also be expected to document your individual progress in the unit through a series of student profiles. At any point in the lesson you may be asked about the decisions you have made, the influences on your work and the impact you are hoping to make. It is vital that these are at the forefront of your mind whilst you are devising.

## How will I be assessed?

This unit is worth 40 per cent of the A2 course, and 20 per cent of you final A-level grade. It will be assessed and marked by your teacher before being externally moderated. The evidence for assessment takes three different forms:

- **Student profile**. Your teacher will complete a document which evidences your involvement during the rehearsal process.

- **Supporting Written Evidence**. This is your opportunity to demonstrate a comprehensive understanding of the work you have explored by documenting the various stages. You will be provided with a series of headings and you will have a maximum of 3,500 words to highlight your contribution.

- **Performance**.

The exam board divides these sections into four different assessment criteria each worth 15 marks, which chart the devising process:

- **Research and exploration**. Marks are awarded for the depth of research and the effect it has on both the practice and performance of the group.

- **Development and structure**. Candidates are actively involved both creatively and imaginatively in the development process, positively impacting on the work.

- **Performance**. Students are marked on their demonstration of skills and their success in communicating ideas to the audience.

- **Evaluation**. Individuals are able to evaluate both process and performance, making links between research, development and performance.

## What role should I take?

The exam board identifies three generic roles students could take in the performance – performer, designer or director. When choosing which role to take, it is important to note the limitations that exist within your own school or college. Poor lighting facilities or a basic set will be self-penalising; you will struggle to communicate your intentions to an audience if your resources are limited. However, you shouldn't be afraid of being ambitious and creative. This can often be the secret of great work.

**Performing**

In Unit 2, a large proportion of marks is earned through performance skill. Candidates are assessed on movement, voice, characterisation and communication. However, in this unit, the performance itself is only worth 25 per cent of the final marks. As a performer you need to be an active member of the devising process; creating a skilled finished product will not be sufficient. You will need to be an intrinsic part of the devising process, making contributions, experimenting with the ideas and evaluating their success.

**Designing**

You had the option of experimenting with different design skills in Unit 2 and if you have been successful in the past, it is definitely worth considering focusing on this area again. Candidates can choose from costume, lighting, make-up, masks, set and props or sound design. Before making your final decision, you will need to understand how your group intend to explore their work. Since most of the groups will create scenes as they work, the demands will be very different from the predetermined expectations of a published script. Would you be comfortable with the evolving demands that this might make?

**Directing**

The exam board gives a detailed outline of the expectations placed on design candidates in Unit 2. If you choose this option, you should look at the list and decide what you are able to include in your Supporting Written Evidence.

Directing is not something for the fainthearted but if you are confident in your dramatic understanding, feel able to lead workshops, and believe you can communicate a strong vision to an audience, then this could be an option which allows you to excel. Inevitably, this will require significant preparation outside of lessons but this in itself may well enable you to demonstrate a high level of understanding in your Supporting Written Evidence.

If you are finding it difficult to decide on just one of the options, then it is possible to focus on more than one area. Naturally, performers can be involved in the directing process and designers can be good actors. However, you want to avoid being overwhelmed by the workload; whatever you choose, make sure your responsibilities are reasonable and enable you to demonstrate your skills.

## Practical considerations

Once you have decided on your role, it is important to look at the various criteria which ensure you are fulfilling the demands of the specification:

**How many can we have in our group?** The minimum group size is three and the maximum group size is six. If students are solely involved in either directing or designing, they are not included in these numbers.

**How long should the piece last?** The performance should last between 15 and 30 minutes depending on the group size. As a general rule, work on the principle of five minutes per performer. Creating more material than this not only consumes valuable rehearsal time but can also add superficial aspects to your work.

**How much rehearsal time will we have?** This will depend on the amount of time allocated by your teacher. As a rough guide, you should expect to spend approximately 10 weeks of lessons working on the project, but the more successful groups will need organise additional session outside of class time in order to polish their work.

**Who is our audience?** The exam board expects you to be aware of your audience when creating your work but who they are is up to you and your teacher. You should make a specific choice about your target audience. It could be a multi-faceted piece which communicates ideas to both young and old. Clearly, this is a decision that needs making at the beginning of the process, as it will influence the form your ideas will take.

## Where do I start?

You must try to see this unit as a shared and collaborative experience for your group. This is not a unit that you are going to be able to tackle or achieve success in alone. It is very important that your whole group feels excited and responsible for the project, and this needs to start at the beginning. Make sure that the whole group knows what the unit will demand and how it is to be assessed. Although you will be assessed as individuals and will receive individual marks from your teacher, the quality of the final piece in performance is perhaps the most telling piece of evidence as to how well you have worked and achieved your objectives. Encourage everyone to feel part of the process of choosing start material and stimuli. Allow everyone to have a voice and to share ideas about:

- What the piece should be about

- To whom it should be performed

- How it should be performed

- What response it will aim to get from its audience.

It's important that your early meetings and lessons give each person the opportunity to put forward ideas, as this will allow everyone to feel part of the team. You then need to go on making it possible for everyone to have an influence over how the piece is shaped and to affect other important decisions. This is very difficult but an important part of the process. There are some very practical ways of ensuring this sense of sharing and collaboration. Try to see the journey of this unit in four clear steps: brainstorming, exploring, structuring and rehearsing.

> **"** I wished we had started working practically earlier. We talked too much and kept disagreeing about what to do even before we had tried to do it. In the end we almost ran out of time. **"**
>
> A former drama and theatre studies student.

### Brainstorming

Brainstorming is a two-phase process.

- **Phase 1** should decide the stimulus that you are going to use. Your teacher may already have made this decision, or you may want to choose your own stimulus in negotiation with them. When deciding your stimulus, be aware that you need to find something that is going to trigger your imagination, get you excited, give you the opportunity to research and develop ideas, have the potential to become good drama, and interest an audience. Use these points to structure your debate and decision.

- **Phase 2** comes after you have decided upon your starting stimulus. You should now get the group to pool as many ideas concerning the stimulus as possible. Each group member could be encouraged to present ideas in a formal discussion, in the form of key words, pictures, photographs, music, or other related stories.

Do not start deciding how you are going to perform the stimulus yet: at this stage, just try to work in terms of abstract concepts and words, and related information. Try to collate all these ideas on a very large piece of paper, perhaps in spider-chart or mind-map form.

Look at the example below of ideas on the stimulus of a newspaper article: 'The place of guns within our society'.

The objective of brainstorming is not to decide how the stimulus will be explored and shaped, but to find as many ways as possible of starting to think about it.

### Exploring

Exploring should also be seen in two phases: **action** and **reflection**.

**Action**

The action phase is a practical session in which one of the keywords from the spider-chart is explored through a theatrical or dramatic form. Your teacher may lead these sessions.

Each member of your group should take one of the key words or concepts from the spider-chart. They should then go away and prepare a workshop session based on that concept. The workshop session should try to use improvisation, physical theatre, music, movement and other devices to explore the chosen concept. You need to support this with research into the key words. Consider which particular dramatic forms and genres would best explore and clarify them.

Let's look at various workshop ideas that you could use for our sample stimulus: 'The place of guns within our society'.

 A workshop idea that uses music might follow this pattern:

1. Using the track 'Bang Bang (My baby shot me down)' sung by Nancy Sinatra – on the sound track for the film *Kill Bill* – create a series of still images that show how guns are used differently in the world today.

2. Now look only at the dark side of guns and create a series of images that show how guns are abused and used for evil in the world. Use a different piece of music for this, perhaps one that creates juxtaposition and irony – for example, 'What a Wonderful World' by Louis Armstrong.

3. Now focus on the positive and show how guns are used for control, protection and peace in the world today. Again, use a different piece or genre of music for this to create a mood or atmosphere – for example, Barber's *Adagio*, as used in the film *Platoon*.

---

 A workshop idea that uses a more tangential approach could involve converting the idea into a fairy story in order to create a different perspective.

For example, you could use this outline of a Chinese fable as your starting point:

> There was once an Emperor who was wise and powerful.

> He built a mighty wall around his kingdom to prevent his enemies from invading.

> He then summoned the inventor to create a weapon that would protect the wall and protect his kingdom.

> After much thinking and much work, the inventor returned with a bamboo tube that, combined with special explosive powder, could shoot large stones a long distance and destroy people, houses and walls.

> The inventor was very pleased with himself and awaited his reward.

> The Emperor asked who knew of this invention. The inventor confessed only himself and his family. The Emperor immediately had the inventor and all his family executed, and the invention destroyed and the plans burned.

> The Emperor had realised that if his enemies captured the invention his kingdom would fall.

What does this fable tell you about weapons and what they can do?

How could this type of fable be used to help you develop your thinking?

> Approaching the chosen theme or idea in an oblique way often casts new light on it and helps you to think about the way the idea should be presented.

---

 For a more improvisational and character-based approach, you could perhaps work through role-play.

**Scenario of first scene.** Create a classroom, with your group as the students in the class, awaiting the arrival of the teacher.

Try to play this scene and the ones below for a sustained amount of time in order to allow tension to mount and characters to develop.

**Devising tip**

Try not to plan this role-play or any other development scenes too much. Agree on the location and your role, but beyond that let it just develop and allow your character to experience the spontaneity, immediacy and reality of such a situation, in the safe environment of the role-play.

You or one of your group should burst in brandishing an agreed prop that represents a gun. This person then demands that all the students in the class stand against the wall.

The person who bursts in is the elder sister/brother of a student in the class who committed suicide at the weekend because of sustained bullying.

The person wants to know who in the class is responsible for bullying their brother, because the bullies are going to be 'dealt with'.

**Scenario of second scene.** Change roles and locations. The group should now become on-the-spot TV reporters outside the school, waiting for news on the events within. You or another member of your group should now be the police officer in charge of the situation, and should brief the press as to what is going on in the school, giving details of who is involved and why – but not giving too much away. Try to speak the facts of the events.

**Scenario of third scene**. Keeping the role of the TV reporter, everyone in the group should now take a turn at re-enacting a live straight-to-camera commentary of what is happening in the school behind them.

While one person speaks directly to the camera, the others should become the crew holding the camera and the mike, or staying behind the shot.

**Scenario of fourth scene.** Two members of your group should now become the parents of the children involved in the action. Someone else should become the police liaison officer.

The police liaison officer enters the room and breaks the news to the parents, who have a thousand questions.

This scene is ended with the sound of a distant gunshot.

**Scenario of fifth scene.** Think about how this situation could be resolved.

Choose a drama device to show how it could end. Consider:

- A movement sequence or freeze supported by music

- Returning to the classroom and improvising it through to an ending

- A planned ending where you agree what happens, think about events and dialogue, and then act it through

- As a group, becoming headlines and an article, speaking as a chorus

- A series of thought-tracking monologues in which chosen characters in the role-play speak their inner thoughts to reveal what has happened.

This action phase of exploring is not about rehearsing ideas for performance; rather, it is about exploring ideas and concepts to see if they are relevant or can be developed.

**Devising tip**

Try not to plan this role-play or any other development scenes too much. Agree on the location and your role, but beyond that let it just develop and allow your character to experience the spontaneity, immediacy and reality of such a situation, in the safe environment of the role-play.

A workshop idea using a play text to give you ideas about narrative and structure could be based on the play *Blood Brothers*.

Guns play a special role within the play, in that they are used as metaphors and to reflect on young people growing up.

- Pretend guns are used to show the children at play

- A toy gun is used as a parting gift between Mickey and Eddie

- An air gun is used to show the development of friendship between Mickey, Linda and Eddie

- A real gun is used to show the desperation of Mickey in finding work

- A real gun eventually kills Mickey and Eddie.

Find a prop that could represent a gun, or use a toy gun. Place the gun in a space and get your group to sit around it. One at a time, each of the group has to come to the gun and begin an improvisation so that it is used in different ways by different people. As soon as they begin the improvisation, the rest of the group must join in.

The gun must always be a gun – but the ages, location, history and context of those using it may change.

After each session, or after all the sessions have been completed, there should be a dedicated time for reflection that allows you and the group to comment.

The language of this reflection needs to be positive. You should find ideas that worked and that you may wish to return to when you come to shape your final piece.

Exploring through action and reflection will help to secure the shared vision and collaborative nature of the group, and will begin to create real and practical ideas that can be used in the shaping of the final piece.

## Structuring

The exploring step should have sparked your excitement about your chosen idea and got you thinking about ideas for how the work could be presented in performance. Remember that an important part of deciding how the idea will be presented is deciding the target audience for your piece.

The structuring step is concerned with the decisions that you will make regarding the material you have gathered. Your knowledge of form and structure from the AS year – and from plays you have studied, performed and seen – will help you make decisions regarding what works in what context and what you want to do.

**Reflection**

**Study tip**

For your Supporting Written Evidence, it would be a really good idea to note down what you did in all the sessions, how you did them in terms of drama devices and why you did these sessions, using this section to comment on whether they worked.

Decide early on whether you want your piece to be narrative, episodic or abstract, or a combination of all these:

**Narrative.** Do you want to tell a story? Is the story about someone or something? Does this person/thing/event represent things greater than itself in an allegorical or metaphorical sense? Will the story be told through a series of chronological scenes or will it defy time and order? Will the story have narration or commentary or will it be created through dialogue and monologue?

**Episodic.** Will your piece be a series of episodes that make sense and meaning in their own right? Do you want to mix up your form and content, using a variety of devices and dramatic genres in dealing with a theme or issue?

**Abstract.** Do you want to create something that holds no particular rationale or logic, but debunks the notion of theatrical form and content? Do you want it to keep the audience guessing and thinking?

**❝** Devised work often has a lot of quiet in it – but actors think they have to speak. **❞**

Peter Ellis, actor, quoted in *Devising: A Handbook for Drama and Theatre Students* by Gill Lamden (Hodder Arnold 2000).

### Be a magpie

Take time to think about the plays you have studied, performed and seen, to consider the story and content of those plays. Think about ideas that have caught your interest and that would be appropriate to your chosen idea.

There is no such thing in theatre as an original idea. Do not feel sneaky or guilty about including in your piece ideas, devices or staging that you have seen elsewhere. Great directors are like magpies: they collect ideas from all different art forms, and are able to select and use them to bring new light, meaning and effect.

Use the wealth of experience that you have accumulated from reading, watching and being in plays, but also use your wider cultural experiences of books, music, pop videos, films, advertising, magazines, TV programmes, paintings and photographs.

### Storyboard

Once you have decided on a structural approach, use the experiences that you have had when exploring to start making decisions about what you want to have in your piece. The best way to begin to organise your ideas is to use the filmic technique of storyboarding. Use a large piece of paper to write down idea headings for scenes. Place these scenes in the order that you would like them to follow, and connect them with large arrows.

### Stepping stones

These idea headings will act like units or scenes from a play, and will allow you to begin to see how the piece is shaping up and how the structure is developing. Bringing together your ideas like this will also enable you to create a rehearsal programme and achievable targets. Without units, the project will spread out before you like a river that can't be crossed. Units will build stepping stones.

Underneath each idea heading, try to answer these three questions:

1. What **happens** in this unit?

2. What theatrical style or dramatic **devices** will be used in this unit?

3. What is the **purpose** of this unit in terms of what you are trying to say?

You don't yet have to be exact in your response to these questions, but trying to answer them before beginning rehearsals will ensure a shared vision and collaboration. Having a storyboard laid out in front of you and your group will provide a sense of the overall nature of the piece and allow you to see where it is going. An overall sense of structure is important from the beginning, even if ideas and units change as you work.

## Rehearsing

You need to start working practically as soon as you can do so without taking short-cuts on any of the above. You have talked and discussed enough – you now need to work on the unit.

**Activity is the key to creativity.** Ideas will be most successfully formed in a practical workshop or rehearsal situation. Ideas can be discussed for enormous lengths of time, but you must remember that you are not ultimately being marked on a script: the assessment is based on a practical realisation of an idea which you have also devised practically.

You must spend time working through ideas specific to your unit idea headings, and see if they work. You can continue to use the model of action and reflection at this stage.

As with the Theatre Text in Performance unit at AS, organisation is a very important part of success in this unit. The models that are given as sample projects on pages 18–46 will give you some clear ideas as to how to approach rehearsals specifically, but there are also some general principles that you need to recognise.

## Performing

Your piece can be performed as a one-off to your chosen audience, or as part of a tour or series of performances.

You may choose not to have a full technical support for the show, preferring to avoid a large set, lighting rig and sound equipment, especially if it is a touring show designed for primary schools or places with other logistical problems – don't see this as a drawback. On the other hand, you may decide to create a multi-dimensional technological feast for the show – this is equally valid. Whatever you do in terms of technical support needs to be a conscious decision and worked into the piece in a fully integrated way during the rehearsal process. It is not something you should tack on at the last minute.

While you need to remember that this performance is an exam, it should above all also be a piece of theatre designed to entertain

**66** Be nice to each other. Just be nice. **99**

Lee Simpson, Improbable Theatre, quoted in *Devising: A Handbook for Drama and Theatre Students* by Gill Lamden (Hodder Arnold 2000).

**Tip**

Your supporting written evidence is a very important part of gaining marks in this unit, and you must be consistent and committed about working on it. Different sessions will answer different questions from the record, so try to respond appropriately to the questions after each session.

**Technical support**

and engage a target audience. Your teacher will be looking at how well you communicate feelings and meaning to your audience, and how effectively you use performing skills within the context of the drama.

A really good final way of looking at this unit is not to think of it as an opportunity for individuals, but as an opportunity for you to demonstrate the collective strength and creativity of your group, within which you can excel as an individual.

## An approach model to a source text

## Animal Farm

### The plot

The novel *Animal Farm* was written by George Orwell in 1943, and is set in Manor Farm, which is being poorly managed by Mr Jones. His drunken exploits leave the animals neglected, and they start to plan how they could be released from his tyrannous rule. Led by the pig Snowball, they plot a successful rebellion and the farmer flees in fear of his life. The liberated animals begin by creating a new social order based on the philosophy of Animalism. Commandments are written down, democracy is installed and hope rises. However, a bitter rivalry festers between Snowball and another pig, Napoleon, which ultimately leads to the former being deposed and a new regime being installed. The new order rules through fear; objecting animals are 'removed' and the original commandments are manipulated as Squealer, Napoleon's deputy, uses political propaganda to control the farm. Tired, hungry and with spirits broken, the animals submit and the pigs take control. Their power corrupts their behaviour as they start negotiating with men, the very beings they are supposed to despise. Ultimately, the novel finishes with the image of men and pigs together, and observes 'it was impossible to say which was which'.

Peter Hall's adaptation is a discussion of power. The animals are a natural image of slavery, with man (and subsequently the pigs) as the enemy who abuses his position. On a basic level, this is a metaphor that can be applied to a range of political situations worldwide. It also raises questions about the role of the suppressed masses, and how they appear more willing to accept their fate and follow the majority rather than standing up for what they believe – an approach that ultimately leads to their continued suffering. It is a dark text that serves as a warning about the perversion of power to those who are apathetic or suppress their true feelings.

**Author's background**

George Orwell was born Eric Arthur Blair in 1903 in Bengal, into what he neatly described as a lower-upper-middle-class British family. Orwell's father was a civil servant in British-occupied India, and his position enabled his son to have a privileged upbringing. Orwell's experiences of prep school and Eton were, however, generally unhappy, and he was struck by the endemic arrogance, insincerity and affectation that dominated the behaviour of his peers. Rather than going to university, he joined the Imperial Police Force for six years in Burma. It was a move that he regretted, as

---

**Further reading**

The dramatised edition referred to in this section was adapted by Peter Hall and is published by Heinemann (1993). It contains a good introduction and useful questions to consider.

---

" One day … I saw a little boy … driving a huge carthorse along a narrow path, whipping it whenever it tried to turn. It struck me that if only such animals became aware of their strength, we should have no power over them. "

Orwell, quoted in *George Orwell: a Life* by B. Crick (Little Brown & Co 1980).

---

The exam board expects you to link your ideas to the work of a theatrical practitioner. You could choose to focus on Brecht's political theatre, the work of Peter Hall or look at the style of a company which has produced the play, for example Northern Stage.

the British Empire seemed to emulate the hypocritical behaviour he despised at school. He resigned and returned to Britain in order to write.

Orwell spent a lot of his time mingling with the working class, living in relative poverty and completing menial tasks. He visited different cities, and his first novel, *Down and Out in Paris and London*, recounted his experiences. He wrote under the pseudonym George Orwell, which appeared to be a symbolic rejection of his middle-class past. In 1936, he travelled to Barcelona to write articles on the Spanish Civil War while participating in the conflict. He rose to the rank of lieutenant and was passionate in his fight against the threat from the fascist opposition. He was injured and returned home only to volunteer for active service during World War II, but was deemed unfit to join.

**Poverty and war**

Orwell's thoughts turned once again to writing. In 1943 he completed the novel *Animal Farm* in three months, but struggled to attract a publisher. People were wary of his work during a period of such political fragility. His indirect criticisms of the Soviet government of Joseph Stalin – and the attitudes of British idealists who hailed communism as a solution to hardship – were too threatening to a Europe ravaged by war. However, once the crisis was over, his work went into print and he received great critical acclaim. He followed this novel with *1984*, another harrowing vision of the future which warns against the drift towards totalitarian solutions. He died in 1950 at the age of 46, after a long battle with tuberculosis.

**Writing**

## Contextualising the play

On one level, Orwell's is novel an allegory of the political situation in Russia at the beginning of the 20th century, with Manor Farm representing the country as a whole. The animals represent the enslaved masses or serfs; the farmer, Mr Jones, encapsulates the ruling Tsars. During the revolution of 1917, the Bolsheviks, led by Vladimir Lenin, planned to overthrow the ruling class and take control of their own destiny. Lenin's ideals were influenced by Karl Marx and Friedrich Engels, and his thoughts and philosophies are reflected in the character of Old Major. Orwell's references to Animalism are an allusion to this new regime, communism, where the personal luxuries so desired by Mollie and the distractions of religion advocated by Moses were made illegal.

**20th-century Russia**

### Further reading

To understand the context behind the playtext adaptation of Orwell's novel, you will need to have a firm grasp of events surrounding the Bolshevik Revolution in Russia, as well as the subsequent battles for political power and Stalin's rise to power. Use encyclopedias, the internet and the resources of your college's history department to help you.

The Red Army, created by Lenin's deputy Trotsky, managed to suppress any resistance to the revolution. A communist order was established, with Trotsky (represented in the play by Snowball) leading the way. However, in 1924, Lenin's death led to greater unrest as people fought for positions of power. Stalin was ultimately successful and Trotsky was forced to flee, action that is emulated in the battles between Napoleon and Snowball. During this period, order was maintained by the secret police force known as the Cheka. They controlled through fear, as do Napoleon's dogs, and ensured that rebels were either imprisoned or killed.

**Trotsky/Snowball**

**Stalin's regime**

### Think about...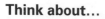

How does Squealer's use of propaganda compare with the role of spin-doctors in modern politics?

*The Lion and the Unicorn*, an essay by George Orwell (1941).

### Further study

Sir Peter Hall is one of the country's leading directors. Research his biography and try to find what you can about his preferred styles of theatre.

Under Stalin's iron rule, attempts at economic and industrial advances were flawed, and Stalin needed to utilise propaganda to convey an image of success. This political spin, controlled in the play by Squealer, employed all forms of media, and the initial communist philosophies were reduced to soundbites fit for manipulation. As Stalin became more desperate to maintain order, the original ideals were abandoned, the regime became more corrupt and ordinary people became victims.

Orwell died while Stalin was still in power; we could perceive his novel as a critique of the corruption inherent in any form of communism. Indeed, his work was celebrated by western culture during the Cold War as a condemnation of the Soviet Union. However, this is too simplistic a view of Orwell's writing. His political views were complex. In fact, his novel serves as a warning about the potential flaws in a system in which he had some faith. He didn't wish to write for a socialist audience about the dangers of capitalism, since this would be something of which they were aware. Neither did he wish to pander to the intellectual British left wing, as he perceived their views to be 'the irresponsible carping of people who never have been and never expected to be in a position of power'. He wanted to present a challenging reality that reflected the insecurities and needs of the people, and the dangers inherent in any political situation.

## Approaching the text

Before you begin to choose which elements of the play you are going to focus on, it is important that you understand the piece as a whole. We've already discussed Orwell's intention, and Peter Hall's adaptation is pretty true to the original novel. The action is essentially the same and only a few characters have been omitted. The only significant change is the extra emphasis Hall places on the ending. In addition to the final image highlighting how power has corrupted both man and pig, Hall makes references to genetic modification and the breeding of humans and animals to make the end product more desirable. This is a theme you may wish to focus on in your interpretation of the text.

Begin by drawing up a table, dividing the play into scenes, giving a brief overview of the action and indicating the characters involved.

Hall, in his introduction, suggests that with doubling the cast could be limited to 12. However, in your production you will be working with fewer actors than this, so it is important when working your way through the scenes that you consider the casting implications.

At this stage, you should also make notes of the musical implications of the scenes you choose – even if you choose to cut this from your version. Your table might initially look something like this:

| Unit | Pages | Description | Cast | Music | Notes and props |
|------|-------|-------------|------|-------|-----------------|
| 1 | 1–2 | Introduction to story Introducing man | Boy and Mr Jones | Jones – 'Who made the cows and sheep so meek?' | Shotgun for Jones |
| 2 | 2–5 | Old Major – introducing Animalism | Boy, Major, Clover, Mollie, Boxer, Snowball, other animals and Mr Jones | Major and animals – 'Beasts of England' | Major may need raised platform? |
| 3 | 6–7 | Pigs explain Animalism | Napoleon, Snowball, Squealer, Boy, Cat, Sheep, Mollie and animals | Pigs – 'No man, no master' | Split staging for the three different pigs? |

Reducing the play to this basic structure will be extremely useful as you start to develop your ideas. The exam board recommends that you allow five minutes' performance time – which is approximately three pages of the text – per member of your group. Bear this information in mind when deciding what material to include in your piece.

It is important that each of these units remains fresh in your mind. There is no point in collecting stale, factual information that simply bogs you down during the rehearsal process. It should save you time and act as a useful reference tool.

In your group, create an abridged version of *Animal Farm* that refers to each of the acting units you have identified. Unlike in your final performance, you can use some of your own words to explain the action, but try to find physical images and key quotations from each section to inform your work. Your version should last no longer than five minutes and should be a fast-paced performance. Think of it as a series of newspaper photographs and headlines that chart the events at Manor Farm.

Like all of the practical units, your performance needs to be governed by a ruling idea. Essentially, you need a theme that is going to be your focus during all decisions. What do you want your production to say to a modern audience? Consider the suggestions below. This is by no means a comprehensive list but it can act as a starting point for your discussions within your group:

- Power and corruption
- Political apathy
- Spin and the use of media for propaganda
- The abuse of animals by humans
- The blame culture – people refusing to take responsibility for their actions
- The effect humans have on their environment
- Greed and envy.

## Further study

The Reduced Shakespeare Company has mastered the art of lively, fast-paced performances. Its topics range from the complete works of Shakespeare to an abridged version of the Bible, and its success stems from its ability to skip through the less central areas with humour and skill, while taking time to explore certain ideas in greater detail. Try to see a live performance or visit the website, which has a lot of interesting information about the company's style: www.reducedshakespeare.com

## Ruling idea

## Further reading

Read a copy of the original novel and note the difference in emphasis. Consider whether the action is different from what you have already imagined in the stage version.

Once you have discussed these ideas, try to find one that could lead you towards making a piece of drama that you will find interesting and challenging. Remember, this unit is testing more than your understanding and application of performance techniques. You will be assessed on your research and exploration, as well as your ability to develop and structure ideas. It is vital that your work is comprehensively considered and has meaning for a contemporary audience.

## Form and structure

There are no limits concerning the form or structure of your piece and you should have encountered a sufficient number of plays during the course so far for you to realise the wide range of possibilities that exist.

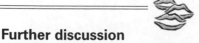

**Further discussion**

Discuss each of the plays you have encountered during the course to date and identify any elements of form or structure that have particularly impressed or interested you. Make a list of the ideas that could prove useful when working on this text.

**Narration**  Hall's script develops the notion of the fairy story through the narration of the boy. The character is a useful tool for describing some of the more complex action, aiding the audience's imagination during some of the more physical sequences. He also helps with the passing of time, allowing days and months to pass quickly when the sense of routine needs establishing. He draws attention to specific moments of interest and helps to establish a subtext for the characters by highlighting their thoughts. In a piece of theatre where you are required to focus on specific elements through the cutting of text, this is an extremely useful form to have at your disposal.

**Song**  The use of song invites comparisons with Brecht's style of political theatre.

**Further reading**

For more information on Brecht's style, see pages 24–31 of the AS companion to this guide (Rhinegold 2008).

The technique can be helpful in creating a more versatile performance, as long as the songs support your directorial concept. They help to prevent the audience from becoming too emotionally involved with the characters, presenting the facts of the situation for their judgement. Even if you choose not to sing the lyrics, you could underscore the action with some of the music, which varies tremendously in style. A simple humming of one of the melodies – 'This isn't what we wanted', for example – could provide the accompaniment to an essential scene change. Although it can be one of the more daunting elements of the piece, do not be afraid of it because it may provide the solution to some of the problems you encounter.

**Design**  In his introduction to the play, Hall outlines the conditions in which his initial production was performed. The stage area was completely black with key elements of the essential set painted with bright colours to resemble a child's toys. Actors were dressed in black apart from brightly coloured signers, which suggested their character through masks, tails and feet. Actors playing animals had crutches attached to their arms to emphasise their four-legged status. Much of the fairy-story feel was created through these oversized characters, and the use of masks helped to dehumanise their behaviour.

**Design factors**

*Animal Farm* is an excellent text for design students: the possibilities are endless. Try to formulate ideas for your vision as you work your way through the exercises. For more on design factors, see pages 28–29.

This physical style of performance will help you to create and define your theatrical world. This freedom should be exciting, since large objects such as windmills can be created physically using bodies in an image, or suggested by a simple prop such as a spinning umbrella. Think laterally and ambitiously; the more exciting the ideas sound to you, the more likely you are to capture the audience's imagination.

**Language**

Hall's use of language clearly helps to define character. After all, language is power in *Animal Farm*: it is no coincidence that the pigs can not only read, but are also the most eloquent. However you choose to edit the script, note how tension and comedy are created through Squealer's use of rhetoric, Muriel's innocent questioning and Boxer's simplistic view of a worker's life. Each animal's dialogue is distinctive: try to keep that style in your final cut.

**Cutting and adapting**

The simplest method of creating your 15–30 minutes of action is by performing a group of consecutive scenes. However, this may prevent you from communicating your message successfully and this in turn could restrict your chances of achieving a high grade. A top-band student needs to show outstanding creative and imaginative input in the devising process. It is now also possible to include some improvised dialogue in your work. Experimenting with unusual scene orders and interspersing segments of dialogue will challenge both you and your audience, and could lead to a more sophisticated performance. Designs for the scenes will naturally become more inventive if you become ambitious with the structure of your piece.

Ultimately, the nature of your performance will be affected by the strengths of your group, the gender balance and the theme you choose to focus on. Over the next few pages, however, we will outline a series of structures for you to consider. Work your way through these and consider whether or not any ideas are appropriate for your performance. Remember, whether you choose to accept or reject each concept, the fact that you have made a decision about your piece is a positive step forward. Try the practical exercises and feel free to experiment with any variations that you find interesting. Creating is always an easier process when you are on your feet. Long-winded discussions about the merits of an idea can be frustrating and fruitless. However, as you work, always keep your ruling idea at the forefront of your mind.

## Getting started

**Key scenes**

If you were to perform the play in its entirety, you would have a production that lasted approximately two hours. The piece would explore complex political ideas and show the subtle development of characters as the action turns full circle, with the pigs and men slowly being presented as increasingly similar beings. Your performance, however, will be no longer than 30 minutes, and it is vital that you select the most appropriate action. This could involve you choosing key scenes and cutting dialogue in an attempt to create an overview of the whole tale, or focusing on one aspect of the play in greater detail.

Look at the table of scenes you created earlier. With your knowledge of the play, which do you think have the most potential to reinforce

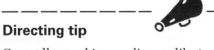

**Directing tip**

Generally speaking, audiences like to identify with the action. If they can recognise their own behaviour in the actions of the characters, they are more likely to remain engaged in the performance. Bear this in mind when structuring the scenes.

your chosen theme? Look at the characters. How might they present the different strands of your idea? Make a new list of the more appropriate scenes and discuss their dramatic potential with the rest of your group.

**Framing the action**

In order to emphasise the meaning of your piece, it would be helpful to frame your performance. Hall uses the boy's narrative as a framing technique to emphasise the fairy story. Rather than making your narrator a boy, you could make him an adult. Instead of reading from a book, he could be making a political speech, or holding a cabinet meeting. It is a clear way to reinforce your directorial concept and help the audience to perceive the work from your perspective.

An example of this device working successfully is in Joe Calarco's *Shakespeare's R & J*, an adaptation of *Romeo and Juliet*. Set in an oppressive boarding school, the play centres around four boys who smuggle in a copy of the Shakespeare play. As they read it, they physically recreate the action, using an edited version of the original text as their main dialogue. In addition to exploring the themes of the text, Calarco's play cleverly conveys the relationship between the four boys, as concepts of love, friendship, fear and violence are re-enacted. The play-within-a-play structure is extremely successful – the audience continually reflects on the action on two levels as the performance switches between the contemporary school setting and Verona.

This style of performance means that some of the actors are often on stage actively watching other members of the cast perform. This demands a high level of discipline and concentration, but the end result is extremely effective. Rather than using frequent entrances and exits, the passive actors are integral to the performance, and the frozen position that they hold outside of the main action complements the work of the other performers. It is an interesting style and is worth experimenting with in the early stages of rehearsal.

### Exploring characters

**Physicality**

You need to consider your characters' physical presence. The original adaptation implied that the animals walked on four legs. There was a clear physical difference between man and beast that highlighted the divide between the two worlds. The beasts themselves were each presented in a different way, with the height of the crutches conveying the nature of their animal gait. As a group retelling the tale to a contemporary audience, you need to consider how you might interpret their physicality. Are they the beasts that Hall imagined or are they a distorted image of humanity – is their behaviour more directly linked to flaws in contemporary society?

**Dialogue**

Look at the meeting on page 16 of your playtext, just after the animals sing, 'Our land was once a forest'. We are formally introduced to each of the groups of animals; their strengths and weaknesses are highlighted by the manner of their speech and their reactions to the formal setting. Look at the dialogue of Squealer, Boxer and the Hen. Choose a few sentences that epitomise their role in this scene.

> **Further study**
>
> Search the internet for further information on this production and try to identify key aspects of the style of the piece.

Ask three members of your group to be each of the characters and speak the lines:

- First, they need to deliver the dialogue as a traditional image of the animals, exaggerating their vocal tone, choosing an appropriate pitch similar to the sound which that animal might make – for example, the snort or squeal of the pig, the neighing of the horse, the squawking of the hen. Accompany this vocal work with relatively literal animal movements.

- Next, imagine the animals as people. It may help to discuss what characteristics they might have. Repeat the dialogue but speak in a very human tone, reducing any traces of animal to a bare minimum.

- Finally, try to find a middle ground between the two forms – half-man, half-beast. What traces of human and animal behaviour might be present in this new form? Perform this version and discuss with your group which approach could be most effective. Consider which elements could help to reinforce your directorial vision.

---

**Monologue**

This technique of selecting the most powerful dialogue for your character can be extremely effective, particularly if you wish to present the story from a particular perspective. In Hall's version, the audience associates with the animals. The characters of Boxer, Muriel, Benjamin and Clover represent our own flaws. Ultimately, we are left to reflect on their mistakes as if we made them, as the pigs continue to manipulate the action.

However, imagine the action presented from Napoleon's perspective; rather than feeling like victims, the audience would feel like the oppressor, looking more closely at how power corrupts than at the consequences of this on the masses. In order to do this, we need to understand Napoleon's thoughts, his morals and the motivation for his behaviour. An easy way of doing this is through monologue. You are allowed to use only the words of the text, but you can take dialogue from any character as long as you remain faithful to its original intention.

Look at Napoleon's dialogue throughout the play. Try to write a monologue that could be used to frame the opening from his perspective. Have him talking directly to the audience, as if he is introducing them to his corrupt world. Although lines can be taken from any part of the play, there should be a logic and fluency to your writing. At this stage, limit your monologue to a maximum of 200 words. Your final version might begin like this:

> **Napoleon:** *(Sat at his desk, surrounded by papers)* I have no schemes, I believe in quiet, conscientious work. We live in dangerous times. We must show solidarity. We must defend ourselves from our enemies. We must look to the future. Our sole wish is to live in peace. But we can't do everything at once.

## Directing tip

Focusing the action on one character does not necessarily mean that there is only one actor involved in the scene. It is important that you perceive your performance as ensemble work, in which the whole group works as a team to convey your intended message. With this in mind, it may be appropriate to use the whole cast in order to create a sense of a particular character. For example, the power of Squealer's propaganda could be enhanced by using choral work to deliver his speeches.

## Directing tip

When presenting an argument between two characters in a non-realistic performance, it is worth experimenting with dislocating the action. Rather than having the two actors facing each other, have them both facing the audience but still imagine the other person is in front of them. This enables the audience to see facial expressions more clearly.

> **❝All dictators try to demoralise and divide their followers because that is the best way of controlling them.❞**
>
> Tony Benn, quoted in the programme for the Northern Stage production of *Animal Farm*.

Try writing similar monologues for other key characters and consider where they might be placed in the context of your piece.

Monologues are a clear way of focusing attention on one character and their personal struggle within the world of the play. However, the same effect could be created without having to select phrases from the entire text. Instead, you could simply remove one of the characters from a duologue. Look at the exchanges between Whymper and Napoleon on pages 38 and 40. Imagine Whymper is removed from the scene. Napoleon's dealings with the outside world are immediately made more abstract. Have the actor performing the lines facing the audience, immediately involving them in his corrupt schemes. We are left to imagine the details of the relationship while focusing specifically on the behaviour of one character.

You could photocopy Squealer's speech on the top of page 44, from 'Comrades! The most terrible thing has been discovered'. Distribute a copy to each member of the group. Ask each person to highlight the five words or phrases that they believe to be the most interesting. While you read the complete text, ask the rest of your group to deliver their five phrases when you come to them. They don't need to worry about synchronising their speech with yours. In fact, it is better if the words are performed at a different pace. Consequently, some lines will be delivered just by you, others by two or three voices that may slightly echo each other. The collage of sound that is created could help to emphasise the disturbing and threatening nature of Squealer's words. Make a note of any lines that are particularly effective. Now rehearse the section, directing when people should speak, applying what you have learnt from the first run-through.

Another variation of this concept is multiple characterisation, where you could choose to have more than one person playing the character in any one scene. In the previous exercise, the focus was on the vocal delivery. With this technique, however, you should focus on the staging of the whole scene, looking at both voice and movement. Look at the argument on page 28, which begins with Napoleon calling Snowball. This is a clear power struggle between the two forces, with the latter eventually losing. Napoleon's attitude is deliberately provocative, challenging Snowball's ideas in front of the other animals. This primitive aggression could be accentuated by having more than one person playing the role of Napoleon in this scene. The introduction of each new Napoleon could symbolically represent the growing strength of his argument.

Look at this extract and imagine that you are gradually going to increase the number of Napoleons in the scene from one to four. The first calling of Snowball begins with just one version of the character on stage. Decide when it might be appropriate to introduce the second, third and fourth versions of the character. Do they speak all of their lines in unison or do they alternate, switching the dialogue across the stage area and emphasising Snowball's confusion. Where might you position the characters in order to reinforce the impact of the scene?

## Juxtaposing scenes

In order to reinforce different perspectives, it may be interesting to place two scenes on the stage at the same time, side by side, to highlight contrasting fortunes. This juxtaposition can remind the audience of the change in a particular character's fate or behaviour. For example, on stage right you could position Boxer and Squealer as the former tries to prove to the latter how hard he has worked at his letters. This could also be followed by some of Boxer's maxims such as 'Comrade Napoleon is always right' and 'I must work harder'. On stage left, however, you could use a different actor to create the image of Boxer collapsing under the weight of his work. He is an image of exhaustion. The resulting effect highlights how people in power can abuse even their most loyal followers.

This technique can be used in a variety of forms – mimes or tableaux can be just as effective in highlighting the change. Squealer's defence of the pigs' behaviour could be contrasted with images either of animal suffering or the pigs wallowing in their luxury. Look back at your list of scenes and see if any moments could be used in this way in order to support your directorial concept.

## Staging moments of conflict

Part of the impact of *Animal Farm* stems from its use of violence – it shows the overthrow of an existing regime and people being threatened into submission. It is an extremely dark aspect of the text, and it can be difficult to recreate, particularly when working with a small cast. The battle of the cowshed between humans and animals is especially challenging due to the physical action that is implied, although the chasing of Snowball with the dogs, the apparent murder of Boxer, or even the show trials in Act 2 all contain problematic action.

If your group feels comfortable with physical work then it is worthwhile spending time trying to structure striking visual images that explore the full horror of the situation. You may find it useful to start with a series of freezes which chart the nature of the battle. These may prove to be effective on their own with blackouts used between each image, as if they are a series of photographs of the events. However, you could also link the scenes together to create a more realistic version.

Alternatively, you could focus on a much more stylised interpretation, in which the political message of your piece is emphasised. Think about images that could be projected behind the action, such as those of modern suffering or animal cruelty. You may wish to link your ideas to a specific conflict or attitude; alternatively, it may be a more general reference to oppression and suffering.

**Directing tip**

Consider how design skills can be used to emphasise the violence of the situation. Music can be very powerful in creating images in an audience's mind without them appearing on the stage. Low-level lighting and shadows can highlight the sense of confusion. Blood could be emphasised by the symbolic image of ribbons being pulled from an animal chest.

**Physical work**

**Political message**

**Designing Animal Farm**

The complexity of your staging may be limited by the size of your performance area, but if you have members of your group who are interested in choosing the design option then this play

**Design tip**

All candidates need to be aware of any health and safety issues that are implied by their design.

provides opportunity for their imagination to run wild. Creating the world of humans and animals can be done simply through physical performances, but, with time and effort, it is possible to create an environment that supports the concept of the fairy story. In an attempt to get your creative juices flowing, we've listed a few ideas for you to consider. Please do not consider these to be limiting – they are simply a starting point for your ideas.

**Set considerations**

- Where are the audience positioned?
- Are you going to create the farm setting literally, and if so, what materials are you going to consider: straw, wooden pallets, metal troughs?
- Is there going to be any water on stage?
- How is the windmill going to be constructed and blown up?
- Will the farmhouse be visible or is it simply implied?
- Where will the commandments be positioned?
- Will they be written or projected?
- Will any contemporary images be used to emphasise the play's meaning to a modern audience?
- Is there a need for different levels?
- Are any props going to be used to illustrate key moments of the play: the raising of the flag, the removal of Boxer in the van, for example?
- Would puppetry help with the more complex moments of the action?

**Lighting considerations**

- How does lighting help to create a sense of location?
- How does it suggest the gradual change in mood during the piece?
- How might the more macabre scenes be emphasised by the colour, position and intensity of the light?
- Which lanterns are best suited for key moments of action?
- Are gobos or projected images going to be used?
- What demands might the method of staging place on your design?
- Does the action ever require you to light key areas of the stage separately?

**Costume considerations**

- How will the costume suggest the difference between animals and humans, and how might the pigs' outfits change during the piece?
- Will you use a literal design, or symbols to suggest which animal is which?
- How might the costume support the physical nature of the piece?
- Is there a clear divide between the four-legged animals and the two-legged man: crutches for legs, bandaged hands to look like trotters and so forth?

- Will you use masks? If so, how and when?

- Does your group wish to use songs, and if so what instruments are needed and how are voices going to be amplified?

- What sound effects are needed in order to create the world of the play?

- Is it necessary to distort voices electronically in order to exaggerate an actor's animal tone?

- Would sound effects of political speeches or mass rallies help to reinforce the communist undertones?

**Sound considerations**

The list of possibilities to consider is almost endless, which is exciting if you are your group's designer. Work closely with your actors in order to create a world that is exciting and liberating, but also practical. Grand pieces of set that limit the acting space and restrict the audience's view will be perceived as a weakness.

## Organising your ideas

Hopefully, in experimenting with the exercises on the previous pages, you will have developed ideas on how your finished piece might look. It is now time for you to pull the different strands together to create a structure for your performance. All of your scenes can be scripted, and it is therefore a good idea to nominate specific people to work on developing each scene. You should aim to type the script in an agreed format, not only because it makes it more legible but because it also makes it easier to amend.

As you are piecing your scenes together, think about how you might order the action. There is no need to follow the chronology of the play, but neither should you mix your scenes at random in an attempt to be unpredictable. Your performance marks focus on whether you are able to communicate your intentions. Always think about what you want your play to say to an audience. Keep this question firmly in your mind and constantly review whether you are being successful.

A final scene structure could look something like this:

Directorial concept: how political ideals are corrupted when people in opposition finally gain power.

1. Napoleon monologue – sat at desk in farmhouse – image of power – finishes with the phrase 'long live Animal Farm'.

2. The principles of Animalism – commandments spoken by whole cast in military fashion.

3. The cruelty of man – animals recount life under Jones using Boy's lines. Leading to the Battle of the Cowshed. Celebrations. Dialogue from page 12 and 13. Discussion of democracy. All cast turn to audience and affirm 'All animals are equal.' The cows are milked – comical physical image. Cast turn to audience to explain milk disappearance.

4. Propaganda – multiple characterisation – several Squealers are used to represent the manipulation of the media. Slightly more human in approach as if being interviewed explaining the disappearance of the milk and other issues.

5. Commandment 'Two-legged beings are our enemies,' spoken in unison. Napoleon and Whymper scene highlighting the corruption.

6. Image of depression. Choreographed movement displaying the hard routine at the farm. Use of Boy's lines to convey depression. Boxer's lines shouted over the top: 'We must work harder'. Boxer collapses. Followed by a script of Muriel, Benjamin and Clover voicing their concerns.

7. Show trials. Split staging. Judgement stage right, brutal killing stage left using images of human torture. Statistics and images of political prisoners projected between two scenes. Commandment 'Animals shall never kill animals.'

8. Narration from page 57. 'Years passed ...'.

9. Song 'On the dusty day when I was born', sung in vaudeville style.

10. Clover, Muriel and Benjamin. Page 59. 'I think the world has been turned upside down'. Finishing with amended commandment.

11. Meeting between pigs and men. Edit dialogue to emphasise political dealings. Finish with Boy's line 'The creatures outside ...', followed by 'Long live Animal Farm,' and a sound montage of political rallies.

## An approach model to devising from a theme

66 One of our most used phrases in the process is 'hold your nerve'. There is no room for neurosis or doubt, these will only undermine the process. Hold your nerve, stay open and delight in the privilege of making theatre. 99

Emma Rice, Kneehigh website on devising and rehearsing.

The existing structures that a ready-made story provides for devising work are one way of approaching the unit. The second is through stimulus material that is broad in range and content but linked together under a specific theme or concept. Once you have a focus then the creative juices can start to flow and ideas can come from any source. Always aim for originality and be careful about choosing an area that lends itself to cliché or a concept that you would not do justice to. Choose an area that can remain fresh and can be explored from different perspectives. Stimulus material is endless – it can constitute one word, an image, a piece of music, a face in the street, something in your mind that started with 'what if...' Alternatively, it could be something more concrete, such as a newspaper article, novel, event or short story. The internet is an incredible place for exploration: personal stories and blogs never fail to raise interest, laughter or tears. The idea is that the stimulus is a starting point; it should trigger the group's collective imagination, using all your ideas to go down several different avenues. At this early stage of the devising process, dismiss nothing and record everything however weird or diverse the ideas may be. The fun and the challenge will come from linking the ideas together and finding different ways of presenting them.

Come to one of the early lessons with each member of the group having written a totally random title for a piece of theatre. This can be taken from song lyrics, your own imagination, poetry or anything. Don't think too much about the titles, be adventurous, abstract and don't worry about them sounding ridiculous; 'The man who never knew his name,' 'Only the good die young,' and 'What if …' would all provide good starting points. Within the devising groups, vote on your favourite title. Each member of the group has five minutes to create an outline for a scene in the play with the title you have chosen. After the time has expired, share your scenes. The challenge now is to create a piece of devised work out of the random scenes that have been outlined by trying to work out a basic structure or storyline. This can then be shared with others in the group. This is a quick, fun exercise that should show how creative you can be when you allow yourself some freedom.

Over the next few pages we are going to take you through the development of a specific devising idea. We will look at how you might explore a concept and develop its dramatic potential. We will use examples to illustrate each point, and you may find it useful to use the sample exercises or adapt them to make them more appropriate for your work. Remember the devising process should be fun, so if you are not enjoying the activity, or if you are finding the suggestions limiting, then move on to the next section. Don't allow your ideas to become stale.

## Stimulus: dream and reality

What are you first thoughts when given the headings 'dream' and 'reality'? Try to focus on your personal responses to the two words; there will be plenty of opportunities to share your ideas with the group.

On a sheet of paper spend a minute recording any ideas that you can think of related to these two words. Don't censor yourself; whatever springs to mind at this stage is good, whether they are images, phrases, music or stories. Ask yourself questions about what the words dream and reality mean. Why do people dream? Are there different levels of reality? After you have finished writing, discuss your words with the rest of the group. Have any common ideas emerged? Did anyone create anything that is an original or a surprising way of perceiving the stimulus? Consider the theatrical potential of the ideas that have been presented.

> 66 We look to surprise each other, to take leaps in the dark but there is no given formula for making the work. If we were to have a manifesto it might include words like generosity, passion, bravery, humility, ambition, instinct and irreverence. 99
>
> Mike Sheppard, company director, Kneehigh.

### Devising tip

From the earliest stage you should keep a note-book to update after every practical session. This will become your bible as the process develops and should be kept with you at all times whenever an idea comes into your head or a stimulus presents itself. Sketches, drawings, cuttings and notes will help you to keep a track of the process and will also be vital in tackling the Supporting Written Evidence document that will be covered in pages 46-60 of this guide. Make a note of ideas that both worked and didn't work, giving reasons why some ideas were accepted and some rejected. Remember the piece will evolve and alter as time goes by, even up to moments before your final performance, and this is an essential art of the process that needs to be recorded. It might be an idea to head up your book with the six guiding questions that the exam board give.

Theatre is, by its very nature, a form that relies on the imagination. As actors and designers, we have the power to take the audience on a journey into a fantastical world. Set, costume, lighting and sound can be extremely detailed, and can be combined with realistic acting to create a naturalistic truth. However, we can also manipulate conventions in order to generate our own world. We do not always need props and sets to create a sense of place. If an actor walks on stage with a bucket of water, points to it and says to the audience 'the Mediterranean Sea', we accept his ideas and trust him. If he sits, takes his shoes and socks off and bathes his feet, we are automatically transported into a different country. Don't limit your piece by always thinking about ideas in a literal way.

### Using the stimulus material

During the AS course, a lot of your practical work would have been heavily influenced by scripted text. At A2, you are expected to take a more inventive approach, generating ideas that will help to shape the piece. In order to help you with this process, we are going to look at three other resources that will hopefully provide you with some ways of accessing the work. Take time to explore each piece of work in turn, and make notes on what you have learnt. Ultimately, they may impact on the form, style and content of your piece, and it is important that you are able to relate your final ideas back to different elements of your research when you write up your Written Evidence document.

### DV8

DV8 Physical Theatre is an exciting and challenging dance company. They use familiar images and extend these into a new physical language that comments on individuals and their role in society. The company often explore ideas of isolation, identity and all of their work, accessible from their website www.dv8.co.uk, provides a rich vein of stimulus material.

> ❝The straightjacket of masculinity defines itself in 'don'ts': don't walk like that, don't talk like that, don't wear particular clothes or colours, or don't show certain feelings. It's not that men don't express feelings – it's just that the feelings they show are not always the ones they actually feel. Men have historically oppressed women, but how oppressive have they been to themselves and one another?❞
>
> Lloyd Newson, director of DV8, quoted at www.dv8.co.uk.

*Enter Achilles* (1996) takes the concept of masculinity and explores it within the contemporary setting of a pub. The traditional images of men propping up the bar, the jukebox, the pool table, the fruit machine and, of course, the alcohol are all present, but are distorted to form a new take on traditional stereotypes. They create a world of group strength and individual vulnerability, where the ability to control both your own emotions and the behaviour of others is a sign of power. The piece touches on a range of quite complex ideas, which are expressed through movement rather than words. Physical images convey ideas and attitudes of mind rather than relying on words. Ultimately, this leaves an ambiguity to the work, but this uncertainty helps to maintain interest.

### Further viewing

The video of *Enter Achilles* (PAL 2708-VI, 1996) and other DV8 productions can be purchased from www.dancebooks.co.uk.

Watch the DV8 video armed with your notebooks. Record anything that makes an impact on you, be it a piece of group movement, the significance of costume, music, and key relationships. There are many complex physical moves in DV8 that you might think you cannot come close to, but if you can isolate a moment or a movement, and then experiment with interpreting it in your own way through physical exploration, then you might be surprised by the results you achieve.

Take the image of the glass as a symbol of male power and control; something that every male aspires to, the prize at the end of a race, the full pint. Set a glass, or symbol of a glass up high in the space; the whole group starts at the opposite end to where the prize is and, in slow motion accompanied by appropriate music that is grand and heroic, start to race for the pint. You might decide on different status levels within the group that would affect how each individual moves in their quest for the pint. Introduce rules: all members of the group must be in physical contact with each other at all times, facial expressions must be exaggerated and cartoon-like, every man running for himself. Play around with speed of movement, freeze the whole image, encourage different levels and clambering over each other to reach the goal. What happens when the prize is reached? Elicit both celebrations and commiserations. Look to exaggerate and mock the stupidity of male behaviour in this scene.

Once you've watched the DV8 video of *Enter Achilles*, think about how its themes can link in to 'dream' and 'reality', with its exploration of suppressed emotion and secret lives. From your initial instinctive notes that you made while watching, you may now want to order them under the following guiding questions:

- What comments were the director and choreographer making about contemporary masculinity?

- How was this meaning communicated through dance?

- How did sound and music create mood and atmosphere?

- Choose three striking images and describe them. Why did they have such a strong impact?

- How might you use these ideas in your devising piece?

## The poetry of Sylvia Plath

Sylvia Plath's poetry is a hugely valuable resource for any piece of devised theatre. As a confessional poet, Plath explores highly personal and sometimes horrific aspects of her life within her work. The graphic nature of her images and material is sometimes violent and confrontational and difficult to understand. The important thing when looking at her work as a piece of stimulus material is that the strength of emotion is vividly conveyed through arresting images that can be adapted and used within the piece. You do not need to understand every phrase that Plath writes in order to use her within your devising work.

Plath was born in Boston in 1932. Her father died when she was eight, an act of betrayal as she saw it and an event that figures heavily throughout her poetry. As a child she showed flair in creative writing and went on to take summer classes at Harvard University. Plath went on to study at Smith College, an independent women's liberal arts college in Massachusetts. It was here that she made

**Plath's life**

### Further reading

Plath's semi-autobigraphical novel *The Bell Jar* (1963) is both disturbing and darkly humourous and provides a real insight into a descent into mental breakdown. General information, resources and essays on Plath can be found at www. sylviaplath.de

### Further viewing

To hear Sylvia Plath read her poem 'Daddy', go to www.youtube.com/watch?v=6hHjctqSBwM

### Further study

Plath's poetry would work well by interpreting it in the light of Artaud's theories and practices. There is lots of common ground in their focus on the expression of emotion and suffering. For further information on Artaud refer to *Edexcel AS Drama and Theatre Studies Study Guide* (Rhinegold 2008), pages 34-43.

66 In this age of gender conflicts, broken families, and economic inequities, Plath's forthright language speaks loudly about the anger of being both betrayed and powerless. 99

Linda Wagner Martin, *The Oxford Companion to Women's Writing in the United States* (OUP 1995).

the first attempt on her life by taking an overdose of sleeping pills and received treatment for clinical depression. Her troubled and complex marriage to the English poet Ted Hughes shaped most of her adult life. The relationship was full of friction and creative and cultural differences. Plath's isolation living in England was further emphasised when her husband had an affair. Her feelings of anger and betrayal are recorded in her poems of the period. In 1962 the couple separated and she moved to a flat with her two children. A year later she committed suicide by gassing herself in the oven while her children slept.

It is Plath's personal struggle with life and relationships that form the centre piece of her poetry. It is the vivid style of her writing that is so appealing to a deviser. Plath's dream-like images clash with the harsh reality of her pain and suffering as she lays her life and emotion bare to the audience. Throughout her poetry she articulates a dark humour that gives another level of interest.

One particular Plath poem that is worthy of further exploration, because it typifies her style, raw emotion and subject content is 'Daddy'. The poem was written in 1962 and deals with the poet's relationship with her father. She re-creates him as a Nazi, with the poet in the role of a Jew, to symbolise the oppressive influence he had on her life. The language is violent and extreme and the repeated, dark words make a strong impact on the reader.

In your devising groups, read through the poem individually. Underline any key words or short phrases that stand out as effective or striking images – no more than two lines, but as little as one word. For the second reading, nominate one person to read it again, but this time any member of the group can join in at random by reading aloud any of the key words or phrases that they have highlighted. Try and get the emotion that Plath is evidently feeling. This should result in quiet a powerful collage of voices of different pitch, volume and tone. Now spilt into groups of four to six and agree on three of the strongest images that you are going to dramatise. Strong examples may include:

- 'I never could talk to you. / The tongue stuck in my jaw. / It stuck in a barb wire snare. / Ich, ich, ich, ich'

  **OR**

- 'They pulled me out of the sack, / And they stuck me together with glue.'

Create a frozen image using your bodies, connecting them in an imaginative way. You are trying to create an abstract sculpture, not a literal creation of the words. Now add the words, play with them through repetition or multiple voices. Once all three sculptures have been created, find a way to move from one to the next without breaking the mood of the performance. Share your work with others in the group and give constructive feedback.

In 1994, the BBC *Horizon* programme documented the story of Genie. Born in California, Genie spent the first 13 years of her childhood locked in a room devoid of human contact in a misguided assumption by her parents that she was being protected from the world outside. The room was bare with the exception of a potty chair to which she was tied to for long periods and an oversized cot. The programme traces Genie's development after her discovery and examines the motivations behind the various scientists who came into her life. Genie's circumstances were seen as a perfect opportunity for scientific research into the delayed development of a child. The nature/nurture argument is examined as is her acquisition of language and her social interaction. The documentary ends with an admission of failure on the part of the scientists with Genie being returned to various care homes where she remains today. The documentary raises a number of very difficult questions about the role of scientific research in our modern world. This truthful account of someone desperately trying to adapt to a new reality is fascinating and emotionally disturbing, verging on the voyeuristic at times. Recreating a story full of moral complexities with which a contemporary audience can associate would be a highly challenging and rewarding process; there are no easy answers and no absolute rights and wrongs.

As a deviser approaching this stimulus there are many areas to consider:

- The documentary style that provides multiple narrative and perspectives on the story; each tells a different version of the truth. Whom do we believe?

- The detached nature of the programme that steps away from emotional attachment with Genie, instead allowing the audience to make up their own mind.

- Was Genie's condition a result of her circumstances (nurture) or was she damaged as a result of a mental condition (nature)?

- Genie's perception of reality; what was normal for her in the first 13 years of her life?

- Genie's attitudes to her mother and father in those early years and to the various scientists and social workers who came in to her life.

- Key images and moments that were significant to Genie – the kite, the balloons, the storing of liquids.

- The way that Genie's circumstances affected her physical movement.

- Genie's dreams and nightmares.

The abstract concepts of dream and reality could still appear a little daunting. You may now have created a range of disconnected ideas that do not link together to make a coherent scene order. Don't panic. Such freedom is healthy at this stage. The more ideas you have the greater chance you have of creating a vibrant and exciting piece of

**The story of Genie**

Genie is not the protagonist's real name but a symbol of the Genie released from the constraint of the magic lamp.

**Further viewing**

The original *Horizon* programme is available to view in six parts on YouTube from manwithaplan999. Alternatively your psychology or English Language department might have a copy. More information about Genie's life can be found at www.feralchildren.com/en/showchild.php?ch–genie. The site contains articles, transcripts and details of books relating to her development and ultimate regression.

**Further viewing**

A cross-reference to Genie's story comes in the 1970 French film *The Wild Child* by Francois Truffaut. Set in the 18th century, it follows the true story of a young boy discovered living on his own in the forest and being taken in by a local doctor who observes his attempts to be integrated into French society. Other films with similar themes are *Greystoke; the Legend of Tarzan* (1984) and *The Elephant Man* (1980).

**Think about...**

Using the bullets as possible starting points for practical exploration, try piecing together fragments from her early life, using frozen images overlaid with a narrative voice. Try writing an interior monologue for Genie at various stages in her life - improvise conversations with the parents, recreate Genie's dreams, take key images as a starting point for physical exploration, such as the balloon as an image of freedom. The possibilities when devising are limitless. One small aspect of the documentary might reach out and grab you.

theatre. In order to ensure you are thinking as diversely as possible, we have put together our own list of ideas on this theme:

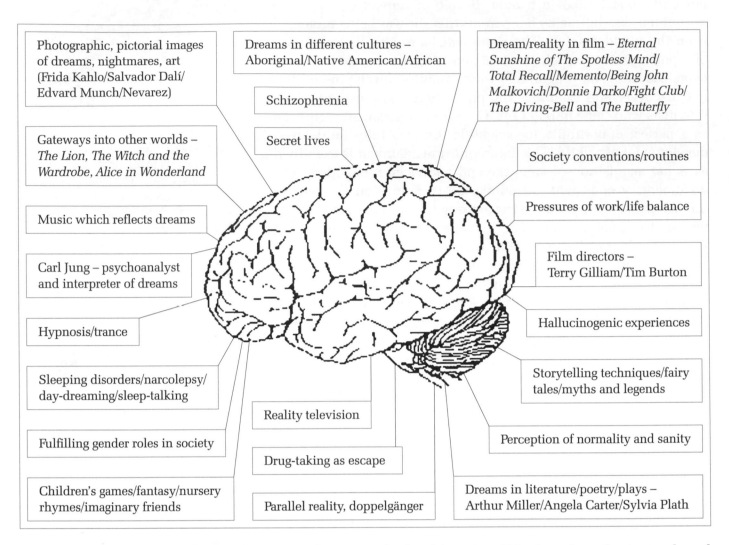

Photographic, pictorial images of dreams, nightmares, art (Frida Kahlo/Salvador Dalí/Edvard Munch/Nevarez)

Dreams in different cultures – Aboriginal/Native American/African

Dream/reality in film – *Eternal Sunshine of The Spotless Mind/Total Recall/Memento/Being John Malkovich/Donnie Darko/Fight Club/The Diving-Bell* and *The Butterfly*

Schizophrenia

Gateways into other worlds – *The Lion, The Witch and the Wardrobe, Alice in Wonderland*

Secret lives

Society conventions/routines

Music which reflects dreams

Pressures of work/life balance

Carl Jung – psychoanalyst and interpreter of dreams

Film directors – Terry Gilliam/Tim Burton

Hypnosis/trance

Hallucinogenic experiences

Sleeping disorders/narcolepsy/day-dreaming/sleep-talking

Storytelling techniques/fairy tales/myths and legends

Reality television

Fulfilling gender roles in society

Perception of normality and sanity

Drug-taking as escape

Children's games/fantasy/nursery rhymes/imaginary friends

Parallel reality, doppelgänger

Dreams in literature/poetry/plays – Arthur Miller/Angela Carter/Sylvia Plath

**Research** Part of your marks for this unit will be based on the research and exploration you undertake. The exact nature of this research can vary tremendously. You may focus on a very personal story where a lot of your work will be spent interviewing an individual about their past and the events that have shaped their life. Conversely, you could focus on an idea of which you have limited experience, such as an aspect of mental health. In this instance, it would be vital that you research the medical conditions associated with the illness and society's reactions to sufferers if you are to create a piece that's fully informed and devoid of stereotypes. A lot of the material that you come across will be sensitive and personal and will need to be handled in a mature and intelligent fashion. However, do not restrict yourself by only researching the final idea. This is limiting and can prevent you from developing the potential within your initial thoughts. It is important that you enjoy learning about different topics and take advantage of this point in the project to explore areas in detail.

Split the group up into smaller sub-groups. It is vital that everyone is given a specific area of responsibility to explore.

If everyone has a sense of ownership of the work then the end result will only be positive.

As a group, highlight the most interesting areas from the brainstorm and then group them into areas of research. Your list might look something like this:

- Reality television culture
- Sleeping disorders, narcolepsy, hallucination
- Artists' interpretations of dreams in film, art, music and literature
- Schizophrenia – including personal accounts
- Institutions – both mental-health and social
- The brain and how it works – looking at strokes and mental illness
- Mental torture, sleep deprivation
- Religion and the afterlife.

Allocate each sub-group a topic and set the task of preparing a 20-minute practical interactive workshop on the ideas that they have researched. Lay down a rule that each member of the sub-group must take an equal role in the presentation of the work. This workshop will be valuable in several ways. Firstly, it helps to generate ideas and pool the personal research that has taken place. Secondly, it allows for the group to bond and to trust each other in the work that they are sharing. Thirdly, it gives every member of the group the opportunity to experience taking the lead in a workshop. Further on in the process it is vital that every member feels confident in leading the group through the various scenes that they have devised or scripted.

Essentially each sub-group will be leading a short drama lesson. It should be structured along the lines of:

> Ideas for warm-up activities and practical exercises can be found in the following pages in the Exploring Ideas section of this guide.

- Warm-up activities and games related to the specific topic (5 minutes)
- Two or three main practical activities that show variety and practical ways in to the topic title (10 minutes)
- A plenary in which the central ideas of the workshop are evaluated (5 minutes).

Each group will need to provide an A4 handout that summarises the ideas covered in the presentation and the practical activities that were undertaken. It may also list useful website addresses or other references for further research.

As you experience each workshop, listen carefully to the ideas they discuss, and start to finalise in your mind which areas are worth focusing on in your piece. You might also look at the way the ideas were presented and gain a good understanding of the ways different people work. Once the presentations have been delivered, share your thoughts with the other members of your group and try to be precise about the sort of theatre you are looking to produce. Use performances that you have seen during the course as a reference point. It is one of the key focuses of the Supporting

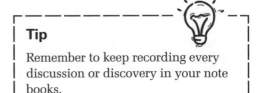

**Tip**

Remember to keep recording every discussion or discovery in your note books.

Written Evidence document that you recognise how existing practitioners, live theatre and playwrights have influenced you.

## Formulating your ideas

You should be in a position where you have discussed a range of ideas and rejected certain topics that lack potential. It is now time to narrow your ideas to a specific area that you can focus on during the devising process. It is essential that you do not try and include too many issues in your piece. This can be confusing for both performers and audience if there is not a clear indication of what you are trying to say in your piece. Do you want to follow the journey of a central character (played at some stage by all members of the group) with which the audience can identify or are you looking for a more collage-based choral piece under a common theme? Remember that you are being assessed both as an individual and as part of a group, so an ensemble approach is vital.

## Structuring your piece

There are many ways to put a piece of drama together. Remember you are performing a piece of live theatre and do not have to be tied to any constraints of chronology or time. Look to surprise your audience and give them the unexpected. Ask questions of them early on and provide hints for the answers elsewhere in your piece. Make them work. Challenge them when you can. When planning a structure be careful not to put similar scenes together. Two monologues one after the other may be too repetitive. Similarly too many realistic scenes side by side will give the audience nowhere to go. Hit them with a surprise. Explode the action with a whole-group movement piece when the audience least expect it. Think carefully about the impact you can make at the very start of our piece and what you want the audience to leave with at the end.

In your group, plan the structure for your piece. Consider key scenes that you might wish to include and how the action might develop. Do not worry too much about listing every scene in your piece, but try to be clear about the direction of the performance and its intended impact on the audience.

Try to formalise your ideas into a directorial concept, a ruling idea that explains what your piece will mean to a contemporary audience. This should be between 100 and 200 words, and should be as precise as possible. Avoid language that sounds pretentious and ultimately means nothing. It should be something you can keep referring back to during the devising process to see if your ideas are still on track.

## Exploring your ideas

It is important to remember that devising should be a fun process. Obviously, at A level you should be interested in learning about

---

**Devising tip**

You must not be precious about the structure that you come up with here. Do not limit yourselves by feeling that you have to stick to the ideas that you have planned. Devised work evolves and changes with new ideas coming in all the time. Just remember to keep recording every change in your note books.

---

Ideas from groups who have completed this unit from a dream and reality stimulus in the past have included:

**Balloon** – Inspired by an image of freedom from Genie, one girl tries to free herself from the multiple personalities that exist within her.

**Haze** – A collage of scenes that look at the highs and lows of alcohol use and abuse.

**Chatting with Charlie** – stuck in a coma and desperately trying to communicate with the outside world, the story is told about a girl's relationship with drugs.

different theatrical genres, but for many people it is the practical work that brings most enjoyment. This unit should be no exception. It is important that you resist the temptation to sit down as a group and spend lesson after lesson discussing ideas without applying them physically. This can be a very slow method of working, and more often than not you will find that ideas that work in theory are not as effective in practice. Try the following exercises as a way of motivating yourselves to create.

### A lively warm-up

Make up a CD of lively and high-tempo, sugary pop songs to get everyone loose and ready for work. Play the music nice and loud. Choose a profession – a chef or a private detective. Ask everyone to think of a mimed movement that goes with that profession – frying an egg/spying from behind a newspaper. Everyone does their own movement in time to the music, repeated like a routine. Ask them to formulate a second movement, then a third then a fourth, dancing all the time. The leader calls out the number and everyone performs their movement associated with the number. The activity can be extended by adding emotions to the movement. Pair up, with each member of the pair at either end of the room. The pairs are in a night club and flirting with each other, still maintaining their dance moves. Speed up the moves and slow them down – have fun with placing the group in different locations. This is a good exercise to release inhibitions and to establish a fun and productive working environment.

### Let's all ...

This is a simple exercise that works on the idea of students accepting every idea that is suggested – an important rule for improvisation. Anyone at any time can call out a 'Let's all ...' instruction, but it must be in an extremely enthusiastic tone. For example: 'Let's all pretend to be on pogo sticks!' or 'Let's all top up our tans at the beach!' The rest of the group must reply with a loud and confident: 'Yes, let's!' This is followed by everyone acting out the activity that has been described. This continues until someone shouts out a new 'Let's all ...'. The game helps to free up the imagination and encourages you to respond quickly to other people's ideas. A variation you could try allows for people to step out of the game if they stop feeling enthusiastic about a suggestion, which means that you are likely to find the most enthusiastic member at the end left performing an activity on their own.

> **Devising tip**
>
> Always try to avoid sitting on a chair unless it is essential for the scene. It can prevent you from acting with your whole body. Think how many teachers actually teach you successfully from a chair. More often than not, they walk around in an attempt to maintain your interest. Similarly, as an actor, you should always work hard to ensure the audience is fully engaged with your performance.

### Yes and ...

This is a storytelling exercise to use in pairs. It is a good way of exploring the potential of scenes, or simply preparing your mind for improvisation. Like 'Let's all', it stresses the importance of accepting your partner's idea, but it also introduces the concept of developing the scene by adding a new idea to it.

The first person begins with an opening statement that contains a sense of action and location. Their partner then states the phrase 'Yes and …', and then continues with a statement of their own. The first person then comes back in with 'Yes and …' once again, before starting another statement. The exercise continues until the scenario dries up. For example:

We nervously walked into my boss' office.

YES AND he was ignoring us.

YES AND his desk was covered with angry letters from customers.

YES AND these letters were all referring to our incompetence.

YES AND you had to say something.

YES AND when I apologised his face turned purple with rage.

On one level, this is a narrative activity involving at least two characters, but you could try adapting the exercise to involve a performance in which the actors physically recreate what they describe – for example, walking into the room or apologising. The game could also be used with two people speaking as one. If your play is about an individual's addiction to drugs, try having two members of the group working as a pair to give one person's viewpoint. For example:

I enjoy being alone in a public place.

YES AND I get great pleasure from ignoring people at bus stops.

YES AND when they ask me some pathetic question I stare back at them.

YES AND I imagine that their faces are melting.

> "After the preview performance, we decided our piece needed restructuring as we had cut many of the linking scenes. We tried to plan the structure of our piece so that we achieved the best response possible from the audience. We did this by drawing a flow chart of our scenes and putting them together in an order so that scenes of a realistic nature separated the non-naturalistic scenes. This meant that the unnerving scenes were more likely to make the audience uncomfortable as if they were all bunched together they would lose their effect as they would become normal and predictable."
>
> Notebook entry from A level Theatre Studies student.

It is important when choosing the appropriate forms for your piece that there is variety within it. A combination of realistic scenes that focus on development of character and emotion should be balanced with more stylised abstract work. This will give balance to your piece.

### Balance

Choosing the most appropriate form for a scene can be difficult, and it is important to avoid being clever simply for cleverness' sake. Students can sometimes search for complicated ideas just because they have a desire to be different. Groups often explain unusual or confusing scene structures by saying that they were looking to challenge an audience's preconceptions. Creating challenging theatre is healthy, and experimentation is important, but you still need to create a coherent performance that communicates your ideas successfully. Sometimes the simplest ideas are the most effective.

It is good to get a balance of tone within your piece. We have already written about the need for balance in structure and form, and it is also true of tone. Don't make your piece consistently dark and full of angst. Like a painting it needs lighter moments to lift the piece and give the audience respite. These moments can be the highlights of your piece. Where the scenes are placed in your piece is very important. Think about providing contrasts for your audience – light against dark, humour against pathos, monologue against choral work, noise against silence. As a rule, if the audience could see the next scene coming, then you haven't worked hard enough.

We list here a range of techniques with which you can experiment. This is not meant to limit your creativity. They are simply suggested forms which may help you to realise the potential of any of your scenes.

**Monologue.** This is an ideal way of providing insight into a character's mind. However, be careful not to be too simplistic. Don't let your character reveal exactly what they are feeling. Use a personal story as a metaphor for their emotional state. A childhood memory of being lost at a funfair could suggest to the audience why they might be unhappy, despite apparently having everything that they need. A simple action such as eating an apple or completing a newspaper crossword can also help to reveal elements of the character and be a very powerful image on the stage.

**Choral monologue.** This is a variation on the idea of a monologue, but instead of having one actor on stage it allows all the cast to speak as one character. The convention will need to be carefully established – perhaps the actor playing the protagonist could speak first and then, once they have been speaking for a few lines, others can join in. The different voices can speak alternately, in unison or even by speaking different lines of dialogue at the same time to reflect the confusion in the character's mind.

**Duologue.** This is an effective way of representing two different perspectives on a complex issue. However, be careful not to patronise the audience by making the dialogue too simplistic. You don't want the characters simply to voice the stereotypical views on your central theme – unless of course this is your intention. Nor does one character need to be persuaded about the other character's way of thinking. Choose carefully which character should be first to enter the stage space and which the last to leave it. This can be a simple way of manipulating the audience's response to the scene. Ensure that you have considered movement within this technique, so that each character moves when the conversation or line dictates.

**Repeated scenes.** These can be used to punctuate your piece, to give the audience something to hang on to or a point of reference. Repeated scenes can highlight the routine of certain characters and come at key points throughout your piece. As they reappear there might be subtle changes within them to illustrate, for example, the degeneration of a relationship. The husband kisses his wife goodbye in the morning and she gives him sandwiches with his

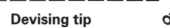

**Devising tip**

Be careful about having a truly realistic approach to your piece. In past years, examiners have commented on realistic performances that appear to be based around a series of monologues simply strung together. Such pieces have the danger of being too much like soap-opera, and even verge on a style more appropriate to film. Always remember that you are devising a piece of theatre to be presented on stage in front of a live audience.

favourite filling; as the scenes are repeated the filling becomes blander and the kiss less warm, until there is no kiss and no sandwich.

**Multiple duologues.** If you are looking to highlight the routine in a person's life, try experimenting with the following idea in groups of four or six. Half of the group should represent the protagonist; the other half should represent this same person in their routine – for example a husband, employer or teenage son – and the two or three actors playing this role will always speak the same lines of dialogue. The aim of this exercise is to have each group of characters speaking in unison, with the lines of the protagonist slightly different for each actor. The lines of Carol 1, 2 and 3 in the example below should be spoken simultaneously.

EMPLOYERS:      Carol, love, you couldn't just do me a little favour?

It won't take long.

CAROL 1:      Of course, Mr Stevens.

CAROL 2:      Of course, Mr Stevens … but … can I just ask about …

CAROL 3:      Of course, Mr Stevens. I would love to do you an incy-wincy, insignificant favour which will be a total waste of my highly pressured time.

EMPLOYERS:      Splendid.

**Dislocating action.** Occasionally, you may find that a realistic duologue lacks action. Consequently, it can be difficult to stage. For example, imagine a scene in which an unwanted guest arrives at the front door. You decide that the scene should be slow-paced with awkward pauses, but you are worried that the actors will spend a lot of time facing each other, which will give the audience a limited view of their facial expressions. Dislocating the action involves both actors facing the audience, but imagining that the other character is actually in front of them. This opens up the scene and allows for greater subtlety. There may be a natural point in the dialogue to stop dislocating – for example, when both characters move into the house.

**Doppelgänger.** This is essentially a literary concept, made most famous in the novel *Dr Jekyll and Mr Hyde* by Robert Louis Stevenson. A doppelgänger is a kind of evil twin, used here it refers to a suppressed side of a person's character that is rarely seen. It is the side that doesn't conform to society's expectations. In a realistic scene, if you want to reveal the hidden thoughts of a character, you will rely on revealing the subtext through subtle changes in tone or expression. However, you could choose to introduce a character's doppelgänger on stage. A simple example could be with a child being told off by a teacher. Instead of having one child on stage, have two actors playing the same character. Initially, they should behave identically, but eventually the doppelgänger should become more and more frustrated, saying what the character really wants to say rather than what the situation dictates that they should say. While they do this, the real child should speak as normal, ignoring their other self. This is a particularly useful device when portraying a character who is finding it difficult to cope with reality.

**Multiple narrative.** It is important to remember that your piece should be an ensemble performance, with all actors working hard to establish the style of the performance. Ideally, no one should leave the stage, and instead you should consider how and where the actors could be positioned when not involved in the main action, in order to contribute to the mood of each scene. By using the group as narrators, you can manipulate time and location by describing what action has occurred between scenes. You may wish to use existing words from literature to act as a metaphor for your central character's mental state. For example, taking some lines from Lewis Carroll's *Alice in Wonderland* could emphasise how a character is looking to escape from their current existence.

**Physical images.** It is important in devised work to realise the physical potential of each scene. Physical images can be used as photographs to reinforce the action implied in a monologue or a piece of narrative. These images can be briefly animated to give the audience a brief sample of a certain event or attitude of mind. However, they could also be used as a backdrop to a scene. An image of poverty could be juxtaposed with a scene about financial dealings. You may even wish to use members of your group to act as walls or furniture.

**Choreographed movement.** DV8's *Enter Achilles* should have helped you to realise the potential power of choreographed movement in a scene. It could be used simply to highlight the routine in someone's life. For example, you could recreate a stylised version of a busy office with repeated movements being synchronised with music. This idea could be extended to the scene changes where the same business-like behaviour could be used during the bringing-on or removing of set items. However, you could look at making the movement more abstract, where it represents an emotion or state of mind. This can be extremely effective, although you must be careful not to let the sequence last too long as it can affect the pace of your piece.

**Multiple locations.** Complex scene and costume changes do little to maintain the pace and flow of your piece. Think carefully about how many props and set you actually need. Can they be represented by one prop that is used in different ways or even better by using the physicality of your actors to create the location? Music can place a scene in a particular place as can a representational prop – refer back to the bucket of water as the Mediterranean Sea. The cleverer your ideas are for switching between locations and settings without disrupting your piece, the more you will be rewarded.

**Multimedia presentations.** More and more theatre companies are experimenting with projections and multimedia work. Well-edited film sequences or powerful images can be visually striking and emotionally intense. However, poor-quality work can be a

" People who say yes get rewarded with adventures. People who say no get rewarded with security. Too much security is boring and too much not knowing is scary. The audience don't want to watch everyone looking terrified. "

Lee Simpson, 'Improbable Theatre', quoted in *Devising: A Handbook for Drama and Theatre Students* by Gill Lamden (Hodder Arnold 2000).

distraction, with complex and unreliable technology ultimately undermining the whole piece. If this is an area in which you feel confident and it would be appropriate for your performance, then use it, but do make sure that you allow plenty of time to rehearse properly with the equipment.

## To script or not to script

As a drama and theatre studies student, you should enjoy the practical demands of creating work in rehearsal. Part of the excitement stems from watching the piece evolve as you experiment with different ideas practically, swapping roles in an attempt to find an appropriate way of presenting your ideas to an audience. This is an essential dynamic of the course and, however you approach the work, it is important that this is kept firmly at the heart of the process.

In order for you to have a firm direction about where the piece is going you need to come to practical sessions fully prepared. This may entail structuring key pieces of information into a monologue or providing a framework in which to tell a particular story. It may be that you decide to completely script a key scene. If you decide to script try and hear the voices of the different characters and consider the specific language they might use. Look at scripts of playwrights who you have encountered during the course to help you achieve your intended effect.

It is important in the early stages to keep your scene order flexible. The dream and reality stimulus gives you freedom to experiment with different patterns of time. If you feel brave, you may wish to leave the scene ordering as one of your last tasks. Write all of the scenes on separate sheets of paper and move them around until you find a well-balanced and interesting piece of drama.

However you choose to rehearse your work, it is important that you are frequently performing your ideas to other people in order to gauge their response. Remember that you should always be focusing on the impact of your work on an audience, and regular showings will help to monitor whether or not you are achieving your aim. You cannot afford to be precious about your work even though you have created it. Listen to the advice that is given, take it in and then decide whether changes need to be implemented.

Unit 3 is a richly rewarding unit, and in devising, many students find themselves. Make sure you remain open and honest with each other throughout the process. Enjoy the experience and learn from both the strengths and weaknesses of your final piece. Having visualised and executed a complete performance you are now in a strong position to approach the next unit in recognising the wide variety of practical approaches that can be applied to a text, specifically those that you will tackle in Unit 4.

### Further study

Two playwrights who are particularly strong on natural dialogue who might be worth referring to are Harold Pinter and Samuel Beckett. Pinter's *Betrayal* plays in reverse which may be of interest when looking at structuring your piece.

### Devising tip

Many local theatres will have examples of devised work for you to go and see. These may even be followed by post-show discussions with the company. Use this as an opportunity to understand how other actors work. The Theatre Royal, Bath regularly stages performances of A-level devised work under the title *Endgames*. Such performances are an ideal showcase for student work and a chance for you to see what you could achieve.

## Supporting Written Evidence

The Supporting Written Evidence document is part of your overall assessment for this unit, alongside your practical involvement in the whole devising process and your final performance. All three stages combine to give an overall assessment based on the areas below:

- Research and exploration

- Development and structure

- Performance

- Evaluation.

In no more than 3,500 words (around 6–8 printed sides of A4) the document traces the journey of your piece from the initial ideas through the various stages of rehearsal to the final performance. You are also invited to offer an evaluation of the process. The document is assessed by your teacher alongside your role in the process and the performance and a sample is then sent for moderation. Although the exam board do not prescribe how the document should be written they do offer six published headings to guide you in the right direction. These appear below:

- How is the initial material being researched and developed at significant stages during the process of creating drama?

- How effectively are you personally exploring and developing your role(s)?

- How did you and your group explore the possibilities of form, structure and performance style?

- How did the work of established and recognised theatre practitioners, and/or the work of live theatre, influence the way in which your devised response developed?

- How successfully did your final piece communicate your aims and intentions for the piece to your audience?

- How effectively did the social, cultural, historical/political context of the piece communicate with your audience?

On looking at these questions, the importance of a note book that is continuously updated with each discovery throughout the process becomes obvious. The note book should be 'evaluative, analytical and reflective' ('Edexcel Getting Started', Pearson, 2007). You must ensure you keep your notebook updated.

As suggested earlier, it might be advisable to head up your note book with the six guiding questions. Date each entry so that you can trace the journey more effectively. Focus on the three core areas of drama writing: **WHAT**, **HOW** and **WHY**.

> Record these assessment headings somewhere prominent in your notebook to serve as a consistent reminder about the way you should be writing.

**Tip**

You should not see the written evidence as six essays, but instead as a living record of the process divided into six areas, complete with notes, plans, script extracts, cuttings, images, all balanced with analytical commentary.

**The process of writing**

**What** you did during the sessions. This can be a moment in rehearsal, a scene or a relationship; a specific piece of research, a prop, a piece of music or a costume.

**How** you did the work. This documents the practical exploration of that moment through its staging, characterisation, movement, entrances and exits, voice or relationships. It also covers alternative approaches, problems that arose during rehearsal and solutions that were found.

**Why** you covered the material. This documents the reasons behind the choice of that moment and its inclusion in your piece, why it changed in form or structure, what it contributes to the piece as a whole, and what it adds contextually to your piece.

It is recommended that you review your notebook regularly to avoid the notes becoming meaningless and the content forgotten. Try to begin to structure them into the demands of the six guiding questions. At this stage don't discard anything. Remember the questions should not be dealt with in any chronological order, with the obvious exception of the evaluation question on your final performance.

Rough drafts of most of the questions should exist in some form before your final performance. The process afterwards is to formalise these drafts into answers that directly address the specific demands of each question. Don't worry if things have changed significantly throughout the rehearsal of your piece. This is an essential part of the devising process and as long as you record why things have changed, scenes being cut and additions made, you will be rewarded. The Written Evidence document should reflect **your** ownership of **your** work. Assessors will be looking to see that you are in control of the material that you are writing about and the decisions that have been made are fully justified in the context of the work

The following pages will go through each question in detail, breaking down possible approaches. We will also give examples of students' own responses with annotations as to the strengths and weaknesses of the writing:

### 1. How is the initial material being researched and developed at significant stages during the process of creating drama?

The research refers both to the stimulus material given to you by your teacher and any individual research that has been undertaken either for specific scenes or as a general way in to your piece. You are also asked to identify 'significant stages' – that is, key moments in rehearsal when practical advances were made in the development of your material and your piece.

The key focus here must be on the practical application of your research and stimulus material. How did the stimulus material influence your piece in terms of plot outline, style of presentation, images or themes? Your personal research might include articles, video and film extracts, blogs, paintings or poetry. The initial presentations that were suggested earlier in these pages might be a good source of information.

When looking at the 'significant stages' refer to your note books. There will be rehearsals that stand out where significant progress was made or a breakthrough occurred. Write about ideas that were both accepted and rejected as a result of exploration, giving full reasons to justify the choices made. Remember to be specific here.

You can see in the following extract from a student's work, how the familiar style of **WHAT**, **HOW** and **WHY** works in this question. Firstly, **WHAT** is identified – 'the narrative' – it is then given a context and the practical description of **HOW** it was executed is highlighted. The final section links directly to the researched material with a specific technique, such as the use of voice and music together, with a clear indication of **WHY** this was successful.

✐ *Extract 1*

> Over the rehearsal period we developed the narrative to our piece, using Adam's voice on top of the ensemble movement, dance and music in many of the scenes. Welcoming Kate into the drug world, Adam narrates a monologue which the group acts out a dance to, with music also playing. The idea of parting the voice and movement came after watching the Genie video as music over voice successfully created a mood of pathos and sympathy for Genie. In our piece we wanted to go with is idea, which we felt was the best way to take the audience on an emotional journey.

What

How

Why

In second extract below, the student's ownership of the work and explanation of how one image from a film can inspire a whole scene and the style of a piece of work comes across very clearly. There is a strong connection with the material and a real understanding of it. The purpose of the scene in relation to the piece and the intended reaction of the audience are also clearly identified.

*Extract 2*

**What**

**Awareness of context**

**How**

**Note detail of practical example given**

**Why**

Continuing this idea of drugs and how they make you feel positively, we wanted take the audience on a journey and through this incorporate the feeling of a hallucination. This is where we decided to integrate the idea of temptation and excitement through child-like stylisation. We decided to focus on Roald Dahl's *Charlie and the Chocolate Factory*. Since the release of the book in 1964 there has been much speculation on its link to drugs and how it insinuates that temptation and greed are in fact representations of addiction of drugs. For example, many complaints were made concerning the song 'Candy Man' as this is also in reference to a drug dealer. Regardless of whether these statements are true or false, the magical world of Charlie and his factory has aided us in the piece. As a group we decided to watch Tim Burton's version of the film and gather ideas from it. As we watched in awe, getting sucked into the fantasy world of delicious, mouth-watering goodies, the excitable children, the temptation, and greed, it completely reflected what we wanted to show in our piece and how addiction to drugs can take over without you even realising it. In creating our fantasy scene, we decided to take inspiration from the film and create our own magical world through verbal dialogue, mime, synchronised movement and dance. As Adam, playing the wizard, walked in and out of the rest of the actors on stage delivering a monologue with enthusiasm, bewilderment and wonder. The rest of the ensemble moved around firstly creating a mime of entering this new and magical world and eventually developing it into a dance. For example, as Adam said a particular line, one actor on stage would portray it through a movement – in my case I had the line 'strawberry-laced vines'. I stretched my arm out wide, as if to reach high, grasped the lace, leant back and circled it round and round as it dangled above my mouth until I engorged the whole thing, all the while keeping an inane grin fixed on my face to convey the pleasure of taste. Here the audience are completely amazed by this fantasy world and are taken with the actors on stage, to share the magical experience. There were seven different images all together; the scene built as we all carried out the movements in unison to create a dance before increasing to the climax where we all drop to the floor in complete exhaustion trying to show how drugs can take over and control your life, reaching a point of destruction. This was a vital scene in our piece as we conveyed a story through dance, as well as showing the audience a positive feeling through the use of drugs.

Note that this question is written in the present tense and hints that your role(s) will continue to develop up until the very moment of your final performance. The ongoing nature of your development must be stressed to fulfil the requirements of this question.

## 2. How effectively are you personally exploring and developing your role(s)?

This question clearly focuses on the two assessment areas of exploration and development. It is a personal response about you and your roles and, as with all the written evidence, it needs to be written in the first person. There are three stages to this question.

i.  To identify early research into your characters.

ii. How your piece practically developed for you both through individual research and through two or three breakthrough moments in the rehearsal process.

iii. To recognise your role as part of a whole piece and not to see it in isolation. Consider how your role(s) complemented those of others and why it might have been necessary to contrast with other characters for the purpose of emphasis for the audience, for example.

> This might have been achieved by exploring different approaches to a scene, through the discovery of a key monologue from the internet or by applying Stanislavskian techniques to unlock the past of a particular role.

Throughout all three sections you need to make sure that you are critically evaluating the work you have done as the question is asking you to make a judgement on 'how effectively' you are working.

In the extract below we can see a strong sense of the role developing, exploration has been undertaken and clear reasons have been given as to why ideas may be rejected. The practical detail is strong and specific and through the whole section there is a strong awareness of the impact of decisions on the audience.

*Extract 1*

The first scene was used to give the audience a prologue and a glimpse of what was to come without giving the plot away. My role in this scene was to play the girl Katie. We decided to have her sitting centre stage on a stool to create a feeling of isolation and discomfort. Immediately the audience are asking themselves who this girl is. At this point the girl is representing her comatose state; initially I had trouble in deciding how to play her. We could have gone down the stereotypical route and had her slouched in the chair, almost dribbling. We decided this was not the best way to portray her and could have offended the audience. Here my role developed as I chose to play her sat upright, stiffening the body to show both her isolation and separation from normal life but also that there was still an element of control inside her. The character then developed even further as the choice of the foot tapping was introduced. This was to show that there was still an element of life left in her and the control of her hallucinations. This reflects that before her drug usage she was completely in control of her life, now the drugs have taken over and they control her life. This is further reinforced by the stylised puppets moving around her. This disconnection between the girl's limbs and the rest of her body is disturbing for the audience, as they are presented with an unnerving dislocated image.

- → Moment identified
- → Identifies problem
- → Explores idea and rejects with justification
- → Practical exploration with justification
- → Awareness of her role in context with their performers
- → Reference to impact on audience

*Extract 2*

In the second extract we can see a very definite shift in emphasis. By making a decision the group have changed the whole dynamic of the scene. She has also found that it enabled a greater freedom in exploring the stage space and delivered a clearer message to her audience.

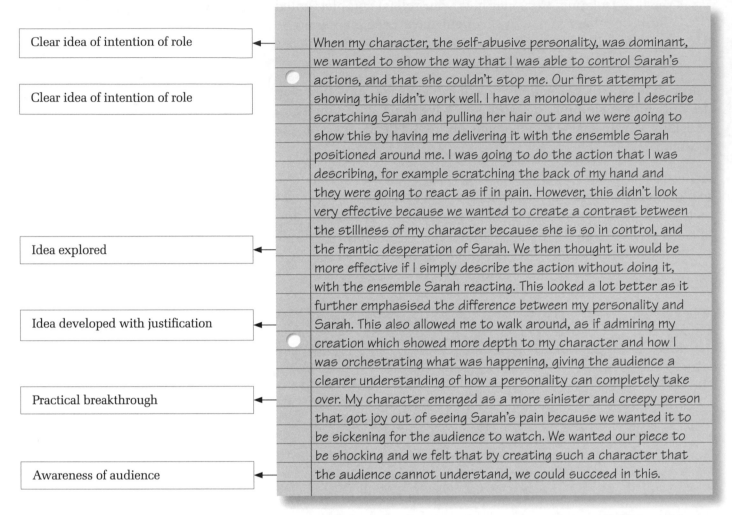

Clear idea of intention of role

Clear idea of intention of role

Idea explored

Idea developed with justification

Practical breakthrough

Awareness of audience

> When my character, the self-abusive personality, was dominant, we wanted to show the way that I was able to control Sarah's actions, and that she couldn't stop me. Our first attempt at showing this didn't work well. I have a monologue where I describe scratching Sarah and pulling her hair out and we were going to show this by having me delivering it with the ensemble Sarah positioned around me. I was going to do the action that I was describing, for example scratching the back of my hand and they were going to react as if in pain. However, this didn't look very effective because we wanted to create a contrast between the stillness of my character because she is so in control, and the frantic desperation of Sarah. We then thought it would be more effective if I simply describe the action without doing it, with the ensemble Sarah reacting. This looked a lot better as it further emphasised the difference between my personality and Sarah. This also allowed me to walk around, as if admiring my creation which showed more depth to my character and how I was orchestrating what was happening, giving the audience a clearer understanding of how a personality can completely take over. My character emerged as a more sinister and creepy person that got joy out of seeing Sarah's pain because we wanted it to be sickening for the audience to watch. We wanted our piece to be shocking and we felt that by creating such a character that the audience cannot understand, we could succeed in this.

3. **How did you and your group explore the possibilities of form, structure and performance style in your piece?**

Exploration and alternatives need to be addressed in this question. This is quite a complex question and ideally should be dealt with in three areas.

The performance style should define your piece and probably be evident to your audience from the opening scene. Don't, however, let the performance style limit you; it may be effective if you use a range of styles and approaches within your piece to keep the audience working. Refer back to the 'directorial vision' that was encouraged in the previous section

The structure, or the construction, of your piece must give the audience the opportunity to go on a journey with the characters, and you must try and take them to places that they do not expect, or sometimes don't want, to go. Refer back to the comments on balance in your piece made earlier.

The form of your piece refers to the whole range of dramatic techniques that you used, from monologue to frozen image. Decide which forms of theatre were most appropriate for the impact that you intended to make and remember to continually justify why decisions were made.

> A full discussion of these took place in the devising from a theme section.

*Extract 1: performance style*

This introduction gives a strong overall sense of what the group are trying to achieve in terms of performance style.

> Our play is not chronological and it doesn't follow a logical time sequence. We use flashback and switch between reality and dream worlds. Some scenes represent something that has occurred over a few hours, and other scenes of a similar length represent things that have occurred over a whole day. The dream scenes are very different from the reality scenes, in that they go inside our main character's, Sarah's, head and they are very abstract. The switching between dream and reality in our piece aims to disorientate the audience and confuse them about what has happened, so that their memories are muddled. This is to let them experience the way that when someone suffers from Dissociative Identity Disorder (DID) their memories are often forgotten and they can suffer from amnesia.

*Extract 2: structure*

Having established the intentions of performance style, this extract goes on to explore the outline structure of the piece, giving strong justifications for ideas.

> The piece was based around a central narrative that followed the character of Helen through her daytime life, as well as the life she experienced in her night terrors. This followed a fairly chronological timeline of events, although at times the action was distanced from this. We chose to have an ambiguous time frame for the piece so that it was more disconcerting for the audience to watch. Even though they were following the story of Helen they were left to wonder how long she had been suffering for and this created questions as to what happened in between each scene. An example of this was the two scenes at the end. They were detached from the main course of time as they were the only scenes that took the audience on a journey out of the bedroom, into the playground and onto the roof. This was intended to show how your dreams can affect you wherever you are; they are not limited to your own bedroom or night time.

*Extracts 3 and 4: dramatic form*

The extracts below show an intelligent response on how to use different forms alongside each other.

> The still images we used portrayed girls in a pornographic magazine, a funeral, and hooligans at a football match. In the fertility clinic scene, we chose to represent the images in the magazine through still image rather than letting the audience use their imagination, to ensure they are confronted with the embarrassment Chris faces. He is at one of the lowest points in his life, and he is required to carry out a degrading activity. The poses we strike combined with the seedy lighting of red from the side, making awkward viewing for the audience in a shamefully familiar way.

> Time manipulation was a dramatic form, which we experimented with while creating our performance. We used a combination of flashbacks to allow the audience to see John as a child: this gave them a chance to see his innocence and enthusiasm for life before his illness, giving the audience a change they could sympathise with. The flashbacks which we used in our final piece were always downstage right, with John looking out over the audience watching his tree outside. This allows the audience to understand every time that it is a flashback, as they become familiar with the technique occurring several times in the piece. The tree is used as a metaphor for John, it grows as he does and starts to rot and decay as he gets ill. The idea of the tree was used as a framing device, linking scenes together carrying John's story. A flash into the future is also used: we used this purely to create emotion on stage. A simple frozen choral image from John's funeral shows the mourning and loss from his loved ones feel when he has passed. A central front light shining onto the freeze allows the chorus to appear in a photograph. This appears to be dream-like and surreal as John watches in on them, the audience can sympathise with his reaction of fear and shock. John's time is limited and so the use of freezes hints at his memories as looks back through his life, the fragmented images seem to flash before his eyes. This is achieved with no unnecessary lines or exchanges; instead the audience are left to respond to reaction and not action, which we felt for this sensitive situation would be more powerful.

**4. How did the work of established and recognised theatre practitioners, and/or the work of live theatre, influence the way in which your devised response developed?**

This question allows you to draw from the wealth of experience that you should have gained since the start of the A-level course. Things you will have seen, performed or studied will have stuck in your mind, or even helped to shape you as a drama practitioner. Again the focus must be on identifying an influence and then practically applying it to a specific moment in your piece. No doubt the practitioners that you used alongside the texts in Unit 1 will have influenced you in either a positive or negative fashion, as would the numerous shows of different styles that you have been to see throughout the course.

> **Tip**
>
> Be careful not to overlap your responses to this question with your responses to question 1.

### Extract 1

The student takes the key elements of Berkoff's theatrical style here and applies them to two key scenes in her piece:

> My group decided to take Berkoff into consideration when we wanted to introduce a physically demanding scene, which advanced the audience's understanding of the story. We had the idea of introducing the idea of the main character's cancer but without dictating his illness to the audience. We wanted to suggest the idea as we explored different movements to portray our message. We decided to look at the idea of mitosis and cell division. Initially we were inspired by Berkoff's range of levels, twists, turns and unusual positions. We then incorporated into this the idea of replication using just our hands instead of our whole bodies. This was a simple action; however, it appeared too abstract for Erica's initial introduction. We instead used this idea from Berkoff in the symptoms scene. While narrating, monologue volumes, tones and pitches were distorted, allowing the delivery to appear threatening and frightening for the audience. This allowed the audience to share John's fear of his symptoms, as he has no control over his body, now they see him exposed centre stage.

### Extract 2

This extract illustrates how live theatre can be inspirational and open up avenues that students would not think were possible. This clear desire to push the boundaries of experience is one of the keys to success in this process.

> I went to see *Nights at the Circus*, which is a piece of theatre rich in circus skills, gymnasts, lifts on rope and trapezes. Obviously we didn't have these props, but we wanted to use gymnastics to portray Kate reaching the highest point. The level of risk involved in these actions creates a thrilling and astonishing piece of drama, if they are pulled off, but could cause the piece to crash and burn if one small mistake is made. But our group took this risk and performed a very risky move, holding Alice up so she reached around ten feet above the stage. During the rehearsal period, we had the pleasure of working with Tiago Gambogi who is a director of his own company, The Detonators, and is also a dancer and choreographer. He inspired us and gave us the basic skills we needed to mould our

> piece around choreographed dance and group movement. We
> had a three-hour workshop with him where he taught us some
> basic rhythmic steps and gave us the confidence to believe
> in ourselves with positive feedback. He put us outside of our
> comfort zone and gave us the push we needed to make our
> piece risky and exciting. This gave us the confidence to scrap
> the party scene, where we just did some dancing around the
> stage and as a group did a pathetic dance to a song we liked.
> Instead we enhanced two other dance scenes – welcome to
> our world and the overdose scene – which ended up being the
> two strongest and more moving scenes in the whole piece.

**5. How successfully did your final performance communicate your aims and intentions for the piece to your audience?**

This question obviously has a clear focus on the final performance. One of the most difficult things for drama students to do is to self-analyse, but this evaluation requires you to be balanced and honest in your view of 'success'. The first thing you need to do is to be clear about what your aims and intentions for your piece actually were. Avoid generalisations that mean little. Instead root your answer in the actual performance. Select two or three central scenes to your piece. As a performer you know instinctively how the audience received a certain scene. It may be nothing like what you expected or intended. Laughter, for example, can be found in the most unexpected situations. Remember that their reactions are vital.

Particularly worthy of coverage might be your opening and ending. How did you grab the audience from the word go, and how did you leave them feeling when they exited the performance space?

What more might you have done in terms of scene order, editing, adding new scenes, the way the story was told, changing the staging or the music? Was your central message clear? If not, how would you clarify for future performances?

*Extract 1*

Extract 1 below recognises the need for a range of forms within the piece. The student shows a very clear understanding of the use of monologue and the impact it can have when used effectively and put in the right place in a piece. The intentions of the piece are very clearly laid out here and the moment is well described in context with the rest of the piece.

> As a group, we really wanted our audience to be able to fully
> connect emotionally with the character, so they could clearly
> understand the mother's journey and Sarah's story. This scene
> was our only still scene in which one person appeared on stage
> and remaining chorus members went offstage. We decided
> on this dramatic form as we wanted Sarah's mother to be

centralised and for the audience to focus on the character
to fully understand her feelings towards Sarah. The chorus
member playing the mother broke the fourth wall by directly
speaking out towards the audience engaging them successfully
and engrossing the audience. Little movement occurred with a
few steps taken centre stage, the mother looked into different
parts of the surrounding audience, questioning them for
example, 'Why me? What did we do to deserve such a burden?'
This worked effectively in demonstrating the idea of the audience
having a relationship with Sarah's mother, understanding the
story of Sarah's condition and the effects it has on people.
This also showed the mother's inner feelings and highlighted
one of our main ideas of how society tends to judge people with
mental-health issues and put pressures on those who have to
deal and live with people who suffer from these conditions.

*Extract 2*

Extract 2 expresses an element of surprise in the relationship between actor and audience and recognises the importance of balance in the structure of the piece. Specific moments are again at the core of this response. The response may well have been enhanced by reference to ways in which the impact may have been made stronger.

In the zoo scene we wanted to create an energetic and dream-like
atmosphere, so we used a lot of over-the-top characterisation
because we wanted to show the audience how Sarah feels being
at the zoo. We wanted them to experience her excitement and
laugh with her so they could see what kind of childhood she
could have had without having DID, and this would make the
fact that she had a disorder more upsetting. In this scene we
emphasised facial expressions and we made all of our movement
very large and extended as we wanted the scene to be larger
than life, as though the audience were in Sarah's dream world.
We tried to create the lightness of the scene by using a rose-
tinted wash for the lighting and also bringing in some upbeat
music; a song called 'Send me on my way'. This scene was very
well-received by the audience and a lot of people said that it
was one of the highlights of the piece. Being in the audience,
our teachers said that there was a sense of everyone breathing
a sigh of relief and relaxing for a few moments whereas before
they had been tense. Throughout the scene we had a lot of
laughter from the audience, more so than we had expected, and
we were very pleased that there was some humour in our piece.

*Extract 3*

Extract 3 contains a very honest account that recognises that complex ideas can be a barrier between the deviser and audience in terms of communicating the central ideas. Clarity and simplicity are watch words of the devising process.

> Comments passed on a most visually dynamic scene (the bath scene where we created a silhouette onstage using a shower curtain and back light) were positive because it was very different and effective. However there was a bit of confusion about the storyline for the section. We were trying to show the audience in a flashback how the current events they were watching had occurred and the reasons for them. There was a certain amount of ambiguity about the story and we collectively as a group heard lots of different storylines that the audience had interpreted. This was also a place where our intended impact for the scene did not quite hit the mark. Because all the action was behind a shower curtain and all images were created in shadow, it was unclear who was behind the curtain. We also used a complex sound-effect CD to lead the action from a bath to a car to a hospital and back to the bath. Due to this sudden change in scene all the time it was unclear of the exact detail of the action. For example, it was said that some people thought that it was the wife in the hospital bed and not the husband, which it was. This we think was because of the nature of the scene, where the wife was explaining how she had lost a baby. We realised that this was an easy mistake to make and made sense due to the order in which we had presented the scenes.

> "There is no formula to the way we make theatre. However, it always starts with the story. No, it starts before then. It starts with an itch, a need, an instinct. "
>
> Emma Rice, www.kneehigh.com

> Society relates to institutions and organisations that are created by a group of people, while culture has more to do with practices, beliefs and values within a particular society.

**6. How effectively did the social, cultural, historical/political context of the piece communicate to your audience?**

There must be a reason why your devising piece needs to be performed – a message that you as a group feel the audience need to experience. Your piece will have something to say about the world in which we live, because you have drawn from your experiences of the world around you.

Consider the following questions as areas that might be addressed:

- What makes your piece relevant to contemporary society?

- Why must it be performed now, in the early part of the 21st century?

**Social context**

- What is society's attitude to the topic you have chosen?

- How does your piece explore the relationship between the individual and their place in society?

- What institutions and organisations exist in your piece and how have they been presented?

**Cultural context**

- What different cultural attitudes are represented in your piece and how have they been presented? For example, youth culture, drug culture or the culture of crime.

**Historical and political context**

- How have you used your research and knowledge of the past to inform what you have presented here? What has changed over time?

- Is your piece set in a particular historical period? Why have you made that decision and what point are you trying to make about modern society by doing so?

- If your piece is political (for example, if it set in a fictional dictatorship) what points of view are you representing?

Once these contextual considerations have been made, you are now in a position to evaluate the success of communicating the ideas to your audience by referring once again to specific scenes or moments.

*Extract 1*

In Extract 1 below, the student successfully highlights the contemporary issues regarding society's attitudes to mental health by interweaving a clear viewpoint with the material of her piece. The honesty with which she draws from her own experiences is also evident.

> We thought about the fact that the majority of people do not think about the effects on the family of the sufferer. The family are forgotten in the midst of people fussing around the patient and their troubles are often overlooked. We decided to write a monologue for Sarah's mother in order to give her a voice and let her emotions be heard. In the monologue she talks about how she feels partly responsible and about how everyone around her doesn't understand her and she feels isolated. We hoped this would be an eye-opener for the audience because normally people think that the patient is the one who feels isolated, yet the family also has a lot to deal with and it is difficult for them to confide in people because no one else understands their situation. We wanted to make the audience aware of this and to make them think more about how mental illness can have a major impact on so many people. I am fully aware of this as a member of my family has Tourette's syndrome and this greatly affects my whole family as we all have to make allowances for their behaviour and I had to learn how to deal with it. I am also aware of the preconceptions that people have towards mental illness because some people mock sufferers of Tourette's syndrome due to the verbal symptoms (such as swearing) when they do not understand it and this can be difficult to accept when you know someone personally who suffers from it. We, as a group,

thought that it was very important for us to show through this scene how people's preconceptions can be hurtful and we wanted to make the audience think about mental illness before they judge the sufferers. The mother talks about how she wants her family to be normal, reflecting society wanting everything to be 'normal'. The mother's wants stem from a fear that her family will not conform to the norms of society, and through giving her a voice we want people to question why society pressures people to be 'normal' and challenge this. As this was the only monologue in our piece, and the only time the other actors left the stage, we were asking the audience to focus on the content of the language and give them the opportunity to connect with the mother character. I hope and believe that people were touched by the sensitive delivery of this difficult subject matter and that it did have a strong resonance among the audience.

*Extract 2*

By focusing the piece on aspects of male behaviour, the candidate here makes strong comments about a cultural issue that is universal. The extract ends with an evaluation of the success of the choices that the group made.

The vital role of the Doctor that John's success depends on is female; this emphasises the female power that he has over him. His fate is left in female control; this may feel to John that his manhood is being taken from him as he is taken away from his comfort zone. This idea is reflected by the fact he is suffering from testicular cancer. John displays stereotypical behaviour of men struggling to share their feelings. John isn't honest with his wife, hides from the truth. John feels that he should take the traditional male approach to be the strong half of a couple, where the women are those who need help and support. Roles are reversed in our plot and the audience see John struggling to adapt to his situation; he ignores his illness instead of facing his problems, hiding the truth away from those who most need to know. John has an inability to communicate his emotions towards the people around him, he feels that it is his duty to look after his family and his illness prevents him from financially supporting them. This is probably why we see him sharing his problems only with the Doctor; she plays a detached figure separated away from his personal life. The Doctor does not judge John or answer back to his decisions. With the group of six only containing one male, we hoped to drive the above points home. Our intentions were to expose the issues that some men have with communicating their emotions and I think this was shown to the audience in a number of scenes when John's isolation was emphasised, resulting in him withdrawing in to himself.

When looking at all the student sample material in the section there are a number of common points that ensure success:

- Looking closely at the wording of the guiding questions

- An openness and honest appraisal in the approach to the work

- Distinct and specific practical examples linked to research material

- A continuing focus on the key words from the assessment criteria – research, explore, develop and evaluate.

With these areas in mind, alongside a detailed notebook that covers the whole process and is updated continually, success in the Written Evidence Document will be assured.

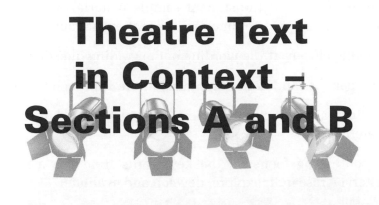

# Theatre Text in Context – Sections A and B

Make sure you are using the correct edition, as specified by Edexcel.

## What do I have to do?

If your performance for Unit 3 is a chance to galvanise your practical skill, then it is important to see this unit as an opportunity to demonstrate your theatrical understanding through your writing. During the Drama and Theatre Studies course, you will have developed a detailed knowledge of different playwrights and genres that will have helped you to formulate your own ideas. You should have a clear sense of which style of theatre most interests you and how this could be realised in performance. Section A of this unit is a chance to celebrate this understanding and apply it to one of three texts – *Lysistrata* by Aristophanes, *Dr Faustus* by Christopher Marlowe or *Woyzeck* by Georg Büchner.

The play you study will need to be approached from a director's perspective. As you work on the text, you will need to understand how the piece was originally performed and how it could be made relevant to a contemporary audience. You will be given a copy of the text, which you should annotate extensively as you explore ideas through practical exercises, discussion and personal research. This text can be taken into the exam, so you should ensure that it contains plenty of ideas that will support you when writing under timed conditions.

## Assessment

These sections of the exam will test you in two different ways. In the first question, the extract you are given will focus on your ability to direct a specific section of the text in detail, recognising the demands of the piece and the impact it will have on the audience. This requires not only a comprehensive understanding of the whole play but also an ability to communicate precise information about the shaping of a scene in rehearsal. You will be asked three short questions worth four, six and ten marks respectively, and it is important that you use your time effectively in order to ensure that you give a balanced approach.

For examples of questions and student responses see pages 89–95, 116–122 and 154–159.

The second question requires a more structured response. You will have a choice of two questions that will require you to explain aspects of your individual production. These may focus on a specific element of design or direction, or may ask for a more general response focusing on a theme or quotation. The key to success in this section is the ability to select the most relevant parts of your production in order to demonstrate a thorough response without exploring irrelevant areas.

Essentially, the exam board requires you to focus on the following areas:

- The social, cultural and historical context of the play, and its possible relevance to a modern audience

- The structure of the play in terms of plot, language, form, character and stagecraft, and how these areas communicate meaning

- Your directorial concept and how you might use production techniques in order to realise your aims

- How you might structure a rehearsal with your actors in order to explore character, meaning and design.

Your teacher will choose the playtext you are studying and give suggestions on how to approach the work. However, always remember that you are trying to establish an original directorial concept. Use the prompts in the margins as a way of extending your understanding and ensuring that you are able to convey a thoughtful and unique response.

## Lysistrata by Aristophanes

### Plot summary

Written and set in approximately 411 BCE, *Lysistrata* focuses on the eponymous character's frustrations with the state of Athenian society. The city is gripped by the damaging effects of the Peloponnesian war and thousands of men are being killed in what she considers to be a pointless battle. She devises a plan to force the men to adopt a more diplomatic solution to the problem. All of the women of Athens and their enemies go on strike, refusing the sexual advances of their husbands. In addition, they take control of the Acropolis and all of the funds within. After a series of comic situations, where the frustrations of both sexes are explored, the men finally capitulate and peace is secured.

The play is a bawdy comedy, full of sexual innuendo. The absurd nature of the situation leads to a series of exaggerated scenarios which expose primitive human desires. As a result, the tone of the scenes are relatively simplistic but Aristophanes manages to contain within them the essence of truth, a truth which invites us to laugh at the both the characters and ourselves.

### Aristophanes

There is little firm information about Aristophanes' life and the evidence that does exist has been pieced together from a variety of sources.

It is generally believed that he was born in 456 BCE into an affluent family. He was probably educated in Athens and took an early interest in the performances at the festival of Dionysus. His first play, *The Banqueters*, which was produced in 427 BCE, was

> 66 Lysistrata is the megaphone through which we assail the war du jour. 99
>
> Mark Adamo in his programme note to *Lysistrata*, or *The Nude Goddess*.

**Further study**

For more detailed information about the traditions of Greek Theatre, look at pages 8–11 of the *Edexcel AS Drama and Theatre Studies Study Guide* (Rhinegold 2008).

> ❝ The worst that could happen to man in war is a glorious death, for a woman it could mean decades of misery as a bereaved wife or mother or even the prospect of not having the chance to become a wife or mother in a society in which the unmarried woman has no role and no place. ❞
>
> Alan H. Sommerstein in his introduction to *Lysistrata and Other Plays* (Penguin 2003).

**Web link**

For more information on the Peloponnesian War visit http://en.wikipedia.org/wiki/ Peloponnesian_War

> ❝ A consistent attitude towards war and politics runs through all his plays … unlike great conflicts of the past and despite grand and noble achievements, the Peloponnesian War is a disaster. It is destroying the greatness of Athens, is against the interests and wishes of ordinary people and is kept going only because generals and politicians are too incompetent or corrupt to end it. ❞
>
> Kenneth McLeish in the introduction to *Lysistrata*, translated by Patric Dickinson (Nick Hern Books 1996).

### The traditions of Greek comedy

awarded second place and the following year he came first with *The Babylonians*. Both of these plays have since been lost.

As a child, Aristophanes experienced Athens as a glorious empire. However, as he grew older, the city began its decline. A range of factors which included the Peloponnesian war, a devastating plague and the death of their great leader Pericles, all contributed to its demise. As a result, Aristophanes used his comic writing to question and ridicule the behaviour of the political leaders. However, a law was passed to curb the satirical work of playwrights and as a result, Aristophanes turned to more social concerns.

During his life, he wrote at least 40 plays and won many first prizes although only eleven have survived. His works often contain a simplistic and traditional sense of virtue, celebrating the qualities of the once great Athens and ridiculing the focus on more intellectual pursuits. Socrates and Euripides are both criticised in his work. However, he, like many Athenians, was not adverse to excess. According to Plato's *Symposium*, he indulged in food, drink and good conversation. He died in approximately 380 BCE.

### Contextualising the play

Aristophanes was writing during a period of social and political upheaval in Athens. He wrote *Lysistrata* in 411 BCE when the future of Athens was in threat. The Peloponnesian war was in its 21st year and beneath his comic style lies an anguished message from a playwright grieving for the thousands of soldiers who had died in a battle.

It is important to note that this is referred to by critics as one of Aristophanes' peace plays, but it would be wrong to call him a pacifist. The audience would be mostly men and they would consider the whole concept of women controlling the city laughable. He is however proposing a different approach – by negotiating with their neighbours they would prevent unnecessary bloodshed, preserve Athens and live to fight another day. He was offering a logical and practical solution to the troubles of the time.

It may appear strange to consider such a strong political message being performed as part of the festival of Dionysus. Although the theme has more resonance when one has a greater understanding of the ceremonies which took place. The critic Sommerstein, in the introduction to his translation, explains that one of the traditions appeared to unintentionally reinforce his writing. 'A parade was held of those young men … whose fathers had been killed in battle, and they were presented with a set of armour at the public expense.' The act of mourning the dead and introducing the new generation to the conflict would have acted as a vivid context for his work.

The performances were staged in large open-air theatres, which seated approximately 14,000 people. Since there was no lighting, mood and the time of day needed to be created through the use of language. The size of the audience meant that the padded costumes needed to be bold and the masks that were worn, which covered the face and the head, exaggerated the features of the character.

The notable addition to the costume of the male characters was a leather phallus which often hung loose, although in the latter half of *Lysistrata* it is unusually erect. Traditionally, all the protagonists were performed by four male actors playing many parts. The Chorus of 34 members supported the action, remaining on stage throughout the performance.

Aristophanes is the only surviving exponent of Old Comedy and was generally considered to be the master of the form. The style is fantastical and absurd, whereas the later writers of New Comedy tended to be more realistic and looked at the nuances of human nature. All old comedies usually followed the same structure:

- **The Prologue.** A scene where the main character and the concept are introduced and the action begins.

- **The Parados.** The entrance of the Chorus.

- **The Agon.** A series of scenes containing the plays central debate (or Agon). This argument was a formal presentation of two opposing ideas and was often introduced by choral song.

- **The Parabasis.** A direct address from the Chorus with no other characters on stage, in a different form to their usual delivery.

- **A mixture of scenes and choral songs (Stasimons).**

- **The Exodus.** A final act of resolution and celebration.

Practically, women would not be able to organise a meeting with ease. Freedom of movement was restricted. Women had to be escorted places by a slave when in public. Coordinating a meeting between other warring factions would be hugely problematic. However, it is the farcical image of women in power which in turn emphasised the absurdity of the long-running war.

The dominant theme is that of war. In ancient Greece, it was crippling society and it is clear that within the play there is a loud cry for greater diplomacy and common sense. A contemporary production could choose to set the play in a specific modern conflict or in a fictitious country. Either has the potential to reflect the universal tragedy that war creates. As Blake Morrison observes in his Guardian article entitled 'A 2,500-year-old sex ban':

> 'These days it seems less absurd. Women have staged sex strikes in recent years in Colombia, Turkey, Poland, New Zealand, the Netherlands and Sudan, seeking variously to stop drug wars, combat repressive legislation, conserve their environment and turn their carnivorous partners into vegans. As for women entering a male sanctum and seizing power, this too has a famous modern parallel: Greenham Common in 1981, when a group of women took up residence around an American military base in protest against cruise missiles.'

Clearly, therefore, it can also be seen as a play about the wisdom and power of women. Within the play, they demonstrate the power to bring about change and the play has been adopted by a group

In Greek tragedy the limit was three actors.

## Old Comedy

Shakespeare's comedies traditionally follow the style of New Comedy, although plays such as *The Tempest* and *A Midsummer Night's Dream* contain elements of both forms.

In *Lysistrata*, the Agon is hardly a debate, as Sommerstein observes, 'The magistrate is hardly allowed to get a word in edgeways.'

*Lysistrata* replaces the parabasis with the debate and ensuing violence between the two different choruses.

## Themes

"The sexual theme is just an attention-grabber ... The comedy neatly inverts spaces and boundaries ... the women turn the city into an extended household and seize control ... not as 'intruder' but as reconcilers and healers ... women's visions and concepts surpass the fractious politics and warfare of the men."

Ian C. Storey's review of David Konstan's *Greek Comedy and Ideology* (http://ccat.sas.upenn. edu/bmcr/1995/95.11.11.html).

called the Lysistrata Project who use the concept as they attempt to bring about world peace in a post-9/11 society.

In addition to this, it ridicules the political structure and the men in power. The male Chorus appear totally incompetent and the magistrate's attempts to dominate the crisis only appear to highlight his inability to communicate with the ordinary members of the city. In a society which is wary of political spin and increasingly apathetic towards the democratic process, the play is a humorous reminder of the power that we all have to facilitate change.

Before we proceed to study each scene in turn, it is important that you begin the process by reading the text in silence on your own. Being able to hear the words of the text in your head and to imagine stage action are skills you will need to acquire if you are going to be successful. As you read, have a pencil in your hand. Underline any interesting phrases and make a note of any sections you do not understand. The nature of the language is such that you may need to reread sections several times before you comprehend the idea being communicated. Whatever happens, do not panic if you are confused by key areas of the text. You are going through a process, and with each new play it takes time to understand the style and the context of the material.

During the following pages, we will work through the play in sections, looking at the dramatic significance of the scene and practical suggestions for exploring the text. Remember, the written examination will be testing your skills as a director so many of the exercises will be focused on how the text can be rehearsed. As each idea is discussed, keep your production at the forefront of your mind. Make notes on any ideas you have on the staging of the piece. Towards the end of the chapter, you will be given suggestions on how to draw these ideas together into a clear directorial concept and ultimately shape your response into written answers. You will find this difficult if you have not made detailed notes along the way.

## Key sections

### Section 1

Lysistrata and Calonice

Pages 3–9

The prologue begins traditionally with the entrance of the central character, Lysistrata. Having organised a meeting for the women of Athens, only Calonice, her neighbour, has bothered to arrive on time. She is furious but not surprised by their behaviour. Lysistrata stresses that she needs to discuss 'big and meaty' matters which could lead to the 'salvation of Greece'. Her aim is to stop the conflict that ravages the land and she has invited representatives of the different factions to help her in her task. As the frustration builds, the women start to arrive from different directions.

**Analysis**  The opening of the play would have traditionally set the comic tone of the piece. The women, who originally would have been played by men, are frustrated at the unreliable nature of their own gender. The absurdity of the exchange is further emphasised by Lysistrata's belief that she can resolve a conflict that has lasted 21 years. More contemporary interpretations may be able to instil within Lysistrata a greater and more serious passion but it is impossible to ignore the comic and subversive tone that is provided by Calonice in Sommerstein's translation of the text.

---

### Exaggerating the fury

Lysistrata's opening line of the scene highlights her frustration at the apathy shown by the women. Work on this exercise in pairs, with one as Lysistrata delivering the line 'Just think if it had been a Bacchic celebration they'd been asked to attend' with the other person playing the role of the director sat on the floor. Lysistrata delivers the line emphasising her fury and the director must respond with praise explaining what was liked. However, they should always conclude with the phrase '… just one criticism, you need to make it bigger.' Repeat the line many times, making each performance bigger than the last. The exploration of the line will have one of two effects. It will either increase the ridiculous delivery of the text, establishing the comedy from the opening line or set a more serious tone by accentuating Lysistrata's despair at the women. Swap with the partner and try to explore the alternative interpretation of the text.

---

**Creating the total life of the characters**

Stanislavski suggested that an actor should use the given circumstances of the text and their imagination to create a total life of the character. As a group, discuss the conversations that Lysistrata and Calonice may have had in the past. Has Lysistrata always been obsessed by the war or has she been preoccupied by different social concerns? What might they have been doing while discussing these matters? Eating food or walking through Athens, perhaps. Try improvising these scenes in order to flesh out their relationship. Consider how the scenes could be altered by the different levels of anger shown by Lysistrata.

**Changing perspective**

In order to ensure the comedy is fully explored in the text, it is important that the director explores the humour within the actions and the characters. In threes, with a director and two actors, create two different versions of the play. The first should flatter Lysistrata with Calonice as a slightly bumbling friend with limited awareness of the world in which they live. The second should focus on Calonice, and how she is trying to tolerate the radical ideas her friend often has. Consider how the scene could be staged in order to emphasise the different interpretations. Placing characters nearer the audience or having them alone on stage at either the beginning or end of the scene is a good method of earning the sympathy of the audience. Changes in tone and projection can also manipulate their response. The style of the play could also support moments where a character looks at the audience without the other character knowing. Rehearse the versions and perform them one after the other. Discuss what the directors intended and what the audience felt was achieved. What did the actors learn about the scene through performing the extract? Note what you have learnt in your text, indicating particular changes in movement and voice on the script.

**Defining the friendship**

To prepare you for a possible examination response, in your group try to define the relationship between the two characters and give two short precise examples of how this might be revealed in performance. You could focus on movement and voice separately or hone in on moments of the scene. Write this response on paper in 5 minutes. This will help you to simulate the pressure you will be under at the end of the year.

Lysistrata, Calonice, Myrrhine, Lampito, Isemnia, Scythaena, Corinthian and Spartan women

Pages 9–33

The tradition of Greek comedy was to use four male actors to deliver all of the main characters in addition to the Chorus. Although this rule would not restrict a modern interpretation, it does explain why there are many characters mentioned in the stage directions who do not speak.

## Section 2

When the women finally arrive they make their acquaintances before Lysistrata begins to present her argument. The initial question of whether the women miss their husbands is replied with increasingly comic examples of their despair. The second which concerns whether they are prepared to 'put a stop to the war' is unilaterally agreed. However, when Lysistrata hesitantly explains they need to renounce sex, panic ensues. The raise concerns about how the men will react and the fact they will still have the money to conduct war. The secondary tactic of occupying the temple is announced and after some debate the women devise a ritualistic oath through which they swear their loyalty to the cause.

**Analysis**

The disparate nature of this scene highlights both Lysistrata's leadership and the skill of Aristophanes' comic writing. She is the first positive female role in Greek theatre and her separation from the other characters is important. She appears to have no sexual desire and the only positive comment she appears to make about the appearance of anyone in the play is in addressing Lampito as 'ravishing'. An ancient Greek audience would have enjoyed the male actors playing women who appear to struggle with every aspect of the decision-making process. However, within this scene, Aristophanes is also ridiculing the over-elaborate and corrupt democratic system run by the Athenian males at the time.

### Sculpting images

In order to develop the characters from the different regions, a director might ask his actors to begin by focusing on the physicality of the roles. Working in pairs, allocate one person to be the sculptor while the other is a blob of clay. Start with the image of Lysistrata. How might a sculptured image encapsulate her confidence and determination? After two minutes, show this image to other members of your group. Ask them to comment on what they understand of the character from her physical appearance. In your group, create a definitive image of Lysistrata before repeating the exercise with the other characters in the extract. Make notes on the final images. You may find it useful to draw stick figures in your copy of the text. Have different members of your group recreate each of the images and illustrate them with one line of dialogue from the scene which epitomises the character.

---

 **Developing accents**

In the translations the exam board have chosen to use, Sommerstein deliberately writes the Spartan woman Lampito's lines phonetically to emphasise the need for an accent to suggest she is not from the area. There are no changes to the language of the Athenian women although a modern production could make use of regional accents to emphasise the scale of the problem facing the women. In your group, discuss what alternative accents could be used and how they could appropriately add to the comedy.

---

**Reciting the oath**

The ritualistic reciting of the oath provides a strong image of the women's dedication to their causes. Lysistrata suggests they should all take hold of the cup, which in performance would present the audience with a striking image of their solidarity, with actors bunched tightly together. As a group, try to recreate this image. Once this is completed, experiment with the humour in the oath. Choose someone to perform the role of Lysistrata and provide them with the lines of the oath. As the words are delivered, one line at a time, the actor should illustrate each line with a gesture – the group holding the cup should then echo the line and the movement. Experiment with the oath gradually becoming more serious as it progresses. Rehearse the scene with other members of the group directing the action. Make a note of the decisions that have been made in your text and explain why you think they could be effective in a contemporary production.

---

It is important to note that in a contemporary production a director will need to quickly define the four main characters in this opening section. Although, some of this may be established through costume and possibly masks, one will also need to advise the actors on how the differences may be evident in their performance. Individually, begin by making a list of the differences you might expect to see in performance. Allow yourself two minutes to do this. Once this is complete, discuss the ideas as a whole group. You may raise notions such as age, pace of delivery, use of gesture and the status of the women. Now consider possible ways of experimenting with these through rehearsal. Try the exercises overleaf.

**Portraying the difference in personality**

## Experiment with status

Using numbers from 1 to 10, with 10 being extremely powerful, allocate a number to each of the characters depending on the power they have in the scene. Consider how this might be evident in their movement and voice. Make a decision and read through the extract. Now allocate the same numbers but to different characters. What effect does this have? Experiment with numbering other concepts, for example their libido, their fear of their husbands or their attention span.

## Focus on the age difference

There is a suggestion that they are women of a similar age. How might the scene be performed differently if there was a difference of twenty years between the oldest and youngest? The fact that Lysistrata and Calonice are neighbours doesn't mean they are the same age. Consider how maturity may contrast with the naivety of youth. Decide the age of each character and in groups of five run the scene with one individual directing the differences in portrayal.

## Experiment with proxemics

Assuming that initially the characters have very little in common, ask your actors to demonstrate a physical distance as they begin the scene. How might this be sustained without the scene becoming static? When might you expect them to come nearer to each other and why? Do they ever hold eye contact?

Men's leader

Pages 32–41

**Directing tip**

Ask the actors to write a character profile for a member of the Chorus. This could include their age, role in the city and general details about their involvement in battle. Small decisions like these will help to colour the choral work where characters are in danger of becoming two-dimensional.

## Section 3

The Chorus of old men enter carrying logs, a torch and coals. They are clearly incredulous that a group of women have captured the Acropolis and promise to beat them; an apparently hollow statement since they struggle to walk on stage. They outline their plan to batter down the doors or even set fire to them but they appear thwarted by the smoke that keeps blowing back into their faces. They conclude with a plea to Athena Nike, the goddess of Victory.

The slow pace at which the men enter, combined with their fragile physicality, is the key to the humour in this scene. The image is mirrored in the successful BBC situation comedy, *Dad's Army*, which follows the exploits of the aging Home Guard. Look at excerpts from the series and note how the characters struggle with routine tasks. Make notes on the actors' portrayal of the figures and try to apply some of the ideas to these characters. You will probably find it easier initially to ignore the script and focus simply on the entrance of the chorus.

**The power of youth**

A possible interpretation of this extract is through providing the audience with an image of the army's former glories. On page 37, the first three stanzas identify how they successfully removed Cleomenes from the Acropolis. A director could choose to present this as a flashback. As a group, devise five images that reflect the action in these stanzas. Create tableaux of young soldiers in their prime as an individual recites the lines. As the action returns to the present, look at how the characters could move from young and competent to old and fragile.

One of the key debates in any contemporary production of a Greek text centres on the delivery of the choral odes. Some interpret the Chorus as a symbolic mass of people, representing a certain state of mind. Others present them as a microcosm of society with a range of characters reacting slightly differently to the events of the play. Look at the four stanzas on page 35. As a group, read the passage in unison and discuss the impact it could create on an audience. Now, read the passage round the circle, changing speaker every time there is punctuation or a line finishes. What is the effect of creating individual voices? Finally, ask each member of your group to underline five short phrases or words that are particularly effective. Ask one person to act as the Chorus leader who will read all 16 lines; the others speak in unison with that person when their line is delivered. Which version is more effective? Make notes on your preferred style of performance in your text.

**Solo or unison**

### The use of choral limericks

Although the limericks reveal how the men are struggling to cope, Sommerstein presumably used this form to encourage the audience to laugh at the men. Each member of your group should take a limerick and practise performing it in order to elicit laughter from the audience. If you have a large group, you could experiment with some rehearsing a section in pairs whilst others look at the stanza individually. After ten minutes, perform the work and note the response. Use this to inform a discussion on what makes an audience laugh.

## Section 4

> The image of the old men crouching is in contrast to the old women who arrive in a hurry carrying pitchers of water on their heads. Stratyllis, the female chorus leader, is dismayed by the proposed actions of the men and challenges the nameless leader of the men. As their bickering builds to a crescendo, the women throw water over the men.

Stratyllis, women, men's leader

Pages 41–49

The comic bickering between the two factions highlights the benefits of Aristophanes' decision to divide his Chorus of 24 into two distinct groups. The Chorus effectively arguing among themselves and the lack of respect shown for each other emphasises the need for a protest for peace and a revision of gender stereotypes.

**Analysis**

**Giants, gnomes and wizards**

Split your class into two distinct groups who should stand on opposite sides of the room. They are effectively two warring tribes who can choose which tactic they choose for battle. They could opt to be a giant, a gnome or a wizard. Giants put their arms above their heads as they shout, 'Fee, fi, fo, fum'. Gnomes kneel on the floor with index fingers as antennae and say 'Wibbly, wibbly, wibbly'. Wizards take a stride forward with a swing of the arms as if casting a spell and say the word 'K-pow'. Effectively, it is a more physical version of paper, stones, scissors. The two groups meet in the centre of the room, standing facing each other. They hit their fist three times into their palm before performing their action. Giants win by treading on wizards, wizards win by making gnomes vanish, gnomes win by tripping over giants. When they realise which form the opposition are taking, the group either run back to their base before being tagged (if they lose), chase the opposition attempting to tag them before they reach home (if they win) or simply shake hands (if they are the same). Group members who are successfully tagged before reaching home swap sides. The game continues until a tribe is defeated. The purpose of this game is for the actors to enjoy the humour and suspense in the conflict. It is meant to be fun and by bearing this in mind, the group should be able to find more humour in the scene.

 **Pace and action**

The argument between Stratyllis and the men's leader is structured as a series of one line exchanges, a technique called stichomythia. Intended to be performed quickly, it emphasises the wit of the characters and in this case amuses the audience through the speed of each character's response. In doing this, however, movement can be lost and as a result the exchange can be less effective. In pairs, focus on the barbed exchange on page 47. For each line of dialogue, the actor needs to imagine an action that could be performed at the same time. Rehearse the exchange with actions to illustrate lines. Perform the extracts to the rest of the group, identifying which movements complement the meaning of the text.

**Exploring tone and emphasis**

Similarly, the subtle variations in vocal delivery can be hampered by the pace of this section. Rather than exploring the whole extract look at small groups of lines. Begin by focusing on the four-line section at the bottom of page 45 beginning, 'If you don't keep quiet' and concluding with 'my teeth'. In pairs, consider how the violence and humour could be emphasised by the vocal delivery. Decide on a starting position and perform the section without rehearsal. Once complete, they should return to their starting positions and begin again, this time emphasising a different aspect of the text. The actors are not permitted to discuss what they are planning; they must simply keep repeating the structure, varying the delivery. After a few minutes, discuss the work and what was learnt about the characters. You could also experiment with removing the last line of the extract so that the actor playing Stratyllis has to invent a different act of violence each time.

---

### Throwing water

As the climax of the scene is reached, the women throw the water from their pitchers at the men. A difficult section to explore literally, a group of actors should experiment with the physicality of this moment before soaking each other. Working as a whole group, break the action into four tableaux based on the following section from page 49:

- 'Go on, set her hair on fire!'

- 'Water do your duty!'

- '[All the WOMEN fling water over the men.]'

- 'Help, I'm soaking!'

Rehearse different methods of staging the throwing of the water. Is it ritualistically performed or more spontaneous in nature? You could ask one member of the group to direct the sequence before someone else attempts a different interpretation. Discuss the potential impact of the different versions and note what you have learnt in your text.

---

## Section 5

Magistrate, men's leader, Lysistrata, first old woman, second old woman, Stratyllis

Pages 51–65

The section begins with the grand entrance of the magistrate, flanked by slaves and policemen. He begins with a lecture about the nature of women and appears to control the situation until Lysistrata enters. A comic confrontation between policemen and old women ensues before the men run away from a potential beating. Stripped of his guard, the magistrate asks Lysistrata her intentions; when she explains she is going to save him, he boils with rage. The extract concludes with Lysistrata explaining that she has been silent too long and she is in now going to act in the best interests of her city.

Athens had been a highly democratic city. A council of 500 members had been responsible for the decision-making process. However, after the massive defeat in Sicily, they were temporarily replaced by just ten officials. The magistrate would have been one of those ten.

### Analysis

This section follows an interesting journey from absurd comic action to serious social comment. The buffoonery of the magistrate and his policemen is eventually undermined by Lysistrata appearing to criticise her own past. Her observations about how she was denied a voice in her own marriage and the society in which she lives adds a moment of poignancy to the scene which is developed when she explains how few men are not at war. Although this is an image of feminine wisdom undermining masculine arrogance, it clearly relates to the silent majority who feel they are unable to affect the decision-making process in contemporary politics.

In pairs, discuss different possible ways of staging the entrance of the Magistrate. Where might the characters be positioned on stage? Share the ideas with the rest of the group. Debate the impact that each entrance would have on a contemporary audience.

### The entrance of the magistrate

**Further reading**

In Germaine Greer's and Phil Wilmott's contemporary translation, the policemen enter in SAS style through trapdoors in the stage (*Lysistrata – the sex strike*, Aurora Metro Press, 2000).

 ### The magistrate's innuendos

The second of the magistrate's passages is filled with sexual innuendo. The stories of the Goldsmith and Shoemaker are deliberately written in order to create humour but what form does this take? As a whole group, rehearse each of the following interpretations of this section:

1. The magistrate realises his use of innuendo and uses it to ridicule the women.

2. The magistrate is unaware of the innuendo but it is noted by his soldiers. They try to keep their composure.

3. The magistrate and none of his party recognise the innuendo but the women are aware of what is being said.

4. Nobody on stage recognises the innuendo and it is staged so that the audience are the only people to appreciate the humour.

After rehearsing the four versions, discuss which is the most appropriate. What effect would this have on the magistrate's status in the scene?

### Rehearsing images of violence

The humourous image of the women beating up the policeman should be staged in a way which is comically subversive. After all, it is an image of the oppressed conquering their oppressors. Divide your class into four groups and independently rehearse an image which shows the old women battling a policeman. How might their age affect the manner in which they fight reflect or even defy their age? Perform two groups at a time to create a sense of the comic chaos of this moment in the scene. Look at which movements are particularly effective and why. Consider underscoring the action with the soundtrack of a silent movie to highlight the slapstick nature of the action.

### Swapping roles

For the actors to fully appreciate the impact that their character's behaviour has in a duologue, a useful rehearsal technique is swapping roles. This enables performers to identify individual lines or actions that are particularly powerful whilst learning from another performer's interpretation. In pairs, look at the section of stichomythia which begins on page 59 with the magistrate questioning Lysistrata's actions. Rehearse the scene for ten minutes and discuss with your partner what you have learnt. Now swap roles and rehearse for a further ten, exploring ways in which the status difference can be emphasised. In preparation for an exam question, write two different ways the actors could emphasise the relationship between the two characters.

For the majority of the play, Lysistrata appears to defy her sexuality. She is first and foremost an articulate protestor fighting for her cause; conversely, the women that surround her appear to constantly behave in exaggerated image of femininity. However, at the end of this extract there is a suggestion of the relationship she has with her husband. Look at the lines that begin near the bottom of page 63 with the words 'I will …' and discuss as a group what you feel life might be like with her husband. In pairs improvise the scene where her husband returns home from the Assembly and they discuss the decisions made. After ten minutes of rehearsal, perform the work to the group. How did this affect your understanding of the role and how might it affect the portrayal of the role?

**Lysistrata and her husband**

## Section 6

Lysistrata, first old woman, Stratyllis, women, magistrate, second old woman

Pages 67–75

> The magistrate's previous request to 'let me die' is positively received by the women as he is dressed in Lysistrata's veil and given a work basket. The women affirm their commitment to the cause and Lysistrata proclaims that they will be known as the 'Liquidators of War'. The Chorus recount stories of intimidating soldiers in full uniform entering the market place before Lysistrata uses wool as a metaphor for resolving the conflict. She goes on to emphasise the effect that husbands being separated from their wives may eventually have on the population of Athens. The women sing to the magistrate as they dress him as a corpse before he finally exits the stage fuming.

**Analysis**

The traditional *Agon*, or conflict between central characters, is deliberately subverted by Aristophanes. He uses the form to show how the supposedly powerful magistrate is undermined by a woman. He struggles to have his voice heard and is man-handled by the elderly women. The term liquidator of war is used deliberately. It is a literal translation of Lysistrata's name and is similar to the name of an important priestess in Athens at the time – Lysimache – whose name means liquidator or releaser of battles.

 **War invading society**

The image of the overdressed soldiers walking through the market and intimidating others is interesting because it conveys a sense of war permeating the everyday existence of the common Athenian. Begin, in groups of five, by looking at the following as a series of tableaux:

- A man with a shield buying minnows

- A long-haired cavalry captain arriving on horseback buying porridge and storing it in his helmet

- A Thracian brandishing shield and javelin – woman on fig stall fainting in fright.

Each of the images is slightly more ridiculous than the last. Now try extending these images to a short scene which explores the arrogance of the soldier and the fear of the women. Despite the apparently absurd nature of the action, keep committed to the reality of the performance. Like any modern comedy, the situation is one in which the audience not the characters should find humour.

 **Choral monologue**

Critics often note that during the wool analogy, Lysistrata suggests the importance of including all citizens. However, Aristophanes stops short of suggesting men and women. The explicit inclusion of women would have been laughable and would have undermined the social comment he is making. However, the language of his metaphor is powerful. This should be explored thoroughly in rehearsal by experimenting with different tones. In groups of between six and eight, read the speech that begins 'Imagine the citizen body …', changing speaker every time punctuation is used. This could mean that some people only speak one word at certain points in the text. Having made a note of the phrases each person speaks, create a performance with the group stood close together as a chorus acting as one voice. Actors should be encouraged to vary the tone while still communicating the meaning of the extract. Rehearse and perform this and then repeat the speech with just one person performing all the different voices and movements. What effect might this have on an audience? What might you learn about how the actor should deliver this section?

**Mothers and sons**

Aristophanes' play emphasises the futility of conflict and in particular the Peloponnesian War. On page 71, Lysistrata remarks that the women have had to send their children off to fight. In pairs explore this image practically. Create a scene without dialogue which recreates the moment when the women say goodbye to their sons. After five minutes rehearsal, perform them to the rest of the group several scenes at a time to highlight how this moment would be repeated in families across Athens. As a group, discuss how this image could be suggested by the women of the chorus as Lysistrata's words are delivered.

## Section 7

Men's leader, men, Stratyllis and women

Pages 75–83

Left alone on stage, the chorus of old men and old women continue the battle between the sexes. The men presume the women have joined forces with Sparta and threaten them with violence. The women respond by addressing the audience, explaining how they have served the city loyally, since the age of seven, before Stratyllis stresses the men's incompetence as decision makers. The men's leader attempts to rally his troop by emphasising the threat the women pose and unsuccessfully he attempts to seize Stratyllis. She avoids his grasp and in turn she threatens the Men with violence. The men accept defeat, momentarily, before exiting the stage.

**Analysis**

The traditional Parabasis is replaced with a war of words between the two choruses. Traditionally, their role allowed time for the audience to reflect on the action and their behaviour in this section emphasises the central debates of the play. However, the message is comically undermined as both sides remove clothing in preparation for conflict.

### A manly discussion

Imagine the old men are sat discussing women. Using the information in the text, in groups of four, improvise a scene which identifies their frustrations. Rehearse the scene for 10 minutes allowing different characters to highlight their individual concerns. Now improvise a similar scene between the women focusing on the weaknesses of men. Perform the work and ask the audience to identify which characters are particularly interesting and discuss how these could be reflected in the choral work.

**Images of youth**

Both choruses allude to their devotion to Athens when they were considerably younger. The women discuss how they have served in a variety of forms from the age of seven (page 79). The men, in a vaguer reference, attempt to summon the strength of youth (page 81). Individually, create a short scene which presents a moment from one of the characters' pasts. Stanislavski referred to this as creating the total life of the character. His theories may initially appear to be irrelevant in a superficial comedy but they will help to provide an element of truth to the pain the people of Athens have suffered.

**Further study**

For further information on Stanislavski, look at page 15–23 of *Edexcel AS Drama and Theatre Studies Study Guide* (Rhinegold 2008).

### Creating the ensemble

Since the structure of this section tends to focus on each group in turn, it is possible to rehearse each gender separately. Split your class in two, with one group looking at the men's lines, the other the women's. Rather than rehearsing the entire text, work with a maximum of 50 words each time the focus passes to the group. Within this section, each group will have two passages to rehearse.

Look at the positioning of the actors and experiment with different images to emphasise the text you have chosen. After 20 minutes' rehearsal, perform as a whole group, switching the action between the two groups. Discuss what was learnt by rehearsing separately and the impact of being verbally attacked by the other group.

Stratyllis, Lysistrata, first woman, second woman and third woman

Pages 85–93

## Section 8

A despondent Lysistrata emerges from the gates of the temple; she, like all the women, is sexually frustrated. This point is emphasised by the three women who enter and claim they need to return home for various reasons. When the third is discovered to be falsely claiming to be pregnant, Lysistrata urges all of the women to be strong. She reveals an oracle which emphasises the need for the women to remain true to their cause if they want to keep their reputation in tact. This has the desired effect and the women re-enter the Acropolis.

**Analysis**  This farcical interlude to the action illustrates the effect of the sex-strike on the women. The ancient Greek audience would have assumed that it would be harder for women to remain true to the oath and there would be humour in watching them succumb to their sexual desires. The invocation of the oracle, real or invented by Lysistrata, highlights two issues which apply equally to the ancient and modern societies. The first is the blind faith shown by some to obscure religious writings. The second is how those in power can easily manipulate others.

### The difference in Lysistrata

The image of Lysistrata looking agitated at the beginning of this scene is partly for comic effect; her outburst at the bottom of page 85 would be far less effective without it. However, it is a rare moment of truth in a character who often presides over humorous situations. In pairs, look at the Stanislavskian technique of emotion memory. With one acting as a director/questioner ask the actor playing Lysistrata to recall a time when she felt let down by those around her. Ask her to explain how this made her feel and encourage her to recall how this affected her movement and voice. Having discussed this information, rehearse the first two lines on page 85 with Stratyllis delivery being relatively neutral but Lysistrata's delivery being invested with the emotion. Perform these brief extracts and observe how the actors playing Lysistrata vary their vocal tone and physicality.

### The different visions of desperation

The attempts by the three women to leave the Acropolis have a familiarity about them. Essentially, they are individuals who are attempting to avoid a task. In groups of four, improvise the following scenes, taking it in turns to play the character in authority:

- Three Year 7 students explaining to their PE teacher why they can't take part in cross-country running

- Three teenage children explaining to their parent why they won't be able to attend their grandma's sixtieth birthday

- Three employees who explain why they will not be able to attend their boss' annual work barbecue.

Having explored the scene in a modern context, revisit the original text, using what you have learnt to inform your portrayal of the characters.

 **Lysistrata writing the oracle**

Although it is unclear whether the oracle is genuine, assuming that Lysistrata composed the words herself, it creates an interesting rehearsal opportunity. In pairs, with one person acting as a director, create a scene where Lysistrata is alone in the temple trying to compose the oracle's words. She should talk to herself and perhaps become excited or frustrated with the task. You could even identify whether the scene should be humorous or serious. Perform the short scenes and discuss how this might affect the performance of the role in the scene. How might an actor show to the audience that the words might not be genuine?

## Section 9

Men, men's leader, Stratyllis, women

Pages 95–99

> The men begin the section by recounting the tale of Melanion who they believe to be wise because he detested women. The women counteract this with a story of Timon who detested the wickedness of men but adored women. After additional threats of violence and sexual taunts, the choruses leave the stage.

**Analysis**

The second of the choral battles between the scantily-clad old people still contains within it a threat of violence but also the first hint of reconciliation. Despite appearing to be frustrated by their behaviour, the men's leader asks Stratyllis for a kiss. The brief flirtation momentarily alters the mood and the status difference between the two groups appears more equal.

 **Men's story versus women's story**

The choruses represent two conflicting stories of men. In order to bring these to life it is useful to imagine that the class is a theatre-in-education company, who are going to perform the two tales physically to an audience of Year 6 children. Divide the group in half, with each group focusing on a different story. Consider how the audience might affect the nature of the performance. Use physical theatre to create a sense of location with exaggerated characterisation to emphasise the tale. Rehearse the scenes, bearing in mind the audience. Perform the two pieces and then discuss what amendments are needed if any are needed in order to make it appropriate for the performance.

## Moment of flirting

Considering the men's leader appearing to flirt with Stratyllis. In pairs, consider how the line 'Old thing, I want to kiss you' could be staged: seductively, in an intimidating way, or innocently? Create three different versions considering the physicality of both characters. Note the different interpretations on your text, using precise drama terms.

Lysistrata, Calonice, Myrrhine, Cinesias, baby, Manes, men and women

Pages 99–121

## Section 10

Lysistrata enters urgently dismayed by the arrival of a man, Cinesias, who is revealed to be Myrrhine's husband. As he enters, Lysistrata exacerbates his sexual frustration by saying how much his wife is missing him. Myrrhine initially appears on the ramparts but is persuaded to come closer when her husband shows her that he has brought their child with him. She cuddles the baby but refuses any physical contact from her husband. A farcical sequence follows where Calonice attempts to seduce Myrrhine, only for his wife to keep finding excuses to temporarily leave. Eventually she abandons him and he moans about the cramps he is experiencing from being denied sex. A Spartan herald arrives and is ridiculed by Cinesias because of his erection. The former brings news of a similar revolt by the women of Sparta and those of their allies.

**Analysis**    The playful torturing of Cinesias is more subtle than some of the previous action. His name derives from Greek slang words for sex and as the scene develops slowly, it is clear that this is his preoccupation. His erect phallus will be a constant reminder of this. Once he is abandoned, Sommerstein's translation has him pleading through song. This is unusual behaviour for a protagonist in this play. Therefore, it could further highlight his frustration and, depending on the music used, it could allow for a moment of sympathy form the audience.

## A love letter

Cinesias is a comic fool, a desperate man who is ridiculed by the women. However, his desperation, albeit for sex, could make the character appealing. Imagine he has decided to write a love letter to his wife to leave at the Acropolis. Individually, write these words on a piece of paper using the information given in the text. You might begin like this:

My beautiful Myrrhine, I write this letter
as a symbol of my love. I miss …

Having written the letter, join with a partner. Decide who will play Cinesias and who will play his male friend. Improvise a scene where the friend discovers the letter before Cinesias enters the stage. The former should tease the latter about its contents and end up tearing up the letter. Does this victimised portrayal of Cinesias appear appropriate for the role or should he be a more arrogant character?

### Removing the words

The exchange between Cinesias and Lysistrata relies on both verbal and physical comedy. Working in groups of four, divide yourself into pairs, with each pair performing a different role. However, one person will be responsible for the lines of the character while the other will perform the movement. The two physical performers should stand in the space whilst those responsible for the vocal delivery stand at the side. The aim is to spread the workload of the performer. As the lines are read, the physical actors focus on their stature and gesture, performing on stage while having the luxury of listening to the lines. Initially, divide the two elements, asking the actors to read the lines before the movement is performed. However, after a few rehearsals, experiment with the two parts being performed in synchronicity. A further stage could be asking one performer to present the vocal and physical ideas for each character.

### Acting apart

When Myrrhine and Cinesias are initially 'reunited', it is over a distance. She is stood on the ramparts while he waits loyally down below. On stage it may be difficult to create the sense of space so try the following exercises in pairs. Begin by rehearsing in the open air, standing approximately 20 metres apart. This should help to ensure the voice is well-projected and the gestures are grand. It may also make the event more public as the actors may well be watched during this aspect of this rehearsal. If this is the case, this should add to the embarrassment that the actor playing Cinesias feels. Having rehearsed this so the actors are familiar with the appropriate performance style for this distance, bring the action back onto the stage. Stand the actors next to each other. They should both face out towards the audience with Myrrhine looking down and Cinesias looking up. The actors should now image that the other person is still 20 metres away and behave appropriately. This dislocating of the action can be particularly effective in presenting the situation to the audience. As a group, discuss the benefits of dislocating this scene or any other scenes in the play.

### Acting on a chair

There is a tendency to overcomplicate the action in rehearsal with complex movements, which can distract you from the true meaning of the text. In pairs, sit opposite each other and allocate roles for the scene between Myrrhine and Cinesias starting on page 109. Read the entire scene to each other, with the script on your laps. As each line is spoken, the actors must hold eye-contact reading the motion of each other's facial expressions. Obviously, in order to complete this exercise, the actor needs to memorise each sentence or phrase in turn before it is delivered. There is a tendency to deliver this quickly, cheating by looking up half-way through the exercise. Speed is not the priority; the actors must focus closely on the text. The actor playing Cinesias could also look at how his increasing sexual frustration could be shown through sounds as well as words. Note any successful aspects of the delivery in your text.

### Saucy sea-side postcards

In order to maintain the bawdy nature of the play look at the same section between Myrrhine and Cinesias but condense into a series of seaside postcard images. Exaggerate the flirtatious behaviour of the woman and the physical frustration of the man. You may find it useful to work in threes, using one person to sculpt the images.

**Cinesias' song**

After being abandoned by his wife, Cinesias breaks into song. In groups of three, look at the action on page 119 until just before the Spartan's entrance. Try interpreting the character as an innocent and slightly pathetic soul. Use the tune of 'Greensleeves' to give a melancholic mood to his singing. The other actors should play the role of the male and female chorus. How could this be performed so that a contemporary audience would have sympathy for his character? Perhaps he could even be playing the tune on his guitar. What contemporary music could be used if you wished to present him as a more loathsome character? How might his behaviour change?

Men's leader, Stratyllis, men and women

Pages 125–131

### Section 11

The Chorus return to the stage with the men's leader emphasising the stubbornness of women; an ironic observation since it is Stratyllis who calls a truce and helps him put his tunic back on. She also notices a gnat in his eye and she removes it, they kiss, as do the other Chorus members, which results in the two groups uniting as one. The scene concludes with a song from the united Chorus which mocks the audience with false promises of 'goodies'.

**Analysis**

This section, despite its brevity, sets the tone for the remainder of the play. By uniting the two separate choruses, Aristophanes hints at the harmony that will follow. It also communicates a very simple message. Life is better when people are united in cause.

## Flirting

Stratyllis breaks the defences of the male Chorus leader with flirtatious behaviour. He complains of having something in his eye and a result she is able to get closer than before, make physical contact, which in turn results in a kiss. In pairs, look at recreating this moment in a modern setting. Improvise the dialogue but use the concept of having something in the eye as breaking down the barriers. How might this scene be performed differently if, as in the play, the two characters are old?

## The united Chorus

The joining of the two disparate groups not only changes the tone of their language but their physical appearance should also be different. As a whole group, create a tableau of the two Choruses in conflict, facing each other. Try to suggest a sense of the different characters that could exist. Now, devise an image of the united Chorus facing the audience:

- Is there more physical contact?

- How are they positioned in relation to the audience?

- Are they in couples or one large group?

- How might different levels be incorporated?

## Section 12

A party of Spartan and Athenian delegates approach with their erect phalloi highlighting that 'the crisis is more inflamed than ever!'. The men explain that they are ready to call a truce. Lysistrata emerges with the beautiful Reconciliation who helps to tease the men one last time. Lysistrata, with the men's divided attention, recounts the previous attacks from both sides which have fuelled the crisis. The men enter negotiation, using Reconciliation's body as a map. With help from Lysistrata, they agree to a compromise before exiting to rejoin their wives.

Leader, first Spartan, Spartan, first Athenian

Pages 133–145

In a play that warns against excesses of war, Aristophanes chooses to present his men at the extremes of sexual frustration before offering a resolution to the conflict. By doing this, he reduces the leaders and warriors to base human beings and stresses that they all have at least one thing in common. By using Lysistrata to recount historical events, which demonstrate how Spartans and Athenians have helped each other during times of conflict, Aristophanes emphasises his key message. He is not calling for an end to all violence, simply a truce between two groups of people who have similar interests. He avoids labouring the seriousness of this message by mapping out the terms of the cease fire on Reconciliation's body.

## Analysis

“ Lysistrata has a serious story to tell. But like all good comedies, it knows when to stop taking itself too seriously. ”

Blake Morrison, *The Guardian*, 10th September 2007.
See article online at www. guardian.co.uk/politics/2007/ sept/10/theatre.classics

### The formality of the situation

The arrival of the Spartan and Athenian delegates, representatives of the warring enemies, could be acted in a relatively formal manner. Their entrances could be grand, representing their military might and their reaction to their opposition should be cautious. However, the tension would be constantly undermined by the image of the men's erect phalli. Look at the text on pages 133–135 and in groups of five, with two delegates for each side, try to present both the formality and comedy of the situation. How should the actors use pause and small gestures to indicate their discomfort with the situation? The delegates only acknowledge each other on page 135. How might eye-contact be used up until that point? As a group, you could experiment with miming the whole scene to emphasise the physical subtleties of the scene.

### Creating the total life of the character

Imagine that Lysistrata and one of the other women are talking inside the temple. They have seen the delegations arrive and know that their plan is reaching fruition. It is important that their next actions are successful if peace is to be secured. In pairs, improvise the conversation they have before exiting the Acropolis. Are they nervous or confident? How will this be shown?

### Setting the tone

The language of the men, and their use of Reconciliation's body, need to be presented carefully. The wrong emphasis could lead to the sexist behaviour of the men being unintentionally celebrated. A contemporary version of the play would need to ridicule rather than condone their language. Look at page 141 and as a whole group discuss how the piece might need to be presented. In groups of five, with one acting as a director, try to stage the action so that their desperation, and therefore the weakness of their sex, is highlighted.

---

**Further reading**

Greer and Willmott, in their production, cut the character of Reconciliation, choosing to present the arguments about land through sexual innuendo instead: '*Kinesias*: We'd have to stake a claim to that thickly wooded triangular bit between the legs of Mageara' (*Lysistrata – the sex strike*, Aurora Metro Press, 2000).

## Section 13

Chorus, first Athenian, second Athenian, Spartan, Lysistrata and Chorus

Pages 145–155

> The Chorus through song explain once again that they have very little of anything before the doors of the Acropolis open and two drunken Athenians enter the stage. In their slightly confused state they threaten to burn the Chorus before explaining that the world appears a lot simpler through drunken eyes. Spartan delegates appear through the doors of the Acropolis and one sings a celebratory song which outlines past battles and concludes with a commitment to peace. Lysistrata, accompanied by the women, enters the stage and instructs the couples to unite, reminding then that all citizens should not 'repeat our errors'. The play concludes with a dance in celebration of the gods.

**Analysis**

Although Aristophanes experiments with the form of Old Comedy, his structure of the Exodus is traditional in style. The two opposing factions of the play, men and women, (rather than Athenian and Spartan) are united as a peaceful solution is established. However, a Greek audience would have found Lysistrata's orchestration of the truce laughable. Women may appear smarter in the play but in society they are not involved in political and democratic processes. Despite this, the different songs emphasise the sense of resolution and harmony, the practical solution to the problems of the war.

### Drunken wisdom

The two Athenians are Aristophanes' final attempt to comment on the ludicrous behaviour of the city. When at war, Athenian soldiers appear to overcomplicate matters when the drunken or simplistic view would be far more successful. In pairs, spontaneously improvise conversations between two drunken people in a pub, beginning with the following lines:

- The problem with the young people of today …
- If I were prime minister of this country …
- The solution to crime is simple …
- As my mum used to say 'Things ain't what they used to be …'

Having experimented with a contemporary setting, look at the text on page 147 and consider how it could be performed successfully.

**Making music**

The Spartan's song, which acts as a confirmation of the truce by the historic enemy, is played on pipes. However, Sommerstein's translation of the section has a clear rhythm and provides a basic structure on which performers can build. In groups of three or four, focusing mainly on the rhythms of the accompaniment, devise a percussion backing for the Spartan's lyrics. If you are musically confident, you may wish to experiment with devising or adapting a suitable tune.

**A celebratory dance**

The traditional use of song and dance in the Exodus helps to conclude the action and gently brings the audience back to reality. Strange as it may appear, it is no different from the role encores play in contemporary musicals. This dance is both a celebration of marriage and harmony among nations and, therefore, this should be demonstrated physically. Consider staging this final dance as a Ceilidh. Research the traditions of the dance and some of the structures within it. You may also discover an appropriate rhythm to use for Lysistrata's song.

## Past and present

The play provides every character with a journey to greater happiness. All characters have benefited from the women's protests, even if they do not fully realise how. In groups of four, choose any of the play's protagonists and create two scenes that reflect their attitude at the beginning and end of the scene. The scenes could directly mirror the action on stage or suggest events that take place off stage. Rehearse for 20 minutes and then show the work to the group. From your knowledge of the play, identify moments in the text where the character begins to move from one state to the next.

## Directorial interpretation

Now that you have read the play and made detailed structured notes as you have gone you should be close to formulating your directorial concept that will carry you through the written examination. The style of *Lysistrata* is firmly grounded in the traditions of Greek comedy but the universal topics of war and sex mean that it has resonances for any era. Conflicts permeate history and protests against moments of inhumanity often punctuate battles. Frustrations with those in political power is a recurring theme and despite its humorous portrayal the play has the power to suggest that action, rather than apathy, is the solution. Can parallels be drawn between the play and modern versions of war? Could the play be successfully be relocated into another period of history? Or does it work better as a play from the past where more subtle resonances are found? Look at the brief extract of the review of Lysistrata at the Arcola Theatre:

Review by Philip Fisher, *The British Theatre Guide* (2005), www.britishtheatreguide.info/reviews/lysistrata-rev

Ranjit Bolt's wildly exciting, updated version of this Greek classic might give the uninitiated the wrong impression. When Aristophanes wrote the play, he almost certainly did not set it in the corner of an underground car park with three, battered cars playing a major part in the action. However, designer Soutra Gilmour, who delights in such settings, knows better. The theme is absolutely up-to-date and could be seen as addressing the war in Iraq today. Therefore Ranjit Bolt can feel justified in allowing the setting and language to reflect contemporary life.

There is a great deal to consider here:

- Do you want to set the play in its original conditions or does it lend itself to a particular period of time or place?

- Do you instead want to make it a timeless or futuristic piece that makes a universal point?

- Who do your central characters represent and what should an audience be picking up in the choices that you have made?

A necessary starting point is to visualise what your production of the play will look like. Choose a venue – indoor or outdoor? Does the play lend itself to performance in front of an audience of 3,000 people or is it more suited to an intimate studio venue? There are justifications for both choices. Where would you like your audience to be physically positioned in relation to the actors? Sketch some ideas or look at existing venues online.

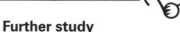

**Further study**

For more detailed reference to staging, look at *Edexcel AS Drama and Theatre Studies Study Guide* (Rhinegold 2008).

## Designing the set

Now that you have a clearer idea about directorial concept, venue and staging you can start to apply it to the specific demands of the text. Work through the text noting the different location and moments of action that exist. It may be worth doing this in table form as below. This will allow you to clearly see where the staging demands occur and what challenges you will have to overcome. Although the location of *Lysistrata* only moves from the front of the house to outside the Acropolis, a modern production may choose to create a range of settings which reflect the mood and action of the scenes.

| Act/scene | Page number | Location | Characters in scene | Key action in scene |
|---|---|---|---|---|
| | | | | |

The initial image of Lysistrata exiting her house reflects the start of her plan. It has an intimacy to it, the suggestion of an idea in its embryonic stages. Will you as a director be looking at a minimalist interpretation of the play with symbolic and significant set pieces or will you be looking to recreate a realistic street scene? How might this location reflect the humbleness of their beginning? The scene begins with them exiting houses but then concludes with them entering the Acropolis. How would you suggest this change in location?

**Turn to the Appendix on page 195. These questions should help to guide you in the right direction and provide a checklist once all decisions have been reached.**

## Tackling the written examination

The examination booklet can be an intimidating document. Remember, all that concerns you is the section on the text you are studying, in our case *Lysistrata*. The page numbers you need to refer to in this booklet will be clearly marked on the question paper.

**Section A** is divided into three questions:

a) is worth 4 marks

b) is worth 6 marks

c) is worth 10 marks.

The paper is worth a total of 20 marks. How much you write for each question should correspond to the maximum marks available.

The chosen extract will cover approximately four to six pages of text. For the purpose of this example we will be looking at pages 99–111, beginning at Lysistrata's line 'Hey! Women, women, come here quickly!' and finishing with Myrrhine's line 'Till then, I've sworn not to.'

**Example question 1**

a) Outline for your performers two ways that they might emphasise the relationship between Lysistrata and Cinesias at the start of this extract. (4)

You first need to consider what that relationship is. How do we want the audience to feel about them at this stage in the play? Lysistrata is the leader about to be challenged not by a political force but by a husband. Cinesias is clearly suffering from the sex ban. Practically, how will you illustrate this to the audience using two clear examples?

For four marks the marking criteria state that 'connections to the demands of the question will be clear' and ask for 'two clear and valid examples supported by reasons'. They ask for 'thinking that is confident, accurate, and clear and rehearsal must be explicit in the response'.

This is an example of a top-band response; the comments in brackets illustrate how the answer corresponds to the criteria.

| | |
|---|---|
| Don't waste space giving needless introductory comment. | I would explore their relationship in two distinct ways. Cinesias would enter upstage left, with Lysistrata already positioned downstage right, linking her to the audience while highlighting the gulf between her and Cinesias. Lysistrata should speak authoritatively with a firm, demanding tone, stressing the consonants in her words. In contrast, Cinesias should stutter, breathing heavily, looking physically insignificant as he shouts in a vulnerable tone the word 'me'. This would immediately establish the status difference and the control the women have. |
| Specific and clear instruction demonstrating awareness of stage space. Clear justification given. | The second way would be through physical comedy. Cinesias should at the beginning of the extract be facing downstage. During their initial exchange he should take tentative steps towards Lysistrata, holding eye contact in desperation. As Lysistrata explains that his is a name they know well, her voice should become softer, more husky in tone, falsely celebrating his masculinity. As he gasps 'you gods' in sexual frustration |
| Again, specific practical instruction to actors, showing an awareness of the development of the action, with clear justification offered. | he should turn to stage right, revealing his fully erect phallus to both Lysistrata and the audience, emphasising the humour of his affliction and the success of Lysistrata's mission. |

Let's now look at a bottom-band response:

> This extract comes at the heart of the play just as Lysistrata's political mission is gathering momentum. She is a woman of great mental strength and it is clear that Cinesias is no match for her. Cinesias enters with a man servant who carries a baby, a fact that will add further complications later in the scene.[1] Cinesias should enter stage left with his enormous phallus fully erect.[2] Males should follow him nervously. They should move towards Lysistrata before listening to her questions.[3] Lysistrata should be acting in a powerful way and the audience should realise this.[4]

1. Needless contextual information that shows no awareness of the question.
2. Simple repetition of stage directions will not be rewarded.
3. Purely descriptive, no evidence of how.
4. Lack of specific reference to how. Not specific and no evidence of rehearsal. Where is the second way as requested in the question? Awareness of impact on audience, justification of decision made.

What comes across most strongly in good responses to the above question are the following:

- Strong PRACTICAL evidence as to HOW the moment might be performed

- Clear reference to WHY the decision has been made

- Awareness that this is a question asking you to explore REHEARSAL

- An awareness of the impact of choices on AUDIENCE.

**Example question 2**

a) Consider THREE appropriate rehearsal techniques that might highlight the difference between the men and women in this extract.                                    (4)

> The first technique I would use to highlight the personalities is an off-text improvisation. In pairs, the men should play the role of a besotted teenager who has been banned from seeing his girlfriend by her parents. The actors should improvise the scene where the boy knocks on the door of his girlfriend's house to see if he could talk to her briefly. This would give the actors an insight into the emotions that Cinesias and Lysistrata are feeling during the enforcement of the ban.
>
> The second technique I would use would be to thought-track Cinesias, Myrrhine and Manes in the section where Cinesias calls up to her. Using additional actors from the company, I would ask them to speak the thoughts of the characters after every line is delivered. Not only will this reveal the subtext in the delivery of the lines but it may also avoid Manes remaining a passive character. I would then ask the actors to perform the scene again, trying to convey what they have previously heard through their physicality and changes in vocal delivery. This should emphasise some of the comic thoughts that underpin the action and the different manners in which the genders approach the conflict.

Technique clearly identified.

Specific practical explanation of technique.

Reason for the choice of technique in context with the performance.

Technique identified.

Practical exploration.

Impact of technique and clear justification for its use.

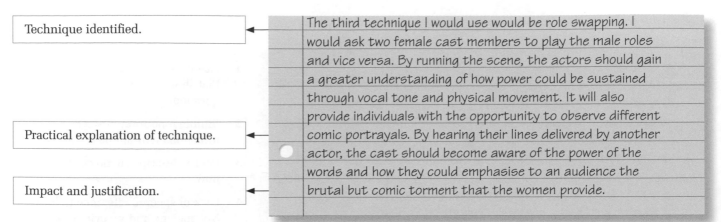

> Technique identified.

> Practical explanation of technique.

> Impact and justification.

The third technique I would use would be role swapping. I would ask two female cast members to play the male roles and vice versa. By running the scene, the actors should gain a greater understanding of how power could be sustained through vocal tone and physical movement. It will also provide individuals with the opportunity to observe different comic portrayals. By hearing their lines delivered by another actor, the cast should become aware of the power of the words and how they could emphasise to an audience the brutal but comic torment that the women provide.

For a top-band response to this question the marking criteria asks for specific examples and balance across the three techniques. A confident grasp of terminology and a clear understanding of purpose in using the ideas are required.

**Example question 3**

b) Explain to your performers how you intend to work on developing an understanding of the character of Lysistrata in this extract and her relationship with other characters and the audience, giving reasons for your approach, supported by clear examples. (6)

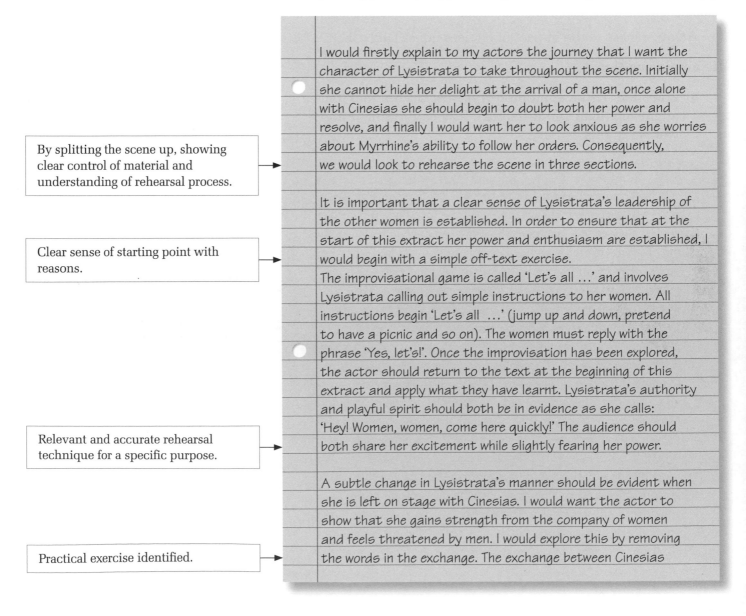

> By splitting the scene up, showing clear control of material and understanding of rehearsal process.

> Clear sense of starting point with reasons.

> Relevant and accurate rehearsal technique for a specific purpose.

> Practical exercise identified.

I would firstly explain to my actors the journey that I want the character of Lysistrata to take throughout the scene. Initially she cannot hide her delight at the arrival of a man, once alone with Cinesias she should begin to doubt both her power and resolve, and finally I would want her to look anxious as she worries about Myrrhine's ability to follow her orders. Consequently, we would look to rehearse the scene in three sections.

It is important that a clear sense of Lysistrata's leadership of the other women is established. In order to ensure that at the start of this extract her power and enthusiasm are established, I would begin with a simple off-text exercise.
The improvisational game is called 'Let's all …' and involves Lysistrata calling out simple instructions to her women. All instructions begin 'Let's all …' (jump up and down, pretend to have a picnic and so on). The women must reply with the phrase 'Yes, let's!'. Once the improvisation has been explored, the actor should return to the text at the beginning of this extract and apply what they have learnt. Lysistrata's authority and playful spirit should both be in evidence as she calls: 'Hey! Women, women, come here quickly!' The audience should both share her excitement while slightly fearing her power.

A subtle change in Lysistrata's manner should be evident when she is left on stage with Cinesias. I would want the actor to show that she gains strength from the company of women and feels threatened by men. I would explore this by removing the words in the exchange. The exchange between Cinesias and Lysistrata relies on both verbal and physical comedy which would be best explored by highlighting the vulnerability of both characters. I would ask two members of the company to work with Lysistrata and Cinesias, speaking their lines for them. The two 'physical' performers should stand in the space focusing on posture and gesture whilst those responsible for the vocal delivery stand at the side, reading the lines. With Lysistrata positioned downstage right, she has the possibility of exposing her frailties to the audience, and I would expect the actor to experiment with this occasionally turning to them for confidence with wide eyes or sharing her insecurities through a nervous stroke of the face and bite of the lip after Cinesias demands Myrrhine to come out to him. After a few rehearsals, I would ask the actors to communicate the vocal and physical subtleties of the role in a manner which proves Lysistrata to be a rounded rather than two-dimensional character.

> Practical ideas linked to intended impact.

In the final section of this scene I intend to expose both Lysistrata's nervous and determined spirit. Rather than

> Directorial statement.

Lysistrata simply passing the onstage focus to Myrrhine, I would like there to be a pause before she appears to exit. She should hold Myrrhine's hands in hers, staring in her eyes momentarily before whispering the line spoken earlier in the scene, 'keep him on tenterhooks'. As Myrrhine nods and walks past her, Lysistrata should follow her with her eyes, doubting the woman's resolve. The importance of this exchange would consequently be drawn to the audience's attention before the comic action dominates.

However, I feel that this scene would need to maintain a sense of Lysistrata's power throughout it and, therefore, rather than exiting, the actor should position herself up stage right, observing the action and enjoying Cinesias torture. Her body should be straight, eyes focused firmly downstage on the couple's battle. She is not a giggling woman observing

> Practical example linked to specific moment of the text.

a playful prank; she is a leader executing her plan and the audience should be clear about her need to see it executed.

> Justification of ideas, audience awareness.

The marking criteria in this section look to see how the candidate establishes relationships between characters and refers to key moments. It is not a character study. Again, they refer to 'a confident and clear grasp of drama', evidence of physical and vocal exploration, evidence of rehearsal techniques, audience impact and a 'clear understanding of the process of interpreting the play in performance'.

## Section B

This section is an extended answer worth 30 marks and should be written in an essay-style format. This section tests your overall understanding of the play and allows you to justify and explore the directorial concept that has been central to all your preparations for this examination. You will have made distinct decisions about how you want the play to be performed and in the previous pages we have done our best to prepare you for this moment. You should see this section as an opportunity to share your vision with the examiner, not as a test that you can fail.

You will be given a choice of two questions and must answer one. What we will do in the following pages is look to see how you might structure a response and then look at the specific marking criteria.

### Question 1

> As a director, explain your approach to the play in every aspect of production. Justify your ideas with clear and well-supported examples. (30)

The first thing you need to make clear in your response is your directorial concept. How do you see the play *Lysistrata*? Is it a modern timeless story that you want to tell or do you feel that you want to do justice to the play in its original performance conditions? Alternatively is yours a vision that combines both aspects? You need to clearly state in your introduction WHY yours is a concept that works for this play.

The next thing to consider is the aspects of every production:

- Acting style
- Interpretation
- Audience
- Performance space
- Staging
- Lighting
- Props
- Performance style
- Sound
- Costume
- Music

This may well give you the structure of your essay. You may believe that some aspects of production are more important than others and therefore worth more coverage within the essay. Work through the aspects of the production section by section, always referring back to how each area supports your directorial approach.

Two words must dominate your response:

- HOW – a practical example of how a particular scene or moment might be staged or audience positioned or costume designed, for example

- WHY – a clear understanding from you as to how this practical example supports your directorial concept and what impact the particular moment will have on your audience.

A good essay can identify the answer to these two words in each paragraph. The more WHYs that you have the greater chance your of achieving high marks.

Conclude your essay strongly by reinforcing the sense of vision that you have been trying to communicate and how within the essay you have attempted to illustrate this.

### Marking criteria

The examiners are looking in the top level 5 (25–30 marks) for the following areas:

- 'An understanding of drama and theatre terminology'
- 'Interpretation and imagination'

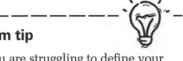

**Exam tip**

If you are struggling to define your interpretation try imagining that your version is in print and you have been asked to write the blurb on the back of the book in exactly 200 words. Start with the line 'Lysistrata is a play about ...'

**Exam tip**

Think carefully about four to five of the key scenes or moments in *Lysistrata* that you will be referring to in any essay about directorial interpretation. Make sure that you do not neglect the minor characters in your choice. Make a brief list of these scenes so that you might be able to refer to them easily when confronted with the essay title.

- 'An understanding of the performance space'
- 'A full understanding of the play'
- 'Supported examples – visually and practically appealing – without losing sight of its original performance values'
- 'Reference to stylistic or historic elements'
- 'Understanding of aesthetic impact complementing meaning and structure of the play'
- 'Confidence … how live theatre could work … a knowledgeable response'.

The following are things you should avoid in your responses – these hints are taken from the marking criteria at the lower level 2 (7–12 marks):

- 'Highly descriptive'
- 'Highly sourced from an annotated script'
- 'Highly imaginative but not able to work in practical performance'
- 'Little sense of justification'
- 'Proposed interpretation not justified in terms of playwright's original intentions'.

Finally using the example answer above alongside the marking criteria for top- and lower-end responses, consider this question and produce a structure or paragraph plan that you might share among your group for the question below:

> As a director, outline how you would portray the character of Lysistrata in order to emphasise the themes of your production. Give supported examples of how your ideas might be achieved in performance.

Although Unit 4 is highly demanding, it is also richly rewarding. The purpose of taking you through every aspect of text and design in the pages above is to thoroughly prepare you for the exam. If you get a sense that you own your interpretation in every way then you will be able to handle any question on any aspect of your production. With a heavily annotated text that you understand and has been put together in an ordered and structured way, the examination should hold no fear for you. You should want to create a sense of ownership and pride in your work born out of a real connection with the play and a personal and intuitive connection with it.

## Dr Faustus by Christopher Marlowe

### Plot summary

*Dr Faustus* follows the tragic tale of a well-respected academic who has grown bored and disinterested with traditional forms of knowledge and is drawn towards the world of black magic. He calls upon a devil, Mephistopheles, and strikes a deal – to sell his soul to Lucifer in return for 24 years of service from Mephistopheles. Despite warnings, Faustus' journey begins. As he travels through Europe he meets figureheads of church and state, all of whom he abuses and disrespects. He conjures up images of historical figures Alexander the Great and Helen of Troy purely to impress the scholars around him. As the final hour approaches the impact of the choice Faustus has made begins to hit home and fear and remorse set in. He belatedly begs for mercy, but it is all too late as the devils enter to take Faustus to hell. The tale ends with a moral epilogue warning the audience of the dangers of excess.

*Dr Faustus* is the story of a choice that an individual makes who through personal greed and dissatisfaction reaches beyond mortal life for something else. He experiences wealth and beauty beyond all imagination and yet fails to recognise the consequence of the choice that he has made. When it is all too late, the realisation of his future dawns and he begs hopelessly for mercy as the devils come to damn him to hell.

Although drawing from other influences as outlined below, there may be much contemporary relevance for you today and you should be inspired to search for a modern perspective to inform your creative and practical decisions in preparation for the written examination.

## The author

Christopher Marlowe (1564–1593) had an incredibly colourful and controversial life that came to a sudden end, aged just 29. His life is littered with rumours of espionage, murder, counterfeiting and public order offences. Most notable are the accusations of atheism levelled against him by Richard Baines, among others, in a libel case submitted in 1593 (BL Harley MS.6848 ff.185-6). Baines accuses Marlowe of having said:

> *That the first beginning of Religioun was only to keep men in awe … That Christ was a bastard and his mother dishonest… That all protestants are Hypocriticall asses.*

and…

> *Into every Company he Cometh he perswades men to Atheism willing them not to be afeard of bugbeares and hobgoblins, and vtterly scorning both god and his ministers.*

In 1593 a warrant was issued for Marlowe's arrest, but before it could be carried out, he was dead, stabbed above the right eye during a fight in a Deptford pub by Ingram Frizar, a man with a shady secret service background of his own. It was said that the fight was over an unpaid bill, but the fact that within a month Her Majesty's Privy Council pardoned the murderer indicates a cover up and links to the rumours of Marlowe's spying past.

Marlowe's biographical details indicate a restless, violent, politically active and intellectual man (a Cambridge graduate) who was willing to rigorously challenge established beliefs and stir up the status quo. It is unavoidable that we as active readers make links between these details and the actions and behaviour of his protagonist, Dr Faustus.

### Further reading

Christopher Marlowe's reputation is built on *Faustus* and three other plays worthy of study: *Tamburlaine Parts I and II* (1587-8), *The Jew of Malta* (1590) and *Edward II* (1592).

## Contextualising the play

The play *Dr Faustus* is itself surrounded by uncertainties of authorship and composition dates. Although it was first published in 1604, eleven years after Marlowe's death, there are records of performances dating back to 1594. A second edition of the play was published in 1616 (known as the 'B' text complete with additional scenes added by other playwrights). The version that we are studying here is the original, known as the 'A' text.

There was a great fascination in the Renaissance with witchcraft and conjuring that tied into a broader theme of exploration. *Faustus* represents the Renaissance man. He has a real thirst for knowledge and an inquiring mind. The late 1500s was an age of exploration and discovery. Explorers such as Francis Drake returned from their travels with amazing stories of other cultures and astronomy was a growing interest. Scientific knowledge and experimentation were taking increasing prominence in society. All these elements are presented in *Faustus*.

A further area worth exploring is the theme of education. Books and learning are the great leveller, since a man from lowly birth can read the same books as those born in to learning. With learning, however, comes a desire for more knowledge and this can lead to an individual acting in blind pursuit of the fulfilment of this desire. Faustus is short-sighted and cannot see beyond immediate pleasure. A true Renaissance man might have logically considered the longer-term consequences of his actions before embarking on such an outrageous journey. We might also question how Faustus chooses to use his power – not to find answers to the unanswerable questions of life but to mock the Pope, flirt with a duchess and kiss the most beautiful woman in the world. Do his choices here betray the kind of man he really is?

The story of *Dr Faustus* comes from a traditional German legend dating back to 1587 and was translated into English by a P. F. Gent. The story of one man selling his soul to the devil was well known and has been adapted throughout history to be a cautionary tale of the dangers of greed and overweening desire.

One can see links in Marlowe's play to the medieval morality plays of the 13th century. Such plays, as reflected in *Faustus*, exhibited temptation, the personification of the devil, the presence of mercy in the form of The Old Man, the seven deadly sins and the death of the sinner who chose the wrong path.

Even further back in theatre history, *Dr Faustus* has links to ancient Greece particularly in some elements of the tragic structure as outlined by Aristotle. Although it does not follow the Unities detailed in Aristotle's *Poetics*, it does have a protagonist with whom the audience can identify, an anti-hero with a tragic flaw, the use of a Chorus, and a strong moral ending that serves as a form of catharsis for the audience. There are also key differences, the most central being the element of choice. Faustus shapes his own destiny where he could have chosen another direction. For

**Further study**

The original company that performed Faustus was the Admiral's Men run by Phillip Henslowe. The lead role was taken by the famous actor Edward Alleyne. These key names are worthy of broader research to gain a greater understanding of contextual performance and style.

**Exploration**

**Education**

**Story**

**Further study**

More detailed coverage of ancient Greek and medieval theatre can be found in *Edexcel AS Drama and Theatre Studies Study Guide* (Rhinegold 2008) in the 'Understanding Theatre' chapter.

tragic heroes such as Sophocles' Oedipus, this was not possible as their fate had been predetermined by the gods from the moment that they were born.

The issues raised in this contextualising section are deliberately written to provoke a practical and creative response in your interpretation of the play. It is vital that before you read the specifics of the next section that you have a clear idea of the Faustus that you want to present. Is he a man that we should love or hate? How is this a story for our times? How as a director can you bring out the themes and issues which you believe to be central to the play?

---

It is vital that you get to know Faustus as a man in order that you can make decisions about directing an actor in the role. The first stage is to identify the journey that the character goes through, where there is change in status, mood or character relationship.

1. Establish how Faustus appears at the start of the play. Find two lines of dialogue that best illustrate their character at the start of their journey. Brainstorm as many key words that describe their character, and provide significant notes on the relationship with other characters

2. What is the first significant moment of change? What has prompted it? How is it identified in relationships, use of language, non-verbal communication, movement or staging? Brainstorm descriptive words that explain Faustus at this point. Select one or two key lines of dialogue to best illustrate his condition.

3. Continue with this pattern throughout the play, following the guidelines in points 1 and 2.

4. Consider carefully the end point of *Faustus*. How does he finish the play?

You should now have identified a series of stages in the development of the character; you should have a number of descriptive words and short quotations for each section.

Draw a flow diagram for Faustus to clarify his journey, and annotate the arrows in as much practical detail as you can to give guidance for performance.

During the following pages, we will work through the play in sections, looking at the dramatic significance of the scene and giving practical suggestions for exploring the text. Remember, the written examination will be testing your skills as a director so many of the exercises will be focused on how the text can be rehearsed. As each idea is discussed, keep your production at the forefront of your mind. Make notes on any ideas you have on the staging of the piece. Towards the end of the chapter, you will be given suggestions on how to draw these ideas together into a clear directorial concept and ultimately shape your response into written answers. You will find this difficult if you have not made detailed notes along the way.

# Key sections

## Prologue

👨👩 Chorus

Page 1

> The Chorus is used as a traditional device in Greek and medieval theatre. In our play the chorus members are increasingly linked to the character of Wagner. The role of the Chorus is to provide a link between the action on stage and the audience, to set the context for the play and to provide some moral guidance and commentary.

**?** Who is your Chorus? In order for you as a director to communicate your concept of the play to the audience you must have a clear idea of who you want the character to be. You must not see the Chorus simply as someone who delivers the context for us, but as a character in their own right. He must have a relationship with the audience in order for us to connect with him. How does he feel about Faustus' actions as the play develops? Does he condemn him for what he does or communicate some sense of sweet temptation that puts us all in Faustus' shoes? Try delivering the opening chorus speech in a range of different tones and moods within the group. Is there an arrogance about a character that is in a position of power in knowing exactly what will happen to Faustus from the very beginning or is he struck with fear about the actions of our hero, knowing that the choices Faustus makes will destroy him?

How will the Chorus be physically represented? Is he an everyman, like every one of us, watching a man fall and helpless to stop him or is he a more sinister representation of fate, a darker conscience that warns us about the consequences of excess? Maybe he is the voice of God, not physical but a vocal presence played through speakers around the audience as we watch Faustus in his study. You need to discuss this important role within the group and explore alternatives. Remember there are no wrong answers if you can justify your choices. Decisions about costume, movement or stillness in this section are important and can be experimented with practically. The decisions you make will shape the overall interpretation of the play that you are communicating to your audience.

## Act 1, scene 1: Faustus in his study

 Faustus

Pages 3–6

> Here we meet Faustus for the first time. Surrounded by books in his study he searches for inspiration from reading the great philosophers, physicians and the Bible but is ultimately dissatisfied. By turning to the 'metaphysics of magicians' he senses that 'these are those that Faustus most desires'.

Again, the primary question for a director is how they want the audience to feel about Faustus when we meet him for the first time and what decisions can we make to influence their reactions. Consider what we know about Faustus already from what our Chorus has told us. Highlight the text with key words that help us to understand the character – 'parents base of stock', 'graced with doctor's name', 'excelling all', 'swollen with cunning', 'self conceit'. Annotate the text with further notes for your actor about how these qualities might be communicated. Try creating some frozen images that capture these key qualities. Bring them to life by experimenting with movement. How does this man walk or sit? Put him in his study before any words are spoken. Get one member of the group to enter his study and make it his own space, picking up books, rejecting them, reading through them, looking for answers. The rest of the group observe the behaviour and provide feedback. Consider the speed of his movement, the ultimate lack of fulfilment that he feels as he works his way through the various texts. Then he finds the answer 'and necromantic books are heavenly'. Ask a member of the group to play the scene again. They enter the room looking for an answer that may be provided in one of 30 books surrounding them. With increasing frustration they eventually find the answer in a particular pile of books and then the mood changes. The pace of the scene changes, communicate the sensual enjoyment of what lines in the pages, almost caressing them, salivating over their content. Give feedback. Now return to the script and in pairs – one director, one actor – rehearse this opening. The reaction of the audience to the character must be at the forefront of the actor's mind.

---

> **Tip**
>
> A lot of answers can be found in off-text work. It is helpful to identify the mood of the scene and an emotional reaction of a character that an actor can identify with. Once this has been established it is then much easier to apply to the words of the text.

Faustus, Wagner, good angel, evil angel, Valdes and Cornelius

Pages 7–13

## Act 1, scene 1

Faustus is inspired by the thought of black magic and summons two experts in the art, Valdes and Cornelius, to teach him. The way that Faustus dismisses the warnings of the good angel reminds us of Oedipus in his dismissal of the Greek gods. We, as an audience, fear for his god-like reaction. The two magicians encourage Faustus in his aim with the condition that he must be 'resolute'. Faustus requests a show of their magical power. Instead they agree to teach him to conjure for himself.

---

We see in this section the resolute nature of Faustus in his determination to conjure. Consider how in control Faustus is at this moment and how his desires and emotions are leading him, as opposed to rational thought ('How am I glutted with conceit of this'). What advice would you give to an actor in communicating this thinking in terms of voice and movement?

There is a practical decision to be made here as director about the portrayal of the two angels. They do serve as Faustus' conscience but enter and exit very promptly. Are they to be presented physically?

If so, where do they come from or are they already on stage and remain there? As a practical activity, place them concealed around the performance space, almost as part of the set. How might they be revealed to surprise the audience? Maybe try giving their lines to Faustus as a kind of possession. Consider how the actor might physically change as the angels within him battle for control. Experiment as a group with this physical change to try and reshape your bodies into evil and good. Do the same with voice.

As Valdes and Cornelius enter, consider how Faustus reacts to them. Ultimately he wants something from them, something that he does not currently possess. Consider how they are brought in to the study and how Faustus reacts around them. Look closely at the delivery of the speech as they enter beginning 'Valdes, sweet Valdes …'.

Highlight the particular choices of language that he uses to persuade them 'odious … obscure … contemptible … vile' and the key line: ''Tis magic, magic that hath ravished me'. How do Valdes and Cornelius react to him? What kind of men are they? Do you want to present them as renowned academics or as figures to be suspicious of or even laughed at? Consider in their vocal delivery the beauty and grandness of the images they conjure to tempt Faustus into their world, balanced with their desire to calm Faustus down and let him see the enormity of his decision.

## Act 1, scene 2

Two scholars, Wagner

Pages 15–19

Two scholars question Wagner as to Faustus' state of mind and whereabouts. Wagner recounts the events of the previous scene, leaving the scholars concerned for Faustus' welfare and determined to seek advice from the rector to save him before it is too late. The scholars provide a reasoned commentary on the behaviour of Faustus. The scene provides a break from the intensity that surrounds it and shows the concern that Faustus' contemporaries show for his move into the 'damned art'. Wagner indulges in some intellectual wordplay to emphasise his superiority that hints at the emptiness of knowledge if it is used purely as a means to establish status.

## Act 1, scene 3

Faustus, Mephistopheles

Pages 19–28

Faustus enters now in possession of the power to conjure. He steels himself before launching into Latin incantation to raise Mephistopheles. A devil appears who Faustus sends away, knowing that his power can conjure Mephistopheles himself. He duly appears stating, 'I came now hither of mine own accord'. Faustus questions him vigorously about the nature of hell. Mephistopheles responds with a note of regret about what he has been denied. Faustus sends him away to deliver his proposal to Lucifer – to give up his soul in return for 24 years to 'live in all voluptuousness'. Mephistopheles leaves to return at midnight with Lucifer's answer as Faustus imagines the joy to come.

As Faustus enters it is vital to create the right mood and atmosphere for what he is about to do. Individually, as you read through Faustus' opening speech in the scene, focus on ritualistic movement and the physical performance of calling the devil. There are hints in the text that this needs to be performed physically: 'Within this circle is Jehovah's name'. Rehearse and share work within the group. The performance might well be enhanced by some well-chosen music to underscore the passage and appropriate lighting. This will be an important exercise for your actors in enabling them to immerse themselves in the world that Faustus is about to enter.

The next challenge comes in tackling the extensive Latin section (page 19) as Mephistopheles is summoned. In small groups prepare a choral presentation of this extract, using the translation printed in the margin. Use a range of voices and group movement. Try and capture the grandness of the dialogue and reflect it in the devised movement.

This is the first time in the play that the audience get a sense of the world of hell. The director's interpretation of this moment needs to be very carefully considered and the impact has to be significant. Don't be tied down by the text and if you feel that this is a moment for choral interpretation, which represents the inside of Faustus' mind, then go with it.

As the devil enters, consider the reaction of both Faustus and the audience. The tension has been built and then dissipates. There is potential for comedy here in the apologetic devil who shuffles on embarrassed. Is this the effect that you as director want to create? Do you want to undercut the intensity of the moment or indicate that Faustus is being mocked? Whatever you decide, the action must build again, as must the intensity leading to the entrance of Mephistopheles. Here a practical decision needs to be made about where the character comes from. Do you want to go for the full pyrotechnics and special effects, flashes of smoke, lighting, with Mephistopheles rising from the ground? Alternatively a more understated entrance. Is he already on stage, concealed about the set, or entering from behind or among the audience? The choice you make will say a great deal about how you view the character. His opening line is not grand, but one of service: 'Now Faustus, what would'st thou have me do?'

" May the gods of Acheron look favourably upon me! Away with the spirit of the threefold Jehovah. Welcome spirits of fire, air, water and earth. We ask your favour, oh Prince of the East, Belzebub, the monarch of burning hell, and Demigorgon, that Mephistopheles may appear and rise. Why do you delay? By Jehovah, Gehenna, and the holy water which I now sprinkle and the sign of the cross which I now form, and by our vows, may Mephistopheles himself now rise, compelled to obey us. "

*Dr Faustus* based on the A text, edited by Roma Gill, Methuen, 1989, page 19.

### Who is Mephistopheles?

 A good opening practical activity is to draw a sketch of him, or a collage pieced together from printed media. What gender is the character? By making her female, for example, you are introducing a whole new meaning to the play with regard to the relationship between men and women. Is he the archetypal devil image with horns and a tail or a little dark-haired man in a grey suit? You want to get the audience asking questions about your choices. Can

### Further viewing

A strong film reference that captures the fear and darkness of this moment in the play is Alan Parker's 1987 horror film *Angel Heart*, starring Mickey Rourke, Lisa Bonet and Robert de Niro as Louis Cyphre. De Niro's portrayal is one of several filmic interpretations of the devil in a non-conventional way. Another comes in Taylor Hackford's 1997 film *Devil's Advocate* with Al Pacino as John Milton.

the character change in his appearance, breaking the audience's expectations by possessing a mixture of different interpretations? Research the internet and once designs are complete take the best bits from all to create the group's image of Mephistopheles.

The relationship between Faustus and Mephistopheles is the central concern of the play and a director must have a crystal-clear idea about what he wants that relationship to be. It is once again important to know as much as we can about the character and he reveals much in this scene. Repeat the same exercise that you did for Faustus earlier by highlighting key words that give us clues as to his character and how he might be played: 'I am a servant … I came now hither of mine own accord … unhappy spirits … this is hell, nor am I out of it … tormented … deprived of everlasting bliss … strike a terror to my fainting soul'. The human elements of the character come over most strongly and he perhaps elicits the warmth of the audience more than Faustus ever does. He is a character who appears in pain, full of suffering and regret.

A further off-text improvisation will serve to gain a greater understanding of Mephistopheles. Stage a *Panorama* programme in which members of the group are invited to send in their questions to Mephistopheles for a serious newscaster to read out in a one-off special: 'The Devil in the Dock'. Prepare the questions thoroughly to make them relevant to the play, draw on the conditions in which Mephistopheles lives and particularly his thoughts on the actions of Faustus.

As a director you need to consider Mephistopheles' attitude towards Faustus on their first meeting. There is a broad scope for interpretation and much comic potential in the way that the devil might be portrayed. Is he tired, bored, full of contempt, unimpressed, polite or eager to please? Make a strong directorial statement in the decision that you make. Within the group you should experiment with different interpretations providing comment on their success.

## Act 1 scene 4

 Wagner, Robin

Pages 29–39

Wagner, having picked up a little of the dark magic, calls Robin, a clown, to him to persuade him to work in Wagner's service for seven years. The pair joke about Robin's poor appearance and that he would sell his soul for a shoulder of mutton. Wagner frightens Robin in to being his servant by conjuring up two devils to take him away. The pair discuss the possibilities of black magic in transforming them into whatever they want.

**Analysis**

This scene exists as a comic counterpoint to the main plot. It is making a comment about education and uses base or low-status characters to illustrate a point about the use of power. Whereas Faustus intends to use his magic for grander aims, Wagner and Robin look to be turned into a flea to gain a greater access to a woman's body.

## Act 2, scene 1

The scene starts with Faustus preparing for the return of Mephistopheles. He has moments of doubt. As he resolves to turn to evil, the good and evil angels reappear to offer final persuasion. They are dismissed by Faustus who focuses on the promise of wealth. Mephistopheles enters with Lucifer's response. By signing a deed in his own blood, handing his soul to the devil, Faustus will get what he desires. Faustus cuts his arm to release the blood. It slowly congeals and Faustus reads this as a sign that he is making a mistake. Mephistopheles provides hot coals to let the blood flow once more. Mephistopheles calls on devils bringing wealth to distract Faustus and the deed is signed.

Faustus, good angel, evil angel, Mephistopheles

Pages 39–51

### Further study

*Faustus* has several parallels here with the behaviour of Macbeth before resolving to kill Duncan. Moments of doubt and the struggle with his conscience are evident in both plays. There are also similarities in the portent of the congealing blood in *Faustus* and the appearance of the dagger in *Macbeth*. For a broader perspective and a deeper insight into the mind of Faustus read *Macbeth* Act 2, scene 1.

In order for an audience to connect with Faustus they must see him as a character that experiences doubt and vulnerability, an aspect of his character that we have yet to see. This scene gives the opportunity for you to explore this as a director. Within the group try reading the scene in two different ways, from the entrance of Mephistopheles to the line: 'I'll fetch him somewhat to delight his mind'. One pair performs the extract with Faustus completely clear, dominant and single-minded in his goal. The second pair plays him as human, vulnerable and full of doubt. Focus particularly on movement and use of pause. The actor playing Mephistopheles will need to react differently to the Faustus that is being played. Is there ever any danger in the scene that Faustus might change his mind and Mephistopheles will return to hell empty handed? Look to explore alternatives.

### Directing tip

There is a further practical consideration in the scene about how the entrance of the devils is portrayed. Where do they come from, how are they dressed and what do they bring in with them? As a director you should have made a distinct decision about your interpretation of the devils in your overall concept.

## Act 2, scene 1

Faustus, Mephistopheles

Pages 53–60

Faustus questions Mephistopheles about the nature of hell and appears to deny its existence ('I think hell's a fable'). He calls for a wife which Mephistopheles provides in the form of a she-devil. Faustus rejects her and asks for books that provide him with knowledge of the world.

A possible examination response may ask you how the relationship between the two characters, Faustus and the she-devil, would be communicated to the audience. In your group, try to define the relationship and give two short, precise examples of how this might be revealed in the performance. You could focus on movement and voice separately or home in on particular moments of the scene. Try writing this response on paper in 5 minutes. This will help you to simulate the pressure you will be under at the end of the year

## Act 2, scene 2

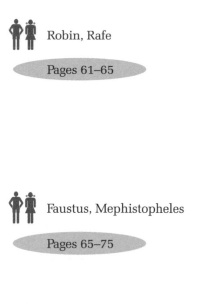

Robin, Rafe

Pages 61–65

Robin enters having stolen one of Faustus' conjuring books. He is mocked by his friend Rafe who points out that he cannot read. Robin promises to conjure Rafe any wine in the world and they leave to get drunk. This scene provides a further comic break from the intensity of the previous scenes and again makes the point about the abuses of knowledge.

## Act 2, scene 3

Faustus, Mephistopheles

Pages 65–75

The scene starts with Faustus questioning the choice he has made and debating whether to 'renounce this magic and repent'. The angels reappear but serve only to strengthen his resolve to proceed. Faustus considers all the glories this new world has given him and questions Mephistopheles about the make-up of the universe. Mephistopheles answers all Faustus' inquiries until the crucial question: 'Tell me who made the world?' Mephistopheles refuses to answer and warns him against turning back to God before he exits. Faustus considers repentance once again.

 The interest in this section for the director comes in the growing control that Mephistopheles has over Faustus. It is worth tracing the journey that the character has taken so far through a flow chart to note the key changes of status in this relationship. There is a distinct mood change in this scene on the question: 'Who made the world?'. Mephistopheles' reluctance to respond here proves God's creative supremacy and this section is worth closer practical exploration. How will you as director manage this mood change, particularly with regard to the use of the stage space, movement between the actors and changes in vocal tone? Faustus' threats to repent once Mephistopheles leaves can be interpreted in several ways. Does it come out of genuine fear or as a childish response to not getting an answer?

## Act 2 scene 3

Faustus, angels, Lucifer, Beelzebub, Mephistopheles, seven deadly sins

Pages 75–85

To re-inspire a wavering Faustus, Mephistopheles enters with Lucifer and Beelzebub. At first they warn him that they have been offended. This frightens Faustus. To impress him they present a show in which each of the seven deadly sins speaks in turn. Faustus is delighted and is given a book by Lucifer himself before he exits.

There are many things to consider as a director in this section. Firstly, the presentation of Lucifer and Beelzebub; they must fit in to your overall directorial concept in line with what you have decided for Mephistopheles. How will you portray their relative status with Lucifer the king, Beelzebub his prince and Mephistopheles their servant? Look back to previous references to Lucifer in the text, the fallen angel, and see how this might influence your decisions. Look at creating a family freeze-frame of the three of them in both formal and informal settings. Use the whole group to alter the freezes to shift the emphasis on different relationships between the three. Strong artists might look to sketch the three's costumes or make collages.

### Presentation of the seven deadly sins

As a warm-up activity the whole group move around the space. When one member of the group shouts out one of the sins, the group freeze in a representation of that sin. Then bring in individual movements related specifically to the sin. How does that sin react when it meets itself around the space? Then finally bring in voice. The entire group make a sound – not words – that expresses that sin. Now bring all three stages together. You can either repeat the process for each sin or, if the group is big enough, get seven groups to move around the space simultaneously, reacting to each other in role. Further warm-up activities might be to create small group freezes of the sins and then see how they can morph from one sin to the next, changing shape and form as appropriate.

A practical consideration as a director is how you will set the stage space in this section. Nominate one of the groups as director. Place the group or individuals around the space to represent the sins. Think about the importance of where each sin is placed and the use of different levels. Start them in a freeze and then bring them all to life, asking each sin to devise a short routine to illustrate their characteristic. Give each sin time to rehearse their lines, focusing on movement and voice. Now consider how Faustus and Lucifer will be brought into the scene. Will it be a show with Faustus as the seated audience or will he be led through by Lucifer as if in some kind of enchanted forest, waking the sins as he passes them by? Rehearse in both these ways and perform. If the group has a strong bond of trust, comment on how the director directed the piece and what alternative styles of directing they might have employed.

## Act 3

Chorus, Wagner

Pages 85

The Chorus returns to describe Faustus' journey – up to Mount Olympus to ride in a chariot drawn by dragons around Europe to see the stars and end up in Rome. The Chorus provides us with narrative that cannot be staged. As a director you need to think about the nature of the Chorus – should the role be played by Wagner or a character more distanced from the action?

## Act 3, scene 1

Faustus, Mephistopheles, Pope, cardinal and friars

Pages 87–96

Faustus begins the scene revelling in his journey around Europe and questions Mephistopheles as to why they have ended up in Rome. They take in Rome's history and beauty and take dinner with the Pope. Faustus sees the opportunity to 'make us merriment' and demands of Mephistopheles that he makes him invisible. A fanfare announces the entrance of the Pope, the cardinal of Lorraine and friars to take part in a banquet. Faustus indulges in some mockery of the holy figures, snatching dishes and cups and then boxing the Pope about the ears. They all flee. The friars re-enter to sing a dirge to curse the figure who insulted them all. Faustus is further inspired to mischief, beats them and flings fireworks at them before they flee.

This scene would have gone down very well with Marlowe's original audience. As England was a Protestant nation, anything that mocked the Roman Catholic Church would have been well received by the audience.

This scene sees Faustus at the height of his powers and is the first in a series of scenes that show his gradual abuse of figures of authority. As a director you need to decide how the audience view Faustus at this stage. There undoubtedly needs to be laughter as this is a physically comic scene. This will bring the audience in to *Faustus*, making them part of his world in sharing his sense mischief. As a modern audience we love to see figures of pomposity brought down to earth. The key is how you decide to portray the Pope and his entourage who are about to indulge in an enormous feast. In order to make the scene work they need to be figures of fun and comic exaggerations of gluttony. As a group you might experiment with their entrance, before any dialogue, and play with the idea of caricature. Do you as a director want them to deserve the disrespect they receive?

As a director this scene needs to be carefully staged to bring out the physical comedy. How will the banquet be brought on? Think carefully about how entrances and exits are handled in the play so that they do not disrupt the flow of the action. Draw a ground plan of the set with Faustus' movement throughout the scene clearly marked. The friars' dirge at the end of the scene is written to mock that particular style of prayer and the juxtaposition of the seriousness of the friars compared to the reaction of Faustus is worthy of physical exploration. How might the final stage direction be performed: 'MEPHISTOPHELES and

**Further viewing**

*Have I Got News for You* and *Mock the Week* both rely on the format of social and political satire and sending up those in authority for their humour, as we see in the Pope scene here.

FAUSTUS *beat the* FRIARS *and fling fire-works among them, and so exeunt*'? Consider how the scene might be cleared in preparation for the entrance of Robin and Rafe.

---

Robin, Rafe, Vintner, Mephistopheles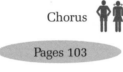

Pages 97–101

## Act 3, scene 2

> Robin and Rafe enter having stolen a silver goblet from the Vintner. He enters demanding its return. He searches Robin and Rafe who pass the goblet between them. They utter stumbling Latin to protect themselves and call on Mephistopheles. Mephistopheles enters and frightens them with explosives. He is irritated by being called by such insignificant clowns and threatens to turn them into an ape and a dog.

**Analysis**    The comic subplot continues with the base characters still misusing the dark powers that they have acquired. There is now, however, a significant similarity in the behaviour of Faustus in the previous scene in boxing the ears of the Pope and the bullying of the Vintner here. Faustus' use of his power is beginning to appear more and more vulgar.

Chorus

Pages 103

## Act 4

> The chorus describes Faustus' return home after his travels. He is met by friends and companions who question him about his experiences. Faustus answers them with great learning and he becomes famed throughout the land. The German emperor gets to hear of his achievements and summons him to his court.

**Analysis**    This choral speech gives context and sets up the action of the following scene. Remember in your approach to the Chorus to be consistent in the choices you have made previously. What is the Chorus' attitude towards Faustus at this stage in the play? Does he share the admiration of the characters he describes or is he more cynical in his descriptions, knowing as he does what is to happen to Faustus? Try experimenting with different vocal tones in the delivery of the speech and make a note of the different impact each choice has.

Emperor, Faustus, Mephistopheles, knights and attendants

Pages 103–111

## Act 4, scene 1

The Emperor praises Faustus for his reputation and achievements. He requests that he sees proof of Faustus' abilities with the reward being praise from the emperor himself. A knight at court continually undermines Faustus' claims to greatness with numerous asides to the audience. The emperor requests that Faustus conjures for him one of the world's most impressive leaders, Alexander the Great, and his paramour. Faustus admits that he cannot reproduce them for they are long dead but can instead create identical versions of them. The knight continues to mock Faustus. Mephistopheles produces the visions of the two characters and the Emperor is highly impressed. The knight is called for by Faustus and he enters with stag's horns on his head as a punishment for his earlier comments. The emperor requests that be are removed and Faustus obliges. After a reference to the passing of time, Faustus returns to Wittenberg.

What has become of Faustus? Look back in the text at the promises Faustus made about the way that he would use his powers. Collect evidence and make a note. Now compare to the way that he uses his powers in this scene. Set up a debate in which Faustus and a number of key characters – Mephistopheles, the emperor, the knight and Lucifer himself – are asked to comment on how successful Faustus has been in the use of his dark powers. Assign two or three members of the group to each character and write a progress report to deliver to the audience. Think about how the characters would react and how honest they would be. This exercise should inform an actor playing Faustus about the increasing emptiness of his actions.

### Directing tip

The very end of the scene reminds us that time is passing. In the space of the play 24 years have passed. Only with the journey reaching its conclusion does the speed of this progression of time become a concerning issue. Time is one of the themes of a play in which 24 years is condensed by Marlowe into three major moments – Rome, the emperor and the Duke of Vanholt scene. How will you as a director illustrate this passing of time? Is their a dramatic device or technique that you might build in to your interpretation to establish the years going by?

## Act 4, scene 1

Faustus, horse-courser, Mephistopheles

Pages 111–119

Faustus agrees to sell his horse to a horse-courser for the sum of 40 dollars. He does so with a warning that the horse must not be led to water. The horse-courser is happy with his purchase and exits. Faustus falls asleep and in a moment of reflection thinks about his damned soul. He consoles himself with the fact that like the thief at Christ's side at the crucifixion, he can repent at the last minute and be forgiven. As he sleeps the horse-courser returns wet and angry. His horse has vanished in a pond and he demands his money back. He wakes Faustus by shouting in his ear and pulls at his leg which comes off. The courser runs out afraid and Faustus leg is restored. He finds the trick he has played hysterical. Wagner enters to announce that Faustus has been invited to the court of the Duke of Vanholt.

**Analysis**   This scene illustrates Faustus' further decline into a cheap illusionist and the joke he plays on the horse-courser is as base as anything that the comic characters have done before. There is a practical consideration about how the pulling of the leg might be staged. The most telling speech in this scene comes when Faustus is alone and faces his situation: 'What art thou, Faustus, but a man condemned to die?' Consider the delivery of this speech and how much Faustus is aware of what he has become. The way he dismisses his predicament at the end of the speech confirms him as a man who has lost what little sympathy the audience may have had for him.

Faustus, Mephistopheles, Duke and Duchess of Vanholt

Pages 121–123

### Act 4, scene 2

Faustus is welcomed to the court of the Duke of Vanholt and his pregnant wife. Faustus asks her to request anything she desires. She requests a dish of ripe grapes, but being winter knows that this cannot be possible. Mephistopheles is summoned to bring the grapes from the other side of the world where it is summer. This he does and Faustus is rewarded by the grateful couple.

 Faustus appears now to be reduced to a novelty act, conjuring grapes for a minor Duchess. As a director do you feel that Faustus knows what he has become? Consider the Faustus character in Act 1, scene 1. Look closely at the speech that begins on page 7: 'How am I gutted ... sage conference'. Highlight the strength of imagery and the passion with which Faustus speaks. Place this speech alongside Faustus' explanation of how he came by the grapes on page 121 beginning, 'If it like your Grace,' which appears to be a bland and flat piece of dialogue. Consider the contrasts in language and delivery. In pairs within your group rehearse both speeches trying to bring out the essential differences between the two Faustuses. Remember 24 years have passed in between the two speeches. Annotate your speeches. Swap over so each actor gets an opportunity to experience the essential differences. Once performances are complete, be prepared to justify your decisions to the rest of the group, using examples of specific lines and moments within the performance.

As a director you might also look at your intended betrayal of the Duke and Duchess. Your interpretation of them should fall into line with how you presented the Pope and the emperor. Are they caricatures of vulgar minor wealth or more genuine portrayals?

Also consider Mephistopheles' role in this scene. The servant of Lucifer himself has been reduced to collecting grapes for a pregnant woman. How does the actor see Mephistopheles at this point? When rehearsing the scene try and play with the non-verbal signals that the character might be giving to the audience concerning his attitude to the characters around him.

## Act 5

Our chorus indicates that Faustus' journey is coming to an end as he has given Wagner all his goods. Wagner admits surprise at Faustus' continued partying with his students. He notes that the banquet has ended as the scholars and Faustus enters.

## Act 5, scene 1

The scholars have been discussing the most beautiful woman in the world, Helen of Troy. They challenge Faustus to make her appear. He obliges and they leave impressed and full of praise for Faustus. An old man enters and offers Faustus salvation. Faustus becomes distraught as Mephistopheles hands him a dagger. The old man repeats his offer: an angel hovers above his head if only Faustus calls for mercy. He asks for time to think and the old man leaves. Mephistopheles warns Faustus against breaking the deal he has struck with Lucifer and threatens to tear him to pieces. Faustus reaffirms his loyalty by cutting his arm once more and asks that the old man be punished. The soul cannot be touched as it is pure, but his body can be afflicted. Faustus requests to see Helen one more time and kisses her. Faustus takes Helen offstage. The old man re-enters and curses Faustus for his choice, although devils enter to punish him, his faith resists them and he returns to God.

Chorus, Wagner

Pages 123

Remember to be consistent in your portrayal of the chorus, carefully considering their attitude to the behaviour of their master and how this might be communicated through tone of voice and movement.

Faustus, scholars, Mephistopheles, Helen, old man, devils

Pages 125–133

Helen of Troy is a famous mythological figure, born to the Greek god Zeus by mother Leda. She had many suitors and was known throughout the world for her incredible beauty.

## Analysis

Faustus is once again performing tricks for the scholars in the appearance of Helen. The practical presentation of the world of academia is worth considering. In all their learning, what most impresses is a beautiful woman. What do you want the audience to feel about these characters? For Faustus himself, the final use of his great power is to satisfy his physical desire. Is this appropriate for a man of supposed great intellect?

## The role of the old man

The old man is a very important character in the play and worthy of close attention for the director. Consider what he represents. Looking back to medieval theatre the character of Mercy always gave the sinner the opportunity to repent. How might the old man be dressed? Is it important to see him as separate from Faustus' world? How might this be achieved in performance? Play with the physicality and voice of the old man. What practical advice would you give to the actor playing him to give him the status he deserves?

The character of the old man reminds us of the all-seeing Tiresias in Sophocles' *Oedipus Rex*. He has grace and poise and remains untouched by the threats of evil around him.

It is at this moment in the play that we see the real force and power that Mephistopheles possesses: 'Thou Traitor, Faustus … thy flesh' (page 129). It is important that you trace the development of Mephistopheles' character as you have Faustus'. As an exercise, try putting together a collage of Mephistopheles' speeches that show the journey he has undertaken throughout the course of the play. There should be 2–3 lines for each stage of his development. Annotate the speech with guidance

**Tip**

In order to prepare for the written examination, it is the process and justification of decisions towards performance that is more important than the performance itself.

to an actor about how the role might be performed. Consider how you will deal with the emotional transitions as the journey proceeds. If each member of the group constructs these annotated monologues, they can then be swapped among the group and directed in performance by the person who wrote them.

Faustus, scholars

Pages 135–139

## Act 5, scene 2

Faustus enters with the two scholars; they are concerned about him and remind him that God's mercies are infinite. Faustus shares with them the deal he has struck with the devil and they are horrified and leave telling him that they will pray for him.

This is the last night of Faustus' life, and as a director it is necessary to create the right mood and atmosphere at the start of this scene to build up to the crescendo of his final moments. From the opening line the scholars are concerned for Faustus. How might the actor communicate his state of mind through the early part of this scene? How might he appear distracted, lacking in focus. The audience must connect with his emotions here as reality is about to dawn. An improvisational practical activity will enhance the emotions of the scene. In pairs, character A is waiting for a phone call about a close family member; the news is feared to be bad. Character B is unaware of the phone call to come and wants to talk about something completely different – the plans for a birthday party. Use this scenario as a starting point to explore the emotional state of mind. The improvised scene should end with the phone ringing.

Faustus

Pages 139–143

## Act 5, scene 2

As the scholars leave, the clock strikes 11. Faustus has 'one bare hour to live'. He calls for time to slow down and calls for his soul to be saved with one drop of Christ's blood. He asks for the mountains and hills to collapse on him to hide him from the devil. A clock strikes again, half an hour left. He calls for God's mercy once more, and curses his parents, the devil and himself. The clock strikes 12 – thunder crashes and lightning strikes. Devils enter to take Faustus to hell. Faustus' last line is 'I'll burn my books- ah Mephistopheles'.

This is the climax of the play and what everything has been building towards. The actor playing the role must be able to immerse himself in the role. The actor can be prepared through improvisation. In a modern context, you could improvise a scene of a prisoner on death row being brought his last meal. His last appeal has been denied and his execution is only an hour away. He has one final phone call. The improvisation ends with the rattle of keys to take him to his death. This exercise should be done without preparation and with the whole group performing at the same time. On the given signal – the rattle of the keys – they must all maintain their emotional state and go straight to the text to perform, beginning with 'Ah Faustus ...' (page 139). By all performing at the same time, you will need to be incredibly focused and also to feed off the atmosphere that everyone is creating. Once the performances are complete, reflect on what you as an actor achieved and try and record on paper the process that you were just involved in.

A second technique is to prepare the actor through use of the Stanislavskian technique of emotion memory. The actor must find a quiet space alone and take themselves to a place in their head when they, not as actors but as people, felt an incredible sense of fear or dread. When they were about to receive some terrible news and after a wait the worst was confirmed. Give the actor time and space to take themselves to that place. You as a director might then give prompts to clarify the emotion by asking the actor, where they were. How did they feel at this precise moment? What did they do the moment after the information was discovered? The actor does not answer your questions but instead feeds them in to his preparations. When you feel the actor is ready you can then return to the text and begin a performance while maintaining the same emotional state.

> Emotion memory can only work in an environment of trust. The boundaries need to be set so that any material that the actor uses in this exercise is not shared with the group and remains private.

Another character that needs to be considered in this final section is Mephistopheles. Faustus' last words are directly addressed to him and might indicate that he is still on stage. Imagine if he were. Consider the relationship that you have decided to create for them throughout the play. As an actor playing the role how will he react to Faustus' final speech? Has he grown close to the man he has served for 24 years? Has he grown to hate him or is it just another job? Consider were he would be on stage. Where would he observe the speech from? Would he be involved more directly?

As an exercise ask each of your actors to record Faustus' final speech. Prepare a non-verbal performance of Mephistopheles played to the soundtrack of Faustus' words. This is a good exercise to focus on non-verbal communication and a reminder to you when writing the exam to focus on all characters and their reactions, not just the ones who might be speaking the dialogue at a given time.

Chorus

Pages 143

## Act 5: epilogue

The final words of the Chorus reminds the audience of what might have been. They implore us to learn from what happened to Faustus and take it as a warning that all of us should not reach beyond ourselves.

**Analysis**

The Chorus completes the play and follows the model of medieval and ancient Greek theatre. How do we feel about our Chorus as the play ends? How does he leave the stage and what point are you looking to make by your choice? Don't forget this is the lasting image that the audience will leave the theatre with and needs to be some final statement about your directorial interpretation.

## Directorial interpretation

Now that you have read the play and made detailed structured notes as you have gone you should be close to formulating the directorial concept that will carry you though the written examination. Although *Dr Faustus* is set in the 17th century, its message is universal in that it can be applied to any era. There will always be individuals who are not satisfied with their lives and are drawn to wider temptations to fulfil their desires. They will be prepared to give up a great deal without considering the consequences in order to satisfy their goals. Look at organised religion in the contemporary United Kingdom. The impact of Christianity has diminished and the god-fearing society of Marlowe's time no longer exists. Does this not make the play even more relevant? Does today's society and culture either advertently or inadvertently encourage the kind of behaviour the Faustus exhibits? What do we value today – beliefs or material possessions? Can a link be made to the current economic crisis and a desire to reach beyond our limited means?

There is a great deal to consider here. Do you want to set the play in its original conditions or does it lend itself to a particular period of time or place? Do you instead want to make it a timeless or futuristic piece that makes a universal point? Who do your central characters represent and what should an audience be picking up from the choices that you have made?

A necessary starting point is to visualise what your production of the play will look like. Choose a venue either indoors or outdoors. Does the play lend itself to performance in front of an audience of 3,000 people or is it more suited to an intimate studio venue? There are justifications for both choices. Where would you like your audience to be physically positioned in relation to the actors? Sketch some ideas or look at existing venues online.

## Designing the set

Now that you have a clearer idea about directorial concept, venue and staging, you can start to apply it to the specific demands of the text. Work through the text noting the different locations that exist. It may be worth doing this in table form as below. This will allow you to clearly see where the difficulties in design will occur and what challenges you will have to overcome. Whether you bring the Pope's

**Further study**

If you look up reviews for the Bristol Old Vic production of 2006 directed by David Fielding on the websites for The Times and The Guardian, you will see an example of a modern interpretation of the play. Note that not every element lends itself to a modern reworking and every idea must be fully justified. The principle behind the interpretation, however, appears a sound one. As Fielding says of the play, 'Its roots may lie in medieval notions of Heaven and Hell but over the years the drama has become a metaphor of personal compromise and instant gratification.'

## Web link

To look at the play in its original performance conditions, visit The Globe website at www.shakespeares-globe.org

**Further study**

For more detailed reference to staging look at *Edexcel AS Drama and Theatre Studies Study Guide* (Rhinegold 2008), pages 45-48.

banquet on- or off-stage, the appearance of the devils and the various explosions that occur in the piece all need practical consideration.

| Act/scene | Page number | Location | Characters in scene | Key action in scene |
| --- | --- | --- | --- | --- |

Faustus' study is the central feature of the set and needs to reflect the concept you have chosen. Will you, as a director, be looking at a minimalist interpretation of the play with symbolic and significant set pieces or will you be looking to recreate the study of an academic in as realistic a way possible? This is Faustus' domain and needs to reflect his personality, his thirst for learning and his interest in the dark arts. Consider how you might build in other locations around this central piece, both internal and external.

 **Turn to the Appendix on page 195. These questions should help to guide you in the right direction and provide a checklist once all decisions have been reached.**

## Tackling the written examination

The examination booklet can be an intimidating document. Remember that all that concerns you is the section on the text you are studying, in our case *Faustus*. You will also get a source booklet with an extract from your text. The page numbers you need to refer to in this booklet will be clearly marked on the question paper.

**Section A** is divided into three questions:

a) is worth 4 marks

b) is worth 6 marks

c) is worth 10 marks.

Adding up to a total of 20 available marks. How much you write for each should correspond to the maximum marks available.

The chosen extract will cover approximately four pages of text. For the purpose of this example we will be looking at pages 135–143 of Act 5, scene 2 up to the exit of Faustus with the devils. Although this is slightly longer than the extract you will receive there is enough variety in the scene to give you scope for practical exploration.

**Example question 1**

a) Outline for your performers two ways that they might indicate the relationship between Faustus and the audience at the start of this extract.                                    (4)

You first need to consider what that relationship is. How do we want the audience to feel about him at this stage in the play? Faustus is a man nearing the end of his life; the reality of the choice he has made has finally hit him. Practically, how will you illustrate this to the audience using two clear examples?

For four marks the marking criteria state that 'connections to the demands of the question will be clear' and ask for 'two clear and valid examples supported by reasons'. They ask for 'thinking that is confident, accurate, and clear and rehearsal must be explicit in the response'.

1 Don't waste space giving needless introductory comment.

2 Specific and clear instruction. Awareness of stage space.

3 Again, specific practical instruction to actor.

4 Awareness of development of the performance, clear reference to specific moment.

5 Strong justification given for rehearsal choice made.

6 Awareness of an alternative interpretation, explored through rehearsal. Hints at interaction with other characters.

7 Practical and specific advice given to actor.

8 Awareness of impact on audience, justification of decision made.

---

1 Needless contextual information that shows no awareness of the question.

2 Some reference to the play and an awareness of what he is feeling, but no practical reference to how this might be shown to the audience.

3 Purely descriptive, no evidence of how.

4 Lack of specific reference to how. No evidence of rehearsal. Where is the second way as requested in the question?

---

This is an example of a top-band response; the comments illustrate how the answer corresponds to the criteria.

I would rehearse the actor playing Faustus in two ways.[1] As the scholars enter I would ask the actor to already be on stage seated DSC leaning towards the audience.[2] His eyes would be staring, head in hands, blank and expressionless.[3] As he says the line 'Ah, gentlemen', I would ask the actor to remain looking outwards, almost as if he has not registered their presence.[4] This would show the preoccupation in the mind of the character, almost as if he has given up on life and is waiting for the devil to take him.[5] The second way I might rehearse the same moment is to have Faustus entering ahead of the scholars who follow him warily.[6] He moves quickly, changing direction as if looking for something, never able to settle, buzzing about as if he does not know where he his.[7] Again this might show the audience the restless mind of a man on the edge.[8]

Let's now look at a bottom-band response:

This extract comes at the end of the play, Act 5 scene 2, just before the devil is about to take Faustus' soul. He has just been given a chance to repent by the old man, but has turned down the chance.[1] Faustus is clearly in a state of shock as he has realised what is going to happen to him.[2] He enters with the two scholars and sits down.[3] They ask him what is wrong and Faustus begins to tell them what has happened to him. I would ask the actor to do this in a sad and upset way.[4]

What comes across most strongly in the responses are the following:

- Strong PRACTICAL evidence

- HOW the moment might be performed

- Clear reference to WHY the decision has been made

- Awareness that this is a question asking you to explore ALTERNATIVES in REHEARSAL

- Awareness of impact of choices on AUDIENCE.

**Example question 2**

b) Consider THREE appropriate rehearsal techniques you might use in order to highlight the personalities of Faustus and the scholars in this extract. [6]

Technique clearly identified.

The first technique I would use to highlight the personalities is an off-text improvisation. Character A is waiting for a phone call about a close family member; the news is feared to be bad. Characters B and C are unaware of the phone call to come and want to talk about something completely different – the plans for a birthday party. This would give the actors an insight into the emotions that the scholars and Faustus are experiencing at the very start of this extract.

> Specific practical explanation of technique.

> Reason for the choice of technique in context with the performance.

The second technique I would use would be to thought-track the scholars. The actor playing Faustus would read out his lines in the speech starting 'But Faustus' offence can ne'er be pardoned'. As he reads, the actors playing the scholars would write down exactly what they are thinking as they hear his words. I would then ask the Faustus actor to read the speech again with the scholars reading aloud their thoughts relevant to what Faustus is saying. This would bring out the reactions of others to Faustus' actions in the play and by giving a different perspective inform the actor playing Faustus of the impact of his actions on others and the scholars' clues as to how they react non-verbally during this extract of the scene.

> Technique identified.

> Practical exploration.

> Impact of technique and clear justification for its use.

The third technique I would use would be to prepare the actor playing Faustus for the emotional intensity of his final monologue. I would take the actor through the Stanislavskian technique of emotion memory. In taking him to a moment in his life when he felt the same emotion of fear or a moment when bad news that he had been expecting was confirmed. When he is in the right emotional state for the scene, I would ask him to rehearse the monologue. This technique would give reality to the emotion of the scene and allow the audience to connect with the pain of the character.

> Technique identified.

> Practical exploration of technique.

> Impact and justification.

For a top-band response to this question the marking criteria ask for specific examples and balance across the three techniques. A confident grasp of terminology and a clear understanding of purpose in using the ideas are required.

**Example question 3**

c) Explain to your performers how you intend to work on developing an understanding of the character of Faustus in this extract and his relationship with other characters and the audience, giving reasons for your approach, supported by clear examples.    [10]

I would firstly explain to my actors the journey that I want the character of Faustus to take throughout the scene. He does need to create a strong sense of impending doom, that the world is about to collapse around him. We would look to rehearse the scene in three sections. The entry of Faustus and the scholars to the scholars' exit, the strike of 11 to the strike of 12 and thirdly the strike of 12 to the final line when he is taken off by the devils.

> By splitting section up, the candidate shows clear control of material and understanding of rehearsal process.

It is important that Faustus enters the scene in a state of emotional distraction as his mind struggles to come to

Clear sense of starting point
with reasons.

Relevant and accurate rehearsal
technique for a specific purpose.

Looking at alternatives.

Awareness of audience impact.

Reference to specific moment.

Clear directorial statement.

Specific reference.

Rehearsal technique.

Firm idea, practically expressed with
justification.

Directorial statement.

Practical example.

terms with what is about to happen. I would be looking to explore a range of off-text activities before approaching the text. I would ask the company to put the actor in as confused a state of mind as possible. One activity you could use to achieve this would be for the actor playing Faustus to stand opposite three other members of the cast (A, B and C) with B standing in the middle. B begins to lead Faustus in a range of simple mirror activities that Faustus follows. They can become increasingly more complicated and vary in pace. At the same time A and C alternately fire questions at Faustus about his character, challenging him in his responses. These questions may be personal, concerning relationships, or ask him to justify his actions. Faustus must answer these questions immediately while continuing to complete the mirror work. One questioner should grow increasingly hostile in their approach to Faustus while the tone of the other should be increasingly supportive and loving. It is in this confused state of mind that the actor can then enter the scene.

I would also experiment with movement in this opening section by rehearsing the opening in two different ways. Firstly I would have Faustus still; try placing him in different positions around the stage, central, still and staring or perched on the edge of the set. The audience would need to get a sense that the character is increasingly in a world of his own, on the verge of madness, detached from the world of the scholars. The second possible staging would be to have Faustus restless around the set of his study, never still, seated and then jumping up, moving to another area, almost as an expectant father waiting for the news of the birth. The actor playing Faustus should deliver the lines in which he outlines his sins starting 'But Faustus' offence can ne'er be pardoned...', as if he is drifting in and out of reality, sometimes murmuring to himself, other times being aware that he has an audience.

The second section should see an increase in the emotional intensity of the scene. The lines are written with short phrases broken up by commas; this indicates the pace that they need to be performed at. Having worked on some emotion memory techniques with the actor I would be looking for him to focus his delivery above the audience in his appeals to time and Christ. This would create the effect that he is searching for an answer, high above him. I would experiment with the actor crossing stage left and right as he appeals to the different elements of nature, climbing the set to create a sense that he is trying to escape from the study and his ultimate punishment.

In the final section of this scene, I plan for the audience to witness the gradual physical breakdown of the character. The sense of helplessness needs to be communicated by the actor. As he delivers the final part of the monologue he slowly falls to the ground, his voice growing weaker and more broken. The 12th strike of the clock should signal the moment of collapse and

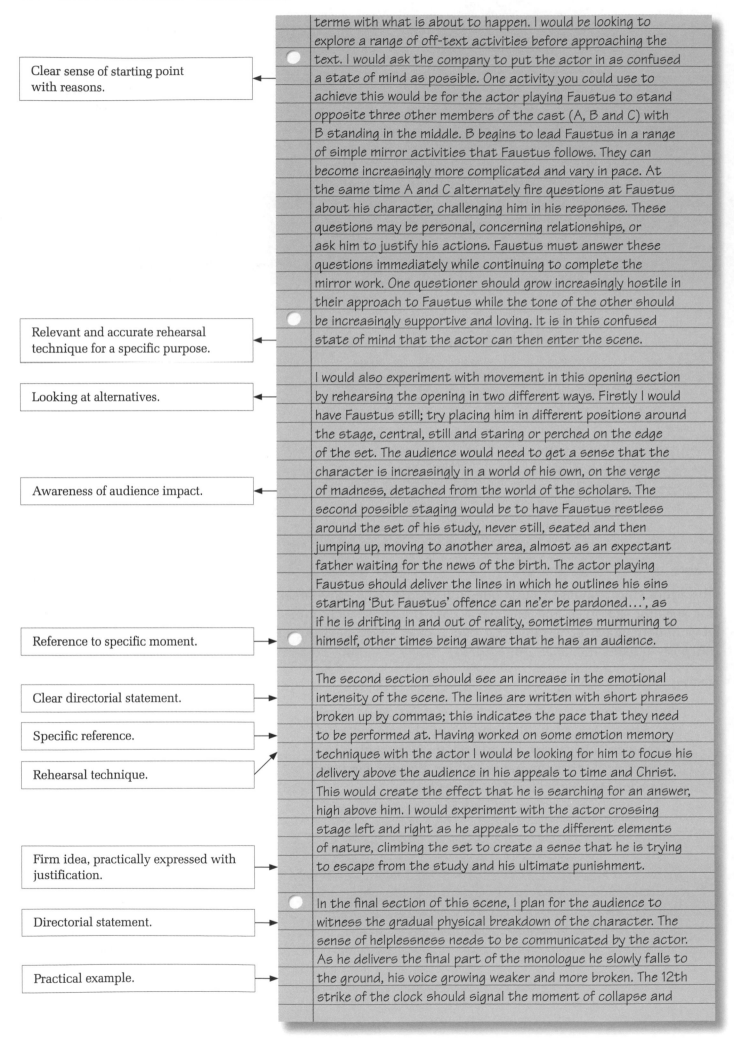

> as the devils enter he has lost his fight. Although the words
> indicate that he is still trying to escape his fate, his body is
> limp and lifeless. The devils carry him off without a fight.
>
> By choosing this ending, I plan for the audience to feel a
> strong sense of sympathy for Faustus. In completely opening
> up his emotions, they cannot fail to connect with the image
> of a broken man, whatever his crime. Only the hardest
> audience member would be able to say 'he deserved it'.

| | |
|---|---|
| Specific moment. | |
| Directorial interpretation. | |
| Justification of ideas, audience awareness. | |

The marking criteria in this section look to see how the candidate establishes relationships between characters and refers to key moments. It is not a character study. Again it refers to 'a confident and clear grasp of drama', evidence of physical and vocal exploration, evidence of rehearsal techniques, audience impact and a 'clear understanding of the process of interpreting the play in performance'.

## Section B

This section is an extended answer worth 30 marks and should be written in an essay-style format. This section tests your overall understanding of the play and allows you to justify and explore the directorial concept that has been central to all your preparations for this examination. You will have made distinct decisions about how you want the play to be performed. You should see this section as an opportunity to share your vision with the examiner, not as a test that you can fail.

You will be given a choice of two questions and must answer one. What we will do in the following pages is look to see how you might structure a response and then look at the specific marking criteria.

### Question 1

As a director, explore your approach to the play in every aspect of production. Justify your ideas with clear and well-supported examples.

The first thing you need to make clear in your response is your directorial concept. How do you see the play *Dr Faustus*? Is it a modern timeless story that you want to tell or do you feel that you want to do justice to the play in its original performance conditions. Alternatively, is yours a vision that combines both aspects? You need to clearly state in your introduction WHY yours is a concept that works for this play.

The next thing to consider is what are the aspects of every production?

- Acting style
- Performance space
- Lighting
- Props
- Interpretation
- Staging
- Sound
- Music
- Performance style
- Audience
- Costume.

This may well give you the structure of your essay. You may believe that some aspects of production are more important than others

> If you are struggling to define your interpretation, try imagining that your version is in print and you have been asked to write the blurb on the back of the book in exactly 200 words. Start with the line 'Dr Faustus is a play about ...'.

---
**Tip**

Think carefully about four to five of the key scenes or moments in Faustus that you will be referring to in any essay about directorial interpretation. Make sure that you do not neglect the minor characters in your choice. Make a brief list of these scenes so that you might be able to refer to them easily when confronted with the essay title.

---

and therefore worth more coverage within the essay. Work through the aspects of the production section by section, always referring back to how each area supports your directorial approach.

Two words must dominate your response: HOW (a practical example of how a particular scene or moment might be staged or audience positioned or costume designed) and WHY (a clear understanding from you as to how this practical example supports your directorial concept and what impact the particular moment will have on your audience). A good essay can identify the answer to these two words in each paragraph. The more WHYs that you have the greater chance of high marks.

Conclude your essay strongly by reinforcing the sense of vision that you have been trying to communicate and how within the essay you have attempted to illustrate this.

**Marking criteria**

The examiners are looking in the top level 5 (25–30 marks) for the following areas:

- 'An understanding of drama and theatre terminology'
- 'Interpretation and imagination'
- 'An understanding of the performance space'
- 'A full understanding of the play'
- 'Supported examples – visually and practically appealing – without losing sight of its original performance values'
- 'Reference to stylistic or historic elements'
- 'Understanding of aesthetic impact complementing meaning and structure of the play'
- 'Confidence … how live theatre could work … a knowledgeable response'.

Things to avoid in your responses – these hints are taken from the marking criteria at the lower level 2 (7–12 marks):

- 'Highly descriptive'
- 'Highly sourced from an annotated script'
- 'Highly imaginative but not able to work in practical performance'
- 'Little sense of justification'
- 'Proposed interpretation not justified in terms of playwright's original intentions'.

Finally using the example answer above, alongside the marking criteria for top- and lower-end responses, consider this question and produce a structure or paragraph plan that you might share among your group.

> As a director, outline your objectives for the character of Mephistopheles in your production of the play. Give supported examples of how your ideas might be achieved in performance.

Although Unit 4 is highly demanding it is also richly rewarding. The purpose of taking you through every aspect of text and design in the pages above is to thoroughly prepare you for the exam. If you get a sense that you own your interpretation in every way then you will be able to handle any question on any aspect of your production. With a heavily annotated text that you understand, and has been put together in an ordered and structured way, the examination should hold no fear for you. You should want to create a sense of ownership and pride in your work born out of a real connection with the play and a personal and intuitive connection with it.

## Woyzeck by Georg Büchner

### Plot summary

Written and set in the early 19th century, *Woyzeck* is the story of a troubled soldier. Crippled by poverty and the restrictions of his social class, he serves those in power respectfully and gives all of his meagre earnings to his common-law wife, Marie, to help her bring up their son. He is haunted by the unnatural; disturbing images and sounds regularly fill his mind. Woyzeck's family appear to provide him with some solace until he discovers Marie has had an affair with the Drum-Major. Her betrayal destroys the mundane routine of his world as he appears destined to seek revenge. Since Woyzeck is unable to compete physically with his rival, he elects to murder Marie before dragging her body to the lake and drowning himself.

The play is a cold and desperate tragedy which, unusually, focuses on a working-class man. Very few characters are given names; even the protagonist's son is anonymous. The text is structured in such a way as to magnify the plight of an impoverished family as they endure a world where they are destined to fail. The middle-class characters manipulate their lives and appear to revel in what they are forced to endure. It is only in death that they find peace.

### Büchner

Georg Büchner was born in Hessen, Germany in 1813. He had a stable childhood and was privately educated. His father, an army doctor, disapproved of his literary interests and quickly engendered in him a critical and logical approach to the world. When Georg turned 18, he began his medical training in Strasbourg. Despite his comfortable upbringing, he became quickly disillusioned with aspects of society and became involved with a group of radical students. He transferred to Giessen two years later to study philosophy and history where he founded the political group, The Society of Human Rights. In 1834, he published *Der Hessische Landbote* ('The Hessien Messenger') which aimed to inspire the working classes to rise against the oppressive forces that constrained their lives.

Büchner's writings were a forerunner to Marx's *Das Kapital* but were significantly less successful. His attempts at widely distributing his document were hampered by the illiterate peasants who received it and he narrowly avoided imprisonment by renouncing his involvement. He completed his first play *Danton's Death* in just five weeks in 1835 and, shortly afterwards, his increasingly

> 66 Have you ever seen nature inside-out? 99
>
> *Woyzeck* by Georg Büchner, translated by J. Mackendrick (Methuen 1979), page 31.

radical behaviour forced him to abandon the country of his birth. Büchner settled in Zürich, Switzerland and decided to convey his political frustrations through his writing. His second play *Leonce and Lena* was a political fairytale which challenged the dramatic forms of the day. He entered it for a literary competition but late submission meant that it was returned unread. He began writing *Woyzeck* in 1836 but in February of the following year as the play was close to being finished he contracted typhus and after a 17-day battle with the illness Georg Büchner died aged 23.

## Contextualising the play

The play has greater resonance when one realises that Büchner based his story on true events which were reported in 1825. Johan Christian Woyzeck, a former soldier and barber, was convicted of murdering a widow, Christiane Woost, in an act of jealousy. He was to be executed but this was delayed following an appeal on the grounds of diminished responsibility. The protracted investigations that ensued suggested that throughout his life he was made to suffer a series of political and social injustices. Both of Woyzeck's parents died by the time he was 13 and so he sought employment through the military. He had a relationship and a child although he was denied the right to marry because he lacked the appropriate identity papers. As a consequence, he was unable to gain future employment and at the time of the crime was reported to be penniless. The psychological investigations into the influences on his mental state took some time but were eventually in vain and Woyzeck was beheaded.

It is important to note that Büchner died before completing the text. There were four drafts in existence. They were kept by his brother before handing them to Karl Emil Franzos in the 1870s. Franzos' aim was to make sense of the different versions of the text, although he was hindered by the faded ink and the illegible handwriting. The original paper had to be treated with chemicals that hampered future investigations and Büchner's scribblings initially led Franzos to refer to the play as *Wozzeck*.

The fragmented nature of the play meant that the scenes from the different versions didn't always follow a logical narrative. In fact, Franzos' initial attempts contained some questionable decisions about the progression of the scenes. However, he did manage to create some sense of order and as a result provide a foundation on which other literary scholars have since built. The version that the exam board has chosen is just one possible interpretation of the text and many contemporary versions of the play exist where the scene order and even the ending is different; in certain editions he is seen returning to the town having disposed of Marie's body.

The predominant theatrical style in the 19th century was Romanticism, with melodramatic behaviour dominating the action. In this respect, Büchner abandoned the traditions and appeared to develop his own form. He admitted to being influenced by Shakespeare's work, although critics celebrate him as being the father of German naturalism, realism and even the modern

> **"Woyzeck is a series of stained-glass windows in a medieval cathedral."**
>
> *Georg Büchner: Complete Plays and Prose, translated by Carl Richard Mueller* (Hill and Wang 1963).

> **"It combines, often in a perplexing reality ... A distrust of the rational, on the one hand, with a commitment to precise, scientific observations and mimesis, on the other."**
>
> John Osborne, *The Naturalist Drama in Germany* (Manchester University Press 1971).

absurdist movement. Artaud and Brecht cited him as influences on their work and many contemporary writers and directors have celebrated the play.

One of the dominant concepts in the play is poverty. The protagonists are dealt with in a realistic manner, while those that act as a catalyst for their misfortune are simply identified by their profession, without even being given names. Büchner challenges the Aristotelian concept that tragedy represents people better than ourselves by presenting a working-class victim of society but he does remain true to central idea of undeserved suffering.

**Themes**

In a contemporary context, *Woyzeck* raises questions about mental health. Despite its period setting, the notion of a loyal servant on the edge of a nervous breakdown due to the pressures of home and work is something with which we can associate. Those in authority appear to provide him with some stability but do not help his deteriorating state; the doctor who should be offering a cure is through experimentation making him worse. Even the natural world provides little comfort and in the scenes where Woyzeck is exposed to fresh air, he actually appears more disturbed. However, this is a world where the natural order appears to be disrupted in his mind.

Woyzeck's loyal and at times passive behaviour acts as a stark contrast to the sexual and violent images that permeate the play. The Drum-Major is animalistic in his passion, particularly when the protagonist appears so devoid of emotion. Marie is clearly excited by the grandness of his appearance and at times emulates his aggressive language which may appear unnecessarily explicit to an audience. A similar response could be induced by the regular threads of violence. From the opening image of heads rolling downs strips of grass to the repeated mention of knives, there is a morbid inevitability about this tragedy. Buchner's juxtaposition of banal routine and extreme brutality is one of the keys to the plays appeal.

Before we proceed to study each scene in turn, it is important that you begin the process by reading the text in silence on your own. Being able to hear the words of the text in your head and to imagine stage action are skills you will need to acquire if you are going to be successful. As you read, have a pencil in your hand. Underline any interesting phrases and make a note of any sections you do not understand. The nature of the language is such that you may need to reread sections several times before you comprehend the idea being communicated. Whatever happens, do not panic if you are confused by key areas of the text. You are going through a process, and with each new play it takes time to understand the style and the context of the material.

During the following pages, we will work through the play in sections, looking at the dramatic significance of the scene and practical suggestions for exploring the text. Remember, the written examination will be testing your skills as a director so many of the exercises will be focused on how the text can be rehearsed. As each idea is discussed, keep your production at the forefront of your mind. Make notes on any ideas you have on the staging of the piece. Towards the end of the chapter, you will be given suggestions on how to draw these ideas together into a clear directorial concept and ultimately shape your response into written answers. You will find this difficult if you have not made detailed notes along the way.

Woyzeck and Andres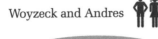

Pages 3–5

### Scene 1

The action begins with Andres, a soldier, whistling his favourite song while splitting sticks in the woods. He is joined by Woyzeck who expresses how unnerved he is despite the apparently peaceful setting. As Andres sings, Woyzeck becomes increasingly alarmed by sounds his friend cannot hear. Ironically, as the sounds in Woyzeck's head become silent, Andres hears the drumming which signals they should return, presumably to the barracks.

**Analysis**

It is often said that a strong opening scene manages to distil within it both the forms and thematic content of the play and this section is a clear example of this. On a structural level, it is a relatively short duologue with economical use of language – a style which is evident in many of the scenes that follow. The location is the woods, a setting which regularly unnerves Woyzeck and the men are simply splitting sticks, an act which immediately undermines their status as soldiers. The use of a knife alludes to the play's denouement and Woyzeck's fragile mental state is emphasised by him hearing noises when all is quiet.

 **Condensing the action**

Imagine you a director wishing to ensure that this opening extract introduces some of the key concepts detailed above. You want your actors to create a series of memorable physical images which could be echoed in future scenes. In pairs, try to recreate the characters of Woyzeck and Andres through a series of five tableaux or frozen images. Each needs to be illustrated with a line from the text and the actors must move smoothly from one image to the next, holding the freeze for as long as they feel is necessary to communicate the mood. Perform the work, discussing which were most effective and then note these images as simple stick men in your copy of the text. Explain what you hope these images will communicate to a contemporary audience.

**Creating the total life of the characters**

Stanislavski suggested that an actor should use the given circumstances of the text and their imagination to create a total life of the character. As a group, discuss the tasks that Woyzeck and Andres may have performed in the past – preparing food, tidying the barracks, Woyzeck cutting Andres' hair. Consider what they may have discussed while doing this – Woyzeck as a doting father, Andres' love life, their lack of money. Try improvising these scenes in order to flesh out their relationship. Consider how the scenes may be affected if Woyzeck's mental health is fragile.

### Changing perspective

If Woyzeck is to earn the sympathy of the audience then as a director, you need to make careful decisions about how it can be elicited. In threes, with a director and two actors, create two different versions of the play. The first should earn sympathy for the protagonist's mental state. However, the second should focus on Andres, and how he is trying to support his troubled friend. Consider how the scene could be staged in order to emphasise the different interpretations. Placing characters nearer the audience or having them alone on stage at either the beginning or end of the scene is a good method of earning the sympathy of the audience. Changes in tone and projection can also manipulate their response. Rehearse the versions and perform them one after the other. Discuss what the directors intended and what the audience felt was achieved. What did the actors learn about the scene through performing the extract? Note what you have learnt in your text, indicating particular changes in movement and voice on the script.

**Defining the friendship**

To prepare you for a possible examination response, in your group try to define the relationship between the two characters and give two short precise examples of how this might be revealed in performance. You could focus on movement and voice separately or hone on moments of the scene. Try writing this response on paper in 5 minutes. This will help you to simulate the pressure you will be under at the end of the year.

### Scene 2

Marie, Margaret, child, Drum-Major, Woyzeck

Pages 7–11

Marie and her neighbour, Margaret, are at Marie's window admiring the Drum-Major's march down the street. As he salutes, Marie acknowledges and once he passes she begins to sing about handsome soldiers. When Margaret comments on how Marie was affected by the man in uniform, the latter takes offence and after a brief exchange Margaret leaves. Marie sings a melancholic song to her child before her common-law husband, Woyzeck, appears at the window. She comments on his wild appearance before he departs and the scene concludes with Marie remarking on the lack of light before exiting hurriedly.

**Analysis**

Just as in the previous scene, the initial physical image of friendship between the named characters is quickly undermined. Marie and Margaret share an initial excitement at the military personnel which could suggest what Marie initially liked about Woyzeck, before she realised he was not as dynamic as the impressive Drum-Major. It also suggests the possibility of infidelity. The sound of drums could be linked to the previous action and indeed suggest the fast pace at which the scenes should move or blur from one to the next. However, the most striking aspect of the scene is the apparent distance between the two protagonists. Although each uses the other's Christian name, there is emptiness in their relationship; Marie observes that 'he didn't even stop to look at his child'.

### Portraying the difference in personality

It is important to note that Büchner describes the two women as neighbours rather than friends, alluding to the trapped, lonely existence that Marie experiences. As a director, it is important that you can communicate to your actors the difference that you would expect in their portrayals. Individually, begin by making a list of the differences you might expect to see in performance. Allow yourself 1 minute to do this. Once this is complete, discuss the ideas as a whole group. You may raise notions such as age, pace of delivery, use of gesture and the status of the women. Now consider possible ways of experimenting with these through rehearsal. Try the following:

> **Develop the concept that Margaret stifles Marie's spirit**. Improvise a scene between the two characters where Marie suggests they should do something, for example going to the village dance, but Margaret points out the dangers of partaking in such an activity.

> **Focus on the age difference**. Rehearse the scene as if Margaret is acting as a maternal figure, tidying Marie's room and even playing with the baby, while Marie ignores her duties in her dream of something better. How might the difference be emphasised through pace and tone of delivery?

> **Experiment with proxemics**. Assuming the characters have very little in common, ask your actors to demonstrate a physical distance as they perform the scene. How might this be sustained without the scene becoming static? When might you expect them to come nearer to each other and why? Do they ever hold eye contact?

### Creation of locale

The scene poses problems in staging; the playwright expects you to create both the inside and the outside of Marie's room, demonstrating the embryonic stages of their relationship. In pairs, discuss two possible ways in which the scene could be staged to show this first meeting. Think about how it might enable the actors to show the flirtatiousness of each character.

## Singing

The use of song is very important to the style and meaning of Büchner's writing. In this scene, Marie uses music to comfort herself and the child. Try rehearsing the song to the tune of different children's songs, for example 'Bobby Shafto', 'Hush Little Baby' and 'Three Blind Mice'. Initially they may appear ridiculous but remember the tune doesn't need to be solemn; Marie could be trying to be positive rather than melancholic. If you have the musical talent, you may wish to compose music to support the mood you are looking to create.

## Scene 3

Marie, Woyzeck, showman, sergeant, Drum-Major, ensemble

Pages 13–17

Unusually, the scene begins with an anonymous voice singing over the 'emptiness' of the fairground setting. Woyzeck and Marie enter the stage as the showman introduces the first of his amazing acts – a monkey who looks like a soldier. Seduced by the promise of other impressive feats, they enter the tent followed by the sergeant and Drum-Major, who explicitly discuss Marie's beauty. The showman introduces an 'astronomical horse' and while demonstrating its powers, lectures to his audience about the lessons that can be learnt from the beast. At the end of the performance, Woyzeck and Marie begin to leave but the former is asked by the sergeant to help the showman. As he does this, the Drum-Major departs with Marie. When Woyzeck finishes helping, Marie cannot be found.

**Analysis**

The grandness of this scene contrasts with the introspective nature of the previous action. The whole company are likely to be on stage creating the escapist nature of the fair. The singing voice sets the mysterious tone for the scene while creating problems for the director as to how this might be staged. Similarly challenging are the animals – the monkey and the horse – because they may well be influenced by the style of performance. Puppets, humans in costume, live animals or even pre-recorded footage could be used to convey the showman's, and therefore Büchner's, questioning of social order.

## The image of the family

The relationship that Woyzeck has with Marie and their child is an important aspect of understanding the character. He is a loyal father in terms of working hard to support the family but how does he show this physically. The scene is potentially the only happy image of the family life and may be essential in earning sympathy for the protagonist's downfall. In groups of five or six, improvise the opening of this scene asking the actors to experiment with as much physical contact as possible between the family. How might the son be suggested?

In Werner Herzog's film, the son rides on Woyzeck's shoulders which not only enforces the love between them but also raises his status as a man capable of supporting his son.

### Creating the tension

The text suggests that the Drum-Major and sergeant come on stage once Woyzeck and his family enter the tent. However, as a director you may wish to experiment with a more complex opening to the scene. Consider how it might be performed differently if the soldiers are on stage from the start. Using the whole group, with one person acting as a director, improvise a modern fairground setting, with traditional stalls for people to win prizes. Ask the actors playing Woyzeck and his family to focus on the excitement of the child while the soldiers should attempt to gain Marie's attention. The rest of the group should create a sense of the crowd. After improvising the scene, discuss what effect this had on the development of the characters and the tension in the scene and make notes on what you have learnt in your text. Consider how the costume and gait of both Woyzeck and the Drum-Major could emphasise this.

**The showman**

The escapism of the fair is combined with a social lecture from the showman. In pairs, look at his speech on page 15 and consider how his physicality and vocal tone might be used to emphasise Büchner's message. What do you think this extract should communicate to an audience? Rehearse the monologue and perform it to the rest of the group. While watching others, make notes in your text, underlining key phrases which are particularly effective.

Marie, Woyzeck and child

Pages 19–21

### Scene 4

> Marie is admiring a pair of earrings she has been given as a gift by the Drum-Major when Woyzeck enters unexpectedly. Marie attempts to explain the gift by saying she found them. After initial suspicion, he believes his partner and gives her his wages before departing. Marie is consumed with guilt and ironically she says that she should cut her throat.

**Analysis**

This is an impressive short scene in so far as Marie fluctuates between mother, adulteress, and wife. In addition to that we are introduced to the dazzling effect that material objects have on her psyche – she is momentarily freed from the drudgery of her everyday existence. Her innocent child looks on at her as she cherishes the moment and, perhaps in a plea for greater privacy, she threatens him with blindness if he doesn't keep his eyes closed.

### Sculpting images

Begin by rehearsing the physicality of Marie in this section. Working in pairs, allocate one person to be the sculptor while the other is a blob of clay. The sculptor needs to shape the clay into an image of Marie. Try to focus on subtle details which might convey one of the different elements of her character outlined above. Show this image to other members of your group. Ask them to comment on what they understand of the character from her physical appearance. Make notes on what they say. Repeat the exercise with a different aspect of her character but swap round so the other person has an opportunity to sculpt.

---

 **Surprises**

Working in groups of three, with one acting as a director, devise a short scene where Woyzeck gives Marie a surprise present. Remember that they have very little money so the gift must be modest. Rehearse the action so that genuine excitement is shown. Perform the scenes to the rest of the group and ask the actors what this reveals about the characters. Now repeat the scene with the same present being given. However, since Woyzeck has given the present in the past, the surprise is undermined and Marie's disappointment should be hidden from him but somehow shown to the audience. Consider how this might affect the staging. Once again perform these and receive feedback from the group making notes on what has been discovered. Try repeating the activity once again but this time a more exciting present has been given by someone other than Woyzeck. How do they react?

---

**Marie's dreams**

Marie's desire for something greater is evident throughout this scene. She is not simply seduced by the Drum-Major's masculinity, or indeed his money; it is the promise of something better or at least a short escape form the routine of her life. Individually, write a monologue for the character where she attempts to communicate her feelings and frustrations. It may begin something like this:

> As a little girl, I used to spend long summer days by the lake, with my friends. We used to stare at our reflection in the water and describe what we saw, imagining we were much older. Some described the pretty necklaces that hung round their necks. Others spoke of the beautiful dresses that swirled as they danced. My image was much more simple ...

## Scene 5

**Captain and Woyzeck**

Pages 23–27

While Woyzeck gives the captain a shave, he respectfully listens to the latter's aristocratic ramblings about time. However, when he passes judgement about the fact that Woyzeck has a son but isn't married, the soldier becomes more vocal and explains how the poor always suffer and are condemned to a virtueless life. His musings appear to tickle the captain who admonishes him for thinking too much.

**Analysis**

This scene is the first of two duologues which highlight how Woyzeck is controlled by those of a higher status. Obviously, the image of the soldier with a razor hints at the violence of his future crime and indeed will conjure images in a contemporary audience of the murderous Sweeney Todd. In order to counteract this, the routine of the shave will probably need to be lacking in emotion, highlighting Woyzeck's subservient role.

### Master and servant

In order to appreciate Woyzeck's downtrodden existence, it is important for the actors to experiment with him performing menial tasks. Your group should divide in pairs, with one person improvising the role of Woyzeck, the other the captain. The latter, sitting down, should ask the former to perform a simple task – fetch him a drink, bring his shoes. After a formal 'Yes, sir', Woyzeck should disappear and then re-emerge with the task completed. However, the captain should be dissatisfied and ask the soldier to repeat the task. Once again, there is a 'Yes, sir' before departing and then returning. The exercise should continue with the captain becoming incredulous at the Woyzeck's stupidity. The soldier should hide their frustrations. After a few minutes, stop the exercise and ask for feedback from each character.

**The daily routine**

Although Woyzeck could appear to derive comfort from his routine, the banality of it will also help a contemporary audience to sympathise with the nature of his existence. Individually, create a mime of Woyzeck shaving an imaginary captain to a slow count of 16. The physical action should be precisely rehearsed and follow an exact timing which could be created digitally as a sound effect or using a metronome. Once rehearsed, experiment with performing the same routine over a count of 32. How does this affect the actor's mental state? Now try completing it to a count of eight. Repeat several times at this pace before immediately stopping and reading aloud Woyzeck's outburst on page 25. How might the frustration of the character be evident in the tone, pitch and pace of delivery?

Doctor and Woyzeck

Pages 29–35

### Scene 6

The scene opens with the image of Woyzeck urinating against a wall in the street. The doctor is dismayed by his behaviour, mainly because it undermines the experiments he has been doing with his patient. The doctor checks Woyzeck is sustaining his diet of peas and in degrading fashion insists Woyzeck tries to urinate once more. The latter declines and asks the doctor if he's seen 'nature inside-out'. The doctor is confused by his statements and, as clarification is given, he simply appears to revel in the deteriorating mental state of his patient. The soldier concludes with a despairing plea for help which is greeted with a simple: 'Keep eating the peas and cleaning your rifle!'

The status of the doctor in this scene is not only created by his social standing and his wealth but also his knowledge. He is able to control Woyzeck, his living experiment, by blinding him with science, using terminology which might even make members of the audience feel inferior. However, unlike the previous scene where Woyzeck was a dutiful servant, this extract begins with him being chastised for his behaviour and a director should consider how he might ask the actor to perform this further lowering of his status.

## Analysis

Herzog sets this scene in the doctor's room after seeing Woyzeck's behaviour in the street. This reinforces how the soldier appears more in control when protected from the haunting images of the outside world. However, this would remove the difficult but powerful image of the character urinating.

### Swapping roles

For the actors to fully appreciate the impact that their character's behaviour has in a duologue, a useful rehearsal technique is swapping roles. This enables performers to identify individual lines or actions that are particularly powerful while learning from another performer's interpretation. In pairs, look at the dialogue on page 29 and the manner in which Woyzeck is chastised for the inappropriate nature of his behaviour. Rehearse the scene for 10 minutes and discuss with your partner what you have learnt. Now swap roles and rehearse for a further 10 minutes, exploring ways in which the status difference can be emphasised. Annotate your script with what you have learnt.

### Acting on a chair

There is a tendency to overcomplicate the action in rehearsal with complex movements which can distract you from the true meaning of the text. In pairs, sit opposite each other and allocate roles for this scene. Read the entire scene to each other, with the script on your laps. However, each actor must on each line decide whether or not they are going to hold eye-contact or stare to the partner's left or right. Obviously, in order to complete this exercise, the actor needs to memorise each sentence or phrase in turn before it is delivered. There is a tendency to deliver this quickly, cheating by looking up half-way through the exercise. Speed is not the focus as this is supposed to help you closely analyse the text.

### Human experimentation

Building on the previous exercise, remove the chairs but insist that Woyzeck remains in the same position on stage, although he may choose to use gestures to reflect his anxiety. Meanwhile the doctor can choose to move about the space. However, once again, the line cannot be delivered until a decision about eye contact and now physical movement is made. The actors should focus closely on the physical checks which may be completed on the patient. Perform this final version to the rest of the group and discuss when the decisions about movement and eye contact were particularly effective.

Drum-Major and Marie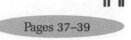

Pages 37–39

## Scene 7

In stark contrast to the sterile emotion of the previous scene, Marie, in her room with the Drum-Major, initially revels in the attention of the military man. He parades for her and she admires his masculinity. As they flirt, Marie is suddenly touched with guilt and the mood changes. She declines the soldier's advances but he persists and she eventually submits.

**Analysis**

The brevity of the scene and the lack of complexity in the dialogue have encouraged some to suggest that it simply serves as a dramatic device to drive the plot forward. The task of the director is to help the actors to create a contemporary meaning to the action, exploring the more subtle shifts of emotion that could exist.

**Engendering trust**

If the emotion in this scene is to be successful, then the performances need to be brave, with the actors trusting each other. Before working on the extract try the following exercises:

**Blind trust**. In pairs, blindfold one of the students and explain that the other has to lead their partner around the room. The exercise could be developed by asking them to explore certain textures or even feeding them food.

**Crab walking**. Standing back to back, the pair must link arms and walk from one end of the room to the other. The exercise can be made competitive by racing against other crabs. Change the exercise slightly so that the pairs now face each other and have to link arms behind their partners back but still must walk using side steps.

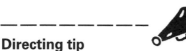

**Directing tip**

In order to make this a modern tragedy, we need to sympathise with Marie's dilemma. Consequently, the appearance and actions of the Drum-Major must be something we admire.

 **Exploring prior action**

Büchner keeps this scene brief in order to maintain the pace of his tragedy. However, the actors need to explore the motivation of the characters in greater depth if they are to be successful. Imagine that the Drum-Major had turned up at the house uninvited. He brought some food and drink to share. Create a scene where the two of them are clearly flirtatious in their behaviour but they are restricted in their momentary embarrassment to simply discussing the food. How do the actors alter their movement and voice to reveal the characters true intentions? Perform the work and then discuss as a director how you when you would expect the flirtatious behaviour to be emulated in the scene itself.

Although the physical violence is the lasting image of the play, the sound of the Drum-Major's sexual advances have an animalistic brutality to them. Look at the exchange on page 37 beginning with 'You should see me Sundays …', concluding on 'Just you dare'. In small groups rehearse this extract focusing on how the emotion of Marie moves from flirtation to fear. What action might trigger this change? The last line of the scene is quite an abrupt change of mind so consider how her submission might be suggested before this. Annotate your script with the physical and vocal decisions made.

## Scene 8

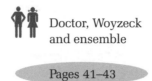

Doctor, Woyzeck and ensemble

Pages 41–43

> The scene begins with Woyzeck acting as a servant for the doctor, bringing in some steps on which the latter stands. The doctor begins by lecturing his audience about the instinct of a cat but quickly makes the crowd focus on his other experiment. At a click of his fingers, Woyzeck returns and is immediately humiliated, being asked to wiggle his ears in front of the assembled crowd. At the conclusion of the meeting, Woyzeck removes the steps and is told to see the captain.

The action effectively mirrors the scene at the fair, with the gathered ensemble admiring the showman, in this case the doctor, as he presents his intriguing beasts. His verbose description of the cat undermines his status and indeed that of his audience who have loyally gathered to hear his wisdom. They are the intellects of the future who are likely to perpetuate the isolation of the working class just as the Drum-Major is looking to spawn more soldiers. However, it is the doctor's inhumane treatment of Woyzeck which emphasises the cruelty of his class and establishes the protagonist as a social victim worthy of our sympathy.

**Analysis**

> Büchner is indirectly ridiculing his employers in this scene. At the time of writing, he was working as a lecturer at Strasbourg University.

 **Blocking the physical action**

Unusually for Büchner, this scene contains a range of stage directions which at times are slightly farcical, emphasising the comic and cruel relationship between doctor and patient. In order to help actors shape the action of the scene, work in groups of three, with one person directing the other two into frozen images of the following stage directions:

- He runs back in as the doctor throws the cat at him, which he catches
- Takes out a magnifying glass to mock examine the cat
- Clicks his fingers. WOYZECK returns
- Teeters almost falling onto the steps
- He prods at glands and points of the thorax
- The DOCTOR goes out, WOYZECK following with steps.

Rehearse the six images and the link between them considering how the actors' position within the performance space may vary. Perform the images to the group and then join the pairs to make sixes, using the most effective images as a basis for the action in the scene.

**The first meeting**

Woyzeck's unwavering loyalty to the doctor is fuelled by a financial incentive on which he depends. In pairs, improvise the circumstances in which the two men first meet. Was the pea experiment the catalyst for their meeting or had they had contact before? Explore the characters' past and perform your ideas to the rest of the group.

Captain, doctor and Woyzeck

Pages 41–45

## Scene 9

Unusually, the scene begins with neither of the protagonists. The doctor enters followed by the unfit captain 'puffing after him.' The captain is anxious about his mental instability and the doctor provides little comfort although the banter between the two men makes him laugh. The mood alters when Woyzeck enters. The captain begins with a few abstract statements which gradually become more blatant. He informs Woyzeck about Marie's affair with the Drum-Major. Woyzeck turns pale and the doctor appears to delight in the soldier's physical reaction to the news. As Woyzeck departs with the doctor following his experiment, the captain remains on stage, praising his own good character.

**Analysis**

The opening of the scene is surprisingly comic as the relatively two-dimensional characters of captain and doctor verbally joust with one another. The ironically unfit captain appears inept and is clearly haunted by imaginings, just as Woyzeck has been. The callous doctor shows no sympathy and attempts to dismiss him through the suggestion of future paralysis. Their exchange highlights the futile behaviour of their class and is a stark contrast to the harsh reality with which Woyzeck is confronted.

### Experimenting with pace

The urgent need for the captain to receive help from the doctor is matched by the latter's desperate desire to escape the former. In pairs, look at each character's lines in turn, focusing on the beginning of the scene and finishing just before Woyzeck enters. Begin with the captain. The actor playing him should read his lines while chasing his partner around the space. He should try to gain the attention and ultimately make the other actor stop and listen to his concerns. Repeat the exercise but this time focus on the captain. He is being chased by his partner. When would he choose to stop and talk to the other person directly in an attempt to make him go away? After rehearsing the characters' lines separately, return to the text as a whole. Look at when the pace may alter and indicate this on your script.

###  Leading with parts of the body

In order to develop the arrogance of both characters, it is important to explore them physically. Ask two members of your group to walk round the space as if they are being led by a piece of string that has been attached to different parts of their body, for example their head, tummy or knees. Look at how this affects their posture and gait and suggest which might be used as a basis for developing the role.

---

Woyzeck has already proved himself to be a loyal servant of both men and has demonstrated appropriate respect for their status in previous scenes. However, when the news of Marie's affair is broken, the language of the text suggests that his usual control disappears. In pairs, using the line 'Yes, sir', choose one person to create the image and sound of the loyal Woyzeck. Now focus on the Woyzeck we encounter in this scene. Repeat the exercise with the line 'Please don't make jokes, sir'. Perform the work to the rest of the group and make notes on the work using specific drama terminology.

**The breakdown in formality**

## Scene 10

The action begins in Marie's room with Woyzeck staring madly at his partner. He asks her about the company she has been keeping, questioning where the Drum-Major stood. She suggests he is delirious. He goes to hit her and she is able to stop him verbally. She ironically suggests she would rather he stabbed her than hit her. Woyzeck departs in a frenzy, questioning whether he can ever be certain about anything.

Woyzeck, Marie

Pages 53–55

The shortness of this scene should not detract from the intense emotion and complex psychology that is present within it. In fact, as a director, it may be appropriate to begin rehearsing this scene first in order to ensure that the actors fully understand the characteristics that underpin their relationship. This skill is to find ways in which you can explore the subtle shades of emotion and action that exist.

**Analysis**

---

### Making promises

Although Marie and Woyzeck were not married, imagine that they have at some point made a verbal commitment to each other. Working in pairs, stand on opposite sides of the room and imagine three promises that Woyzeck or Marie might have to their partner in the early stages of their relationship. Once both members of the pair have planned what they are going to say, improvise a scene by the lake where they are making promises to each other. You could further explore this by improvising a monologue from either character which could take place after this scene. The aim is to reflect on how some of the promises have been broken.

---

### Units and objectives

In order to focus on the subtleties of action, Stanislavski believed that a text should be temporarily broken into units whenever there is a change in the psychological state of the character. In groups

**Further reading**

For more details on Stanislavski, read pages 15–23 of *Edexcel AS Drama and Theatre Studies Study Guide* (Rhinegold 2008).

of three, look at the scene in detail and try to divide the scene into rehearsal units. Each unit needs to be accompanied by an objective for each character. This needs to be expressed in the form 'I want …' and needs to contain within it an essence of action. For example, the opening unit could be the first two lines of text with the actors focusing on the following objectives:

> *Marie*: I want to clean my house.
>
> *Woyzeck*: I want to control my anger.

Once the different units and objectives have been decided and written on your text, two members should rehearse each unit in turn, polishing each extract before moving to the next. The third member of the group acts as a director, ensuring that the objectives are fully explored.

Perform the scene to the rest of the group, seeing if the audience can identify any of the objectives.

---

**Witnessing the betrayal**

**Think about…**

The role the child plays in the action of this scene. Is he ignored or does his presence affect the delivery and ultimately add to the tension of the scene?

Andres and Woyzeck

Pages 57–59

Within the scene, Woyzeck questions where the Drum-Major stood and clearly tries to make sense of the act of unfaithfulness. Try performing scene 7 with Woyzeck on stage watching the action and then run immediately into scene 10 with him now echoing the Drum-Major's position at key moments. Experiment with him trying to force himself on Marie, giving her a passionate kiss just as her lover may have. It would be ironic to present the often emotionally detached Woyzeck so passionately when ridiculing Marie's unfaithfulness.

**Scene 11**

The high emotion of the previous scene is juxtaposed by the relative calming effect of Andres mundanely cleaning his boots and singing. He is interrupted by Woyzeck's preoccupation with Marie and the thought of her dancing with the Drum-Major. The latter appears engulfed by his thoughts and becomes less lucid, eventually exiting to see for himself what is happening.

**Analysis**

As the two friends appear on stage for the second time together, the audience should be able to chart the deterioration in Woyzeck's mental state. Andres' calm exterior acts as a good comparison for the protagonist's fragility. The relatively peaceful setting of the guardroom provides Woyzeck and the audience with a moment to reflect on the events that have occurred.

**The world goes on**

The matter-of-fact nature of Andres' behaviour is important to establish a sense of normality. The cleaning of boots implies a daily routine and the singing demonstrates his relaxed nature. As a group, discuss how this moment should be staged. If Woyzeck is sitting, where is his chair on stage? How are the boots cleaned? Try singing Andres' song to the tune of 'Greensleeves'. The slightly melancholic tone might emphasise the irony of the tale of the landlord's wife waiting until the soldiers come marching in.

The use of the phrase 'What now?' implies that Woyzeck has not been silent while sitting on the chair. He is likely to have been pestering a friend. In pairs, acting out the roles of Andres and Woyzeck, use the essence of the dialogue to improvise around the scene. Use the following structure:

**What now?**

> *Woyzeck*: Andres!
>
> *Andres*: What now?
>
> *Woyzeck*: ... (Woyzeck makes a comment, such as 'It is getting dark')
>
> *Andres*: ... (Andres agrees with Woyzeck, saying for example 'It is certainly less bright').

The actors must experiment with different mimes, physical positions on stage (e.g. lying, sitting or standing) and vocal tones. The actors are not permitted to discuss what they are planning; they must simply keep repeating the structure, varying the dialogue and how it is performed. After a few minutes, discuss the work and what was been learnt about the characters. How frustrated did Andres become?

 **Woyzeck's mind**

In order for the actor playing Woyzeck to understand how the character is feeling, it may be useful to create a sense of his disturbed mind. Sit one person in the middle with the rest of the group sat round them. Look at the line: 'Got to get out. Everything spins round – Dancing, dancing! Her hands'll be hot – Oh damn her, Andres, damn her!'. The person at the centre of the circle should remain silent with eyes closed. The others should try to create a collage of sounds which could reflect Woyzeck's confused mental state. Using just these words and general sounds they need to experiments with tone, pace, projection, pitch and inflection to create the chaos in his mind. After two minutes, ask the person in the middle to explain how the experience might help him to portray the character in this scene.

First journeyman, second journeyman, Woyzeck, Marie, Drum-Major and ensemble

Pages 61–65

## Scene 12

The scene opens with two drunken journeymen entertaining a crowd at the tavern with songs and flippant observations about the world. As the crowd erupts into song, Marie and the Drum-Major are revealed, dancing. Woyzeck appears and is wounded by the sight of the two lovers. The crowd fall silent as he remains in shock at their blatant affection. He collapses and the first journeyman preaches to the crowd. The latter explains that it is within a soldier's nature to self-destruct. Woyzeck comes to and hurriedly leaves.

**Analysis**

The previous group scenes have been used to comment on different aspects of society and indeed the initial exchanges between the journeymen appears to mirror this form. However, Woyzeck's entrance turns the general to the very specific as his private embarrassment and anger at Marie's affair becomes public. This tragic character is being forced to endure his downfall in front of the rest of the town.

**Creating the tavern**

The serious tone of the text is often lifted by the energy that is provided through group scenes. In this section the tavern needs to be particularly powerful in order to further Woyzeck's isolation from society. Begin by creating a tableau as a group which could be the opening image as the lights come up. Consider what this scene says about the microcosm of society on show. Are they happy or are there any suggestions of their own ill-fortune. How could this be shown? Try converting this image into a series of five images which chart the development of the characters in the ensemble.

### The dancing

The image of the lovers spinning has a lasting effect on Woyzeck's mind during the remainder of the play and therefore the audience need to have a similar response. A director would need to consider carefully the style of this dance. As a group, discuss how the characters should dance. How do they hold each other and how do they turn? Is it a traditional dance or simpler and more animalistic in nature? Is Woyzeck's observation of the dance a moment of realism or does it become more stylised? Perhaps the crowd and the dancers could alter their pace as Woyzeck rambles in fevered fashion. Formulate in your own mind how you might direct this section and consider how you might communicate these ideas to a group of actors.

### The journeyman's message

Similar to a Shakespearean fool, the first journeyman, in his drunken and humorous frippery, communicates a truth which needs to be relayed to the audience. The fragmented language, heavy with punctuation, would make his delivery stilted and therefore it may be worth utilising this in rehearsal as a way of exploring his different tones. In groups of between six and eight, read the speech that concludes the scene round the circle, changing speaker every time punctuation is used. This could mean that some people only speak one word. Having made a note of the phrases each person speaks, create a performance with the group stood close together as a chorus, acting as one voice. Actors should be encouraged to vary the tone to emphasise the disjointed delivery while still communicating the meaning of the extract. Rehearse and perform this and then repeat the speech with just one person performing all the different voices and movements. What effect might this have on an audience?

## Scene 13

Woyzeck

Pages 65

This short scene compares the apparently peaceful location of the woods with Woyzeck's fragile mental state. His mind is filled with the rhythm of the dance before a moment of silence suggests that a voice in his head comes with a moment of clarity – 'Stab the she-wolf, dead.' The invasive rhythm returns and he runs out of the scene.

**Analysis**

The challenge as a director is to find a method of presenting this short passage so that it emphasises the brutality of the thoughts in Woyzeck's mind.

**Using sound**

Create a soundtrack which combines a piece of music which could be used for the dance with the sound effects of a woodland setting. As the sounds fade from one to another, discuss as a group when it might be best for Woyzeck to appear. How does he enter the space? In preparation for a possible exam answer, give two possible ways an actor might enter the stage space and explain the effect you are looking to create.

### Conscience alley

As a whole group, form two lines facing each other at the point of Woyzeck's entrance. A volunteer, playing the role of the soldier should slowly walk down the alley. As he passes each group member, they should state what the people at the tavern may have said about his strange behaviour. Repeat the exercise two more times with the ensemble saying what Woyzeck thinks Marie and Drum-Major will be doing and then what he feels about himself. This technique is a way of developing an actors understanding of his role but also creating a sense of the chaotic thoughts in his mind.

Woyzeck and Andres 🚹🚹

Pages 67

## Scene 14

The image of Andres asleep in the guardroom is shattered by Woyzeck's insomnia. The thought of Marie and the Drum-Major still troubles him and the sounds still pervade his mind. Andres' normal tolerance of his friend's troubled state is not present. He insists his friend should let them be, insisting he goes to bed and finishing by calling him a fool. As Andres goes back to sleep, Woyzeck exits.

**Analysis**

In a true reflection of Woyzeck's mind, Büchner uses sleep-deprivation to add to his personal torture. The use of Andres soundly asleep, under the comfort of the blanket, emphasises the difference between the friends.

### 💡 Improvising prior action

Imagine Woyzeck, as he returns to the barracks, is going to confess to Andres about his murderous thoughts. As he is walking, he plans how he is going to express what he is feeling. Individually, improvise the monologue he has with himself.

### 💡 Watching Andres sleep

The stage directions at the beginning of the scene state 'Woyzeck comes in, shakes him.' However, rather than Woyzeck immediately waking his friend, consider the impact of him watching and admiring the peaceful nature of the sleep. Improvise the stage directions, varying the length of time Woyzeck waits before shaking Andres and discuss the impact it has.

**Andres' despair**

Andres' increasing frustration is evident in this scene. As a method of developing the total life of the character, write a monologue which Andres might deliver to another friend about Woyzeck's increasingly bizarre behaviour. Perform the words and discuss how this activity might help you if you were an actor in this scene.

Drum-Major, Woyzeck, second journeyman, Margaret and ensemble 🚹🚹

Pages 69

## Scene 15

The powerful image of the Drum-Major opens the scene with an aggressive declaration of his power. The unstable Woyzeck refuses to drink when the Drum-Major commands and as a result receives a horrific beating. As the ensemble comment on the scene, Woyzeck concludes with the statement, 'One thing after another'.

**Analysis**

This is the only time that we see the two rivals for Marie's affection without her present and the contrast between the two men should be obvious. However, the two extremes appear to make both versions of masculinity undesirable. This is not a

Shakespearean tragic hero proving himself to be a great fighter or tactician; this is a broken man being unfairly punished by the world in which he lives.

### Comparing the two men

Clearly the director of this scene would need to ensure the difference between the men is made explicit. If this was your responsibility, give two ways you would expect the actors to reflect this in performance and the impact you would hope this would have on a contemporary audience.

### Modern interpretation

The physical battle between the two men could be seen as a somewhat clichéd tussle between bully and victim. In pairs, improvise modern versions in which a character similar to Woyzeck could be humiliated at work, school or watching a football match. How might this setting help you to understand the period battle presented in the text.

**Directing the fight**

If you were to write about this scene in the exam, you will need to consider carefully the impact you want the fight to have. Stage directions suggest Woyzeck has a bad beating. However, in Werner Herzog's film the intimidation is more subtle. Once the Drum-Major has demonstrated his superior strength, the humiliated Woyzeck is left alone. In pairs, try staging both versions of the fight and then discuss which you feel is more effective.

## Scene 16

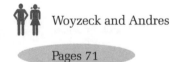

Woyzeck and Andres

Pages 71

> In the guardroom, Woyzeck quizzes Andres about a conversation he'd heard between the Drum-Major and the other soldiers. Although Andres believes it to be irrelevant, he still reveals the Drum-Major's celebration of his sexual exploits. Woyzeck explains he's been dreaming about a knife. As he gathers his kit to depart he refers to the woman he once loved – someone with which Andres appears to have forgotten he had any connection.

**Analysis**

As the pace of the tragedy develops, the scenes between the two friends become more frequent. However, Andres, the once passive listener who resorted to calling his comrade a fool, now reveals details which he knows would unsettle his friend, accelerating his descent.

### Highlighting the conflict

In pairs, stand facing your partner with the script in your hands, approximately three metres apart. Learn each sentence before you deliver it and hold eye contact as you speak. Decide whether each phrase challenges your partner or serves another purpose. Every line which is spoken as a challenge should involve you taking a step forward; all other lines should take a step back. This enables actors to focus carefully on the proxemics of the scene. Once you have been through the script rehearse it in a freer manner, using what you have gained from the exercise as a guide for the difference between the two men.

### The Drum-Major boasts

The scene alludes to action that took place off-stage in the washroom. Begin by discussing as a whole group whether you feel that Andres' comments are a true reflection of what took place. Using what you have discussed, try to recreate the scene with a few members of the group. Did Andres participate in the discussion or did he hover nervously in the background?

### Experimenting with pace and pause

In groups of three, with one acting as a director, look at the pace of the delivery in this scene. The short lines and frequent use of questions suggest that the lines should be delivered quickly. Try performing the scene at a fast pace, almost overlapping some of the lines. Now consider where the pauses might be placed and what this might communicate to an audience. Try rehearsing the extract with some changes in pace and use the director as a guide to what is successful. Mark each pause with a '/' on your script and make notes on why it would be effective.

Woyzeck and Jew

Pages 73–75

## Scene 17

Woyzeck enters a shop to purchase a weapon. He initially enquires about a gun which he discovers to be too expensive. He settles on a knife, which the Jew presumes is to slit his throat. Woyzeck hands over the money and departs quickly.

**Analysis**

The scene serves a simplistic purpose, driving the action forward although Büchner still uses it to emphasise a social comment. More affluent people would be able to purchase a gun, which would achieve a cleaner and potentially more distant death. Woyzeck is forced to settle on a cheap knife. The Jew observes that this makes the death 'economical' but an audience should realise that it is a death from economics – if Woyzeck had more money, he wouldn't be in this situation.

**Creating location**

As a group, create the size of the Jew's shop by standing as the walls of the room. In turn, describe a different aspect of the space until a full mental picture is developed. The exercise may develop as follows:

There is one window to the shop which looks out onto the street. The walls are filled with different weapons. The knives are of varying lengths and some are rusting. The room is lit with candles that flicker slightly. The shadows that they create accentuate the menace of the weapons.

**The relationship between the men**

This is clearly a business relationship and Woyzeck appears uncomfortable in the shop. As a director, identify five different ways an actor playing Woyzeck could communicate this to an audience and then, combining with two other people, rehearse the scene, making these ideas explicit in performance.

## Scene 18

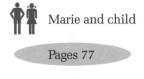
Marie and child

Pages 77

The guilt-ridden Marie is revealed in her room, beside her son's crib. She is reading extracts from the Bible while trying to hold her hands together in prayer. As she reads from the Bible she becomes overcome with her sense of her own sinfulness and wishes she could be granted forgiveness by God.

**Analysis**

Marie's dependence on religion on this scene appears slightly incongruous and yet reaffirms the sense of her complex characterisation. Similar to her husband who she has appeared to have abandoned, she is craving routine – 'Franz doesn't come' – and is beginning to feel the heat.

### Communion

Stanislavski uses the concept of communion as a way of improving the actor's focus. If a range of objects is referenced in a scene, then an individual may be able to radiate feelings, due to their high level of concentration. In this scene Marie communes with the Bible, the crucifix, her son and herself. Individually look at the script and decide where her focus is on each line. Having done this, explore the monologue practically, considering how eye contact and gesture could revel the emotion in the scene.

### The routine of Franz and Marie

If Marie is missing the routine appearances of her common-law husband, then it is worth looking at what form this may have taken. Although there is some evidence of this in the text, Franz is clearly troubled and their home is not as ordered as perhaps it once was. Improvise in pairs the couple's routine. You may choose to focus on the morning, mealtime or their son's bedtime. Repeat the scene three times, with subtle changes to indicate the comfort they may derive from their behaviour.

Woyzeck and Andres

Pages 79

### Scene 19

In the guardroom, Woyzeck appears unusually in control, and in an apparent conclusion to their friendship, he is giving his belongings to Andres. The former discovers a paper which he reads aloud. It identifies his age and position. In a final act of support, Andres encourages his friend to seek medical help.

**Analysis**

The religious pleading by Marie in the previous scene is made more interesting by the subtle suggestion in this scene's action. As the critic John Reddick observed, Woyzeck's age in this scene is identical to that of Christ when he died. He also was born on the feast of the Annunciation, when Christ was reportedly conceived. Rather than ridiculing religion, he is actually making a salient point. Both Woyzeck and Christ had a pre-ordained fate. The eponymous soldier is not mad; he is simply following the path that life has created for him. Therefore, in the previous scene, Marie, it could be argued, is not only praying to the Lord, but also asking for forgiveness from her husband.

> **Further reading**
>
> *Georg Büchner* by John Reddick (Penguin 1993).

**Recreating the bond**

The emotional distance between the friends appears more resolved in this scene as the tragedy nears its denouement. His destiny sealed, Woyzeck appears to have a clarity of purpose which Andres finds a little disturbing. The sorting through of the belongings is something in which they both participate and this will naturally affect the proxemics in the scene. What opportunities are present in the scene for physical contact between the two characters? Indicate on your text when you would expect this to happen and identifying when eye contact might be held.

**The total life of the character**

By emptying his kitbag, we are introduced to the fragments of Woyzeck's life which have until now remained hidden. Using each of the objects as a starting point, divide the group up so that each has responsibility for recreating a scene where Woyzeck first took possession of this object. By imagining these scenarios, an actor should be able to recall the emotion attached to the items and demonstrate this through vocal tone and gesture.

Margaret, grandmother, Marie and Woyzeck

Pages 81–83

### Scene 20

The scene opens with Margaret singing a simple song about people dancing in pairs; a reminder to Marie of her infidelity. When the grandmother suggests Marie should sing, she refuses – a stark contrast to the Marie seen at the opening of the play. The grandmother recounts a depressing tale of an orphan who had nothing and so went in search of things which promised more. However, when he visited the moon, sun and stars, they were not as beautiful as they seemed from afar. As the tale of false hope concludes, Woyzeck enters and insists Marie follows.

**Analysis**

The setting of this scene in the street, without the child present, and the opening song suggest that Marie is no longer to be perceived as a mother but as a whore. Her now primitive existence is emphasised by the dark fairytale which, rather than offering comfort, presents a depressing view of the world. It is perhaps the most poignant of all the stylised monologues which appear to reveal Buchner's voice as it echoes his personal life. Once a man of ideals and hope, his spirit was crushed by society, with the world failing to live up to his dreams.

### The voice of the grandmother

The haunting character of the grandmother is mostly silent in the play, although often present in the ensemble scenes. She appears as a powerful voice drawing focus to the tragedy of the play just as the blind Tiresias does in Sophocles' *Oedipus*. In order to create a sense of age, each member of the group should record a person two generations older than them reading the monologue. Once recorded, they should practise speaking the text, mimicking the pace and rhythm of delivery. This should not only break their vocal habits but also help to establish a different quality in the voice.

**Further viewing**

In Werner Herzog's film, he chooses to give this story to Marie who speaks of a little girl whose dreams are dashed, adding to the complexity of Marie's character.

**The change in characters**

Although the exchange between Marie and Margaret is a little curt in scene 2, the events of the play and the passing time could suggest a difference in physicality. In threes, create a tableau for scene 2 which shows how they behave towards each other. Create a similar image for scene 20 but consider how the position of the grandmother might alter the dynamic between them. As a director, what would you be hoping to communicate to an audience in this second scene?

### Scene 21

> As the couple walk through the woods, Marie appears to be troubled by the darkness. Woyzeck attempts to reassure her by saying that he will save her from sore feet. The couple discuss their past but Woyzeck speaks in riddles as he alludes to her fate. Woyzeck draws the knife and as Marie begs him to stop he stabs her and cuts her throat before running away from the scene.

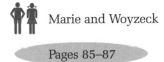 Marie and Woyzeck

Pages 85–87

**Analysis**

Many of the lines uttered by the two characters in the previous scenes have been dominated by heat – the heat of passion, adultery, madness and anger. Here there is talk of cold but only in reference to Marie. Woyzeck is numb to the temperature because he is so focused on the task in hand.

**Highlighting the individual**

There is an hypnotic awkwardness between the two characters as they enter the stage at the start of this extract. They each appear isolated – any connection between them has disappeared and therefore it's appropriate to look at the portrayal of the roles in isolation. In pairs, allocate the two roles and begin with the character playing Woyzeck. The actor should read the lines up to 'Are you cold, Marie' with the other actor responding physically but remaining silent. Repeat the scene but this time focus on Marie's dialogue. Consider how this has focused the performers on the individual's determination or fear. Now perform the section again with both actors talking and consider what was learnt from working this way.

**Making the murder contemporary**

Despite apparently rejecting the Romantic tendencies of the era, this scene would not look out of place in a Victorian melodrama. One of the greatest challenges is ensuring the violence is either subtle or so gruesome that it manages to remove any link to the two-dimensional nature of that genre. Research methods of presenting violence. Look at Tim Burton's film of *Sweeney Todd* and read Martin McDonough's *Lieutenant of Innishmore*. Both contain unnerving violence fuelled by revenge. Using these sources, make notes on how you would stage the murder appropriately.

Woyzeck, Margaret, first journeyman, second journeyman, grandmother and ensemble

Pages 89–91

### Scene 22

The active dancing at the tavern is one which Woyzeck feels he can now enjoy. He sings for the first time and seems full of the energy he has previously seen in others. He encourages Margaret to sing and her words have unusual resonance for Woyzeck as he reflects on Marie's murder. Margaret followed by the crowd of people notice blood on Woyzeck. He attempts to dismiss it as a self-inflicted injury before the haunting voice of the grandmother suggests foul play. Despairingly, he quickly exits.

**Analysis**

Either as an act which attempts to defy his destiny or one which reflects the calmness of his mind, Woyzeck returns to the setting where he witnessed Marie's haunting dancing and received a beating from the Drum-Major. An audience should feel a sense of foreboding with a third visit to this fateful setting and the tension should be palpable.

**Woyzeck's status**

Büchner's text implies that the murderous act has given Woyzeck greater status. Rather than drinking in solitude, he is able to address the whole tavern in an apparently confident manner. As a director, identify three different ways of communicating the status change. You might find it useful to organise your ideas in a table:

| | Scene 15 – lower status | Scene 22 – higher status |
|---|---|---|
| The change in physicality | Woyzeck should be perched on the edge of a bench, not even facing a table. Shoulders rounded, back arched, head bowed down, looking to hide. | Woyzeck stands in the centre of the performance space, straight back and arms stretching upwards, waving slightly in celebration of the twirling dance. |

### The change in Margaret

As a named character, it is important that Margaret doesn't drift into nagging stereotype. In pairs, improvise a scene between her and Woyzeck before the play started. Was she supportive of his attempts to raise money or critical of the lack of physical support he gave Marie? Use this to compare with her reaction to the now confident Woyzeck who dominates the tavern. How might her character change within the scene when she sees the blood?

---

In a realistic portrayal, the reaction of the crowd to the blood could be performed in a believable manner. However, the grandmother's line may also work successfully after a crescendo of noise. As a group, try to create a stylised version of the text on page 91. Consider how the rhythm of the lines or even the rhythm of Woyzeck's heart played over this section, could add to the violent nature of his act. How might the movement be staged to emphasise this?

**The questioning of the crowd**

### Scene 23

> Woyzeck is seen approaching through the woods to Marie's body. In an apparent state of madness, he treats Marie as if she were still alive, discussing her appearance and her need for a wash. He drags her to the pool and in a macabre and romantic image walks step by step with Marie into the pool where they both disappear. The journeymen enter, remarking on the strange sound of someone drowning in the lake. They rush towards it.

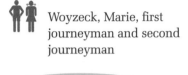 Woyzeck, Marie, first journeyman and second journeyman

Pages 93–95

The controlled Woyzeck of the tavern is immediately undermined as he announces a setting with which we are familiar as 'a strange place'. He clearly is not himself, a fact that is emphasised at his apparent surprise in finding what he believes to be Marie – rather than her dead body. His attempts to wash her clean are clearly symbolic of the act of baptism. They may not be able to afford to get married but they could wash away their sins. Unfortunately, Woyzeck struggles to get clean and he drowns with the body.

**Analysis**

The tragedy of this virtuous man is in the final image we see of him alive. Rather than showing remorse for his act or fighting bravely, he is acting as a loving husband, an act we should admire and detest in equal measure. It is important to experiment carefully with the physical action in order to ensure the tone is appropriate. Begin by working in pairs, with one person acting as the dead Marie. The actor playing Woyzeck should begin by 'holding her like a child' before manipulating her body subtly as if she were alive. Look at how small movements of her arm could suggest a desperate attempt at tenderness.

**Animating the body**

> **Further study**
>
> DV8's *Enter Achilles* begins with a scene with a dancer manipulating an inflatable doll in a futile attempt to make her feel real. Look at the actions used and consider if any of them could be applied in this context.

As Woyzeck stumbles into the water with Marie, there is a tender and encouraging use of dialogue. In pairs improvise a scene where he has encouraged her to do something of which she was scared. Try to create a genuine tenderness in the vocal delivery and a real sense of moral support. Now apply that tone to the final lines beginning, 'Take a step'. By doing this, Woyzeck's final living image should evoke pity for his undeserved suffering.

**The final image**

Doctor, Marie, Woyzeck and captain

Pages 97–101

## Scene 24

In a gruesome and dispassionate conclusion, the doctor conducts an autopsy on the two bodies. For once he appears medically adept and he offers some regret for their death. The pompous captain enters and attempts to undermine the doctor. The two debate their findings over the bodies before the doctor realises that Woyzeck mysteriously has no blood in his body appearing to defy medical science.

**Analysis**

One of the trademarks of German Naturalism is the obsession with the scientific and this scene in *Woyzeck* celebrates pre-occupations with medical matters. However, there is a twist more appropriate to contemporary crime dramas. As an act of final defiance, Woyzeck's body raises questions which nobody can answer and in doing so Büchner undermines the dominant scientific thread which permeates his work.

**A lack of respect**

The doctor, when privately undertaking his duties, appears relatively appropriate in his manner. In fact, Woyzeck is initially shown more respect in death than life. This alters when the captain enters his space, suggesting that he is also affected by the social pressures of his class. In groups of four, with two people acting as the dead bodies, look at the exchange on page 99. Consider how the bodies could be treated in order to emphasise their low status.

 **Directing the doctor**

The doctor's final line of the scene highlights his frustration at his patient. His rhetorical question emphasises the mystery and inhumanity of the situation. Work on this exercise in pairs, with one as the doctor delivering the line, 'Where's the blood, Woyzeck? What's happened to the blood?', with the other person playing the role of the director sat on the floor. The doctor delivers the line and the director must respond with praise explaining what they did that they liked. However, they should always conclude with the phrase '… just one criticism, you need to make it bigger.' Repeat the line many times, making each performance bigger than the last. The aim is not to create a ridiculous delivery but actually encourage the actor to explore the power of the scene.

Andres and grandmother

Pages 103

## Scene 25

In a return to the opening scene, Andres is seen splitting sticks. A haunting whistling is heard and he becomes unnerved by a strange sensation. He becomes aware that gore is seeping through the ground. The grandmother laughs and he runs away, disturbed by the events. The audience are left with the image of the grandmother before she is swallowed by the thickening mist.

The problematic nature of the play is that the final image and, therefore, the playwright's message varies in each edition and as a result it is difficult to assert what Büchner was trying to communicate. In this edition, the blind woman who appears to see and understand more than the other characters directly addresses the audience, involving them directly in the play and bringing the fictitious world into their own.

Analysis

As Woyzeck's personal tragedy concludes, there is a sense that Andres' is just beginning. The calm and rational soldier is unusually spooked by the events in the scene, although it is unclear whether they are really happening or are figments of his imagination. If it is the latter than the stage directions suggest that the audience are also witnesses to this hallucination. As a director, consider how this scene could mirror scene 1, with Andres' action copying that of Woyzeck. What similarities could be noted in their physical and vocal delivery? How might you work with the actor to create a sense of the fear the character is experiencing?

**The cyclical nature of the play**

If the final image is that of the grandmother, then it is important to identify what this could mean to a contemporary audience. Discuss as a group the impact it should have. Is she an image of fate, suggesting it could be our turn next? Is it a warning to those who stand by and do nothing? Is it a simple reminder that life is fragile in a way that we do not understand? Having decided on a concept, decide how the action could be staged in order to emphasise this.

**The final image**

## Directorial interpretation

Now that you have read the play and made detailed structured notes, you should be close to formulating your directorial concept that will carry you through the written examination. The great advantage of Büchner's visionary and fragmented writing is that it doesn't conform to any particular theatrical genre. As a director, you are given the freedom to make the action suit the style of your choice. Thematically, several key concepts need to influence the decision you make. Woyzeck's extreme poverty and manipulation by those with more power should be at the heart of your work. He is the underdog facing a battle against the restrictions which society imposes on him. He is someone with whom an audience should sympathise and his story is so universal that it could be placed comfortably in almost any period of history. Look at the brief extract of a review of Woyzeck at the Barbican Theatre:

> 'Gisli Orn Gardarsson's production has an industrial setting rather than a military one; Borkur Jonsson's design features thick silver pipes and platforms fronted by water tanks and Ingvar E. Sigurdsson's Woyzeck is a boiler-suited factory worker. The doctor who performs cruel experiments on him is a hard-faced female, and her associates, who string him up by his feet, force a catheter into his penis and cram his head into a glass globe which they gleefully fill with water, are menacing hooded figures wearing alien-looking gas masks.
>
> The most striking innovation, though, is the music, by rock star Nick Cave ... Cave's blood-soaked lyricism and noisy trash-can blues lend

> a thrilling extra dimension to the staging — particularly when the Drum-Major dangles dizzyingly from the ceiling to snarl a vainglorious hymn to himself.'
>
> Review by Sam Marlowe, *Times Online.*

There is a great deal to consider here. Do you want to set the play in the early 19th century or does it lend itself to a more modern time and place? Do you instead want to make it a timeless or futuristic piece that makes a universal point? Who do your central characters represent and what should an audience be picking up in the choices that you have made?

A necessary starting point is to visualise what your production of the play will look like. Choose a venue – indoor or outdoor? Does the play lend itself to performance in front of an audience of 3,000 people or is it more suited to an intimate studio venue? There are justifications for both choices. Where would you like your audience to be physically positioned in relation to the actors? Sketch some ideas or look at existing venues online.

**Further reading**

For more detailed reference to staging look at *Edexcel AS Drama and Theatre Studies Study Guide* (Rhinegold 2008), pages 43–45.

### Designing the set

Now that you have a clearer idea about directorial concept, venue and staging you can start to apply it to the specific demands of the text. Work through the text noting the different location and moments of action that exist. It may be worth doing this in table form as below. This will allow you to clearly see where the staging demands occur and what challenges you will have to overcome. The various locations in the play and the different impact of the indoor and outdoor settings on Woyzeck's mental state should be carefully considered.

| Act/scene | Page number | Location | Characters in scene | Key action in scene |
|---|---|---|---|---|
|  |  |  |  |  |

The initial image of Woyzeck and Andres in the woods highlights the peaceful setting and Woyzeck's chaotic states of mind. Will you as a director be looking at a minimalist interpretation of the play with symbolic and significant set pieces or will you be looking to recreate a realistic sense of the town? How might the different locations be implied and how could they emphasise the abject poverty that the protagonist endures? How are you going to stage the ending of the piece and how would it compare to the peaceful opening?

**Turn to the Appendix on page 195. These questions should help to guide you in the right direction and provide a checklist once all decisions have been reached.**

### Tackling the written examination

The examination booklet can be an intimidating document. Remember all that concerns you is the section on the text you are studying, in our case *Woyzeck*. The page numbers you need to refer to in this booklet will be clearly marked on the question paper.

**Section A** is divided into three questions:

a) is worth 4 marks

b) is worth 6 marks

c) is worth 10 marks

Creating a total of 20 marks. How much you write for each should correspond to the maximum marks available

The chosen extract will cover approximately four pages of text. For the purpose of this example we will be looking at scene 9, pages 45-51.

**Example question 1**

a) Outline for your performers two ways that they might indicate the relationship between the captain and the doctor at the start of this extract? (4)

You first need to consider what that relationship is. How do we want the audience to feel about the captain and the doctor at this stage in the play? This is one of only two times in the play where they meet and the previously self-confident captain is undermined by his hypochondria. The doctor maintains his clinical approach. Practically how will you illustrate this to the audience using two clear examples?

For four marks, the marking criteria state that 'connections to the demands of the question will be clear.' and ask for 'two clear and valid examples supported by reasons.' They ask for 'thinking that is confident, accurate, and clear and rehearsal must be explicit in the response'.

Below is an example of a top-band response; the comments in brackets illustrate how the answer corresponds to the criteria.

> I would rehearse the relationship between the captain and doctor in two ways. As the two men enter form upstage left crossing to downstage centre, I would ask the actor playing the doctor to take large purposeful strides, while the captain would be taking smaller steps at double the speed, emphasising his inferiority and his lack of physical control to the audience. The second way the relationship between them will be emphasised is in the change of pace. The initial pleas of the captain should be delivered by the actor in a breathless, high-pitched tone as he states he is 'depressed', almost shouting the line like an angst-ridden teenager to highlight his uncontrollable despair. At this point, the actor playing the doctor should stop and for the first time turn to hold eye contact with the captain, his fierce facial expression softening as the latter, in a relieved and slower pace, utters '… without bursting into tears', suggesting a moment of mutual respect.

Don't waste space giving needless introductory comment.

Specific and clear instruction. Awareness of stage space. Clear justification given.

Again specific practical instruction to actors, showing an awareness of the development of the action, with clear justification offered.

Let's look now at a bottom-band response:

> 1   Needless contextual information that shows no awareness of the question.
>
> 2   Simple repetition of stage directions will not be rewarded.
>
> 3   Purely descriptive, no evidence of how.
>
> 4   Lack of specific reference to how. Not specific. No evidence of rehearsal. Where is the second way as requested in the question?

This extract comes at the heart of the play just as Woyzeck learns of Marie's affair, a fact that preys on his already troubled mind. This very fact earns greater sympathy for the character while accelerating his downfall.[1] The doctor walks briskly down the street with the captain puffing after him.[2] Once they have entered they follow each other round the stage, the doctor asking for help.[3] The doctor should be acting in a desperate way and the audience should realise this.[4]

What comes across most strongly in good responses are the following:

- Strong PRACTICAL Evidence

- HOW the moment might be performed

- Clear reference to WHY the decision has been made

- Awareness that this is a question asking you to explore REHEARSAL

- Finally an awareness of impact of choices on AUDIENCE.

  b) Consider THREE appropriate rehearsal techniques you might use in order to highlight the attitude of the doctor and the captain to Woyzeck in this extract.   (6)

Technique clearly identified.

Specific practical explanation of technique.

Reason for the choice of technique in context with the performance.

Technique identified.

Practical exploration.

Impact of technique and clear justification for its use.

Technique identified.

The first technique I would use to highlight the personalities is an off-text improvisation. In threes, character A is a school pupil, who has been unfairly asked to sit a detention. Characters B and C are teachers who relish the opportunity to make the character feel inferior by tormenting him about his poor work and even exposing rumours they have heard about him from other students. This would give the actors an insight into the vindictive and effectively unprofessional behaviour of the two men as they explore Woyzeck's inferiority. The second technique I would use would be to rehearse the extract through movement alone. The actors playing the doctor and captain should experiment with how their posture could emphasise their status and contrast with Woyzeck's physical frailties. Glances to each other, patronising taps on Woyzeck's shoulder and greater movement than the static soldier should emphasise their superior control. When the text is reintroduced, the actors should have a greater awareness of how non-verbal action reinforces the class difference.

The third technique would focus on exploring the doctor's and captain's thoughts. I would ask both actors to analyse the behaviour of the protagonist in this scene. The former would look at it from a medical perspective whilst the latter should imagine he is writing a reference for the soldier referring to how he deals with moments of pressure. Once written, the two monologues should be spoken at the beginning of the scene, helping the actors to establish a subtext for the delivery of their lines and hopefully communicating to the audience a sense of their dismay at Woyzeck's behaviour.

> Practical explanation of technique.

> Impact and justification.

For a top-band response to this question the marking criteria ask for specific examples and balance across the three techniques. A confident grasp of terminology and a clear understanding of purpose in using the ideas are required.

c) Explain to your performers how you intend to work on developing an understanding of the character of Woyzeck in this extract and his relationship with other characters and the audience, giving reasons for your approach, supported by clear examples.          [10]

I would firstly explain to my actors the journey that I want the character of Woyzeck to take throughout the scene. He begins as victim, avoiding contact with the others, momentarily turns into a loyal and respectful servant before displaying the pain of a betrayed human being. Consequently, we would look to rehearse the scene in three sections.

> By splitting the scene up, the candidate shows clear control of material and understanding of rehearsal process.

It is important that Woyzeck enters the scene trying to 'avoid notice' as he seeks to avoid any further punishment or humiliation. In order to establish the tone of their relationship, I would begin with a simple off-text exercise. I would ask the actor playing Woyzeck to move silently around the rehearsal space, physically, his posture should be cowered but his eyes shoud be wide open. The aim of the actors playing captain and doctor is to make eye contact with him a fate Woyzeck should avoid at al costs. There can be physical contact but Woyzeck is not permitted to struggle. This should not only highlight Woyzeck's fear of personal contact but also encourage the actor playing the protagonist to focus on the eyes of the character and how they portray the vulnerability at the start of this scene.

> Clear sense of starting point with reasons.

> Relevant and accurate rehearsal technique for a specific purpose.

The change in Woyzeck's manner should be evident to the audience when his name is first called by the captain. An initial aspect of formality should be suggested by a salute or bow by Woyzeck; however as the dialogue continues this relationship should erode. I would begin by looking at this through an off-text exercise. In pairs, using the line 'Yes, sir', I would choose one person to create the image and sound of the loyal Woyzeck. The captain will ask him to complete simple tasks and all the time the faithful soldier will apply affirmatively with a polite and respectful tone. Once the actors are comfortable with the exercise I would ask them to develop it with the captain discussing Marie in a lewd manner. Woyzeck should show signs of increasing offence,

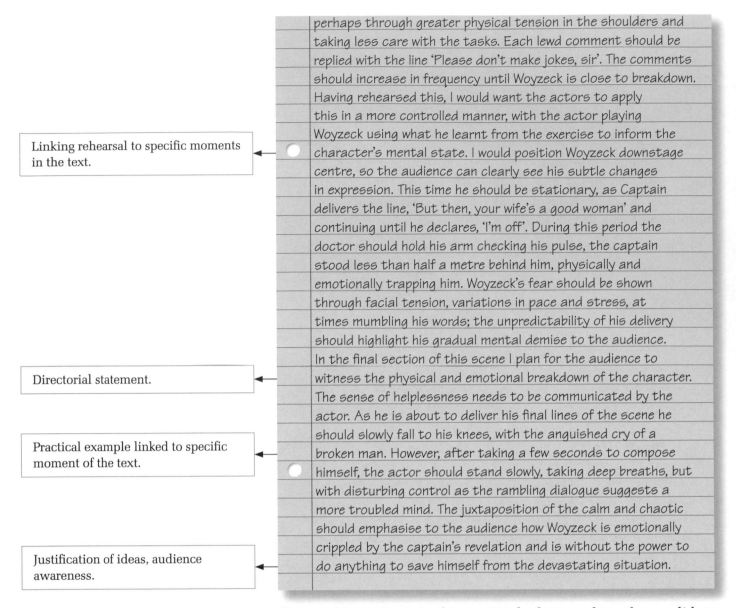

Linking rehearsal to specific moments in the text.

Directorial statement.

Practical example linked to specific moment of the text.

Justification of ideas, audience awareness.

perhaps through greater physical tension in the shoulders and taking less care with the tasks. Each lewd comment should be replied with the line 'Please don't make jokes, sir'. The comments should increase in frequency until Woyzeck is close to breakdown. Having rehearsed this, I would want the actors to apply this in a more controlled manner, with the actor playing Woyzeck using what he learnt from the exercise to inform the character's mental state. I would position Woyzeck downstage centre, so the audience can clearly see his subtle changes in expression. This time he should be stationary, as Captain delivers the line, 'But then, your wife's a good woman' and continuing until he declares, 'I'm off'. During this period the doctor should hold his arm checking his pulse, the captain stood less than half a metre behind him, physically and emotionally trapping him. Woyzeck's fear should be shown through facial tension, variations in pace and stress, at times mumbling his words; the unpredictability of his delivery should highlight his gradual mental demise to the audience. In the final section of this scene I plan for the audience to witness the physical and emotional breakdown of the character. The sense of helplessness needs to be communicated by the actor. As he is about to deliver his final lines of the scene he should slowly fall to his knees, with the anguished cry of a broken man. However, after taking a few seconds to compose himself, the actor should stand slowly, taking deep breaths, but with disturbing control as the rambling dialogue suggests a more troubled mind. The juxtaposition of the calm and chaotic should emphasise to the audience how Woyzeck is emotionally crippled by the captain's revelation and is without the power to do anything to save himself from the devastating situation.

The marking criteria in this section look to see how the candidate establishes relationships between characters and refers to key moments. It is not a character study. Again they refer to 'a confident and clear grasp of drama', evidence of physical and vocal exploration, evidence of rehearsal techniques, audience impact and a 'clear understanding of the process of interpreting the play in performance'.

## Section B

This section is an extended answer worth 30 marks and should be written in an essay-style format. This section tests your overall understanding of the play and allows you to justify and explore the directorial concept that has been central to all your preparations for this examination. You will have made distinct decisions about how you want the play to be performed and in the previous pages we have done our best to prepare you for this moment. You should see this section as an opportunity to share your vision with the examiner, not as a test that you can fail.

You will be given a choice of two questions and must answer one. What we will do in the following pages is look to see how you might structure a response and then look at the specific marking criteria.

## Question 1

> As a director, explore your approach to the play in every aspect of production. Justify your ideas with clear and well supported examples.

The first thing you need to make clear in your response is your directorial concept. How do you see the play *Woyzeck*? Is it a modern timeless story that you want to tell or do you feel that you want to do justice to the play in its original period? Alternatively is yours a vision that combines both aspects? You need to clearly state in your introduction why yours is a concept that works for this play.

> If you are struggling to define your interpretation, try imagining that your version is in print and you have been asked to write the blurb on the back of the book in exactly 200 words. Start with the line '*Woyzeck* is a play about ...'

The next thing to consider is what are the key aspects of any production:

- Acting style
- Props
- Sound
- Lighting
- Interpretation
- Performance style
- Music
- Costume
- Staging
- Audience
- Performance space.

This may well give you the structure of your essay. You may believe that some aspects of production are more important than others and therefore worth more coverage within the essay. Work through the aspects of the production section by section always referring back to how each area supports your directorial approach.

Two words must dominate your response – HOW (a practical example of how a particular scene or moment might be staged or audience positioned or costume designed) and WHY (a clear understanding from you as to how this practical example supports your directorial concept and what impact the particular moment will have on your audience). A good essay can identify the answer to these two words in each paragraph. The more WHYs that you have the greater chance you have of achieving high marks.

> **Tip**
>
> Think carefully about four or five of the key scenes or moments in *Woyzeck* that you will be referring to in any essay about directorial interpretation. Make sure that you do not neglect the minor characters in your choice. Make a brief list of these scenes so that you might be able to refer to them easily when confronted with the essay title.

Conclude your essay strongly by reinforcing the sense of vision that you have been trying to communicate and how within the essay you have attempted to illustrate this.

## Marking criteria

The examiners are looking in the top level 5 (25–30 marks) for the following areas:

- 'An understanding of drama and theatre terminology'
- 'Interpretation and imagination'
- 'An understanding of the performance space'
- 'A full understanding of the play'
- 'Supported examples – visually and practically appealing – without losing sight of its original performance values'
- 'Reference to stylistic or historic elements'

- 'Understanding of aesthetic impact complementing meaning and structure of the play'
- 'Confidence…how live theatre could work…a knowledgeable response'.

Things to avoid in your responses – these hints are taken from the marking criteria at the lower level 2 (7–12 marks):

- 'Highly descriptive'
- 'Highly sourced from an annotated script'
- 'Highly imaginative but not able to work in practical performance'
- 'Little sense of justification'
- 'Proposed interpretation not justified in terms of playwright's original intentions'.

Finally using the example answer above alongside the marking criteria for top- and lower-end responses, consider this question and produce a structure or paragraph plan that you might share among your group.

> As a director, outline how you would portray the character of Woyzeck in order to emphasise the themes of your production. Give supported examples of how your ideas might be achieved in performance.

Although Unit 4 is highly demanding it is also richly rewarding. The purpose of taking you through every aspect of text and design in the preceding pages is to thoroughly prepare you for the exam. If you get a sense that you own your interpretation in every way then you will be able to handle any question on any aspect of your production. With a heavily annotated text that you understand and has been put together in an ordered and structured way, the examination should hold no fear for you. You should want to create a sense of ownership and pride in your work born out of a real connection with the play and a personal and intuitive connection with it.

# Theatre Text in Context - Section C

This section focuses on a live theatre production that you will go to see. This will be chosen by your teacher and will need to be from a different time period from the play that you studied in Sections A and B. For example if you studied Lysistrata then the play you will go to see will have to be from one of the other two recommended periods – either 1564–1720 or 1828–1914.

You are asked to study and research the original performance conditions of the play. The form of study comes in two parts; firstly, to evaluate the ways in which directors, designers and performers have used drama and theatre to interpret the play in a contemporary performance and secondly to relate this through contrast and comparison to the plays original performance conditions.

You will be assessed on this section as part of the Unit 4 examination when you will be required to answer one question from a choice of two in an essay-style format worth 30 marks. This is 38% of the total marks for this paper.

The examination board highlight three key areas of performances that you will need to feel comfortable with:

- Acting techniques including verbal and non-verbal communication

- Design elements including set, staging, costume, make-up, lighting and sound

- The interpretation of the play in performance that you have seen.

Alongside this you will need to have a strong knowledge of the original conditions of the play. How it would have been staged, knowledge of the design elements as they existed, the make-up of the audience, the acting style of the time and the contributing social, historical, political and cultural factors that would have contributed to the writing and production of that play.

You then need to be able to make links between the two time periods – then and now – and carefully consider what changes have occurred in the three key areas highlighted.

In the following pages we will look at each of the three periods using two texts from each period as examples. Each period needs to be approached from a practical perspective focusing on performance conditions and context. You will then be directed to past productions of the plays and similar texts of the periods that might complement your understanding of the time (although your answer should focus on live performances you have seen).

## 525BCE – 65CE

The key developments of theatre during this period can be seen in the theatre of ancient Greece. Three main playwrights of tragedy dominate this period – Aeschylus (525BCE – 456BCE), Sophocles (495BCE – 406BCE) and Euripides (480BCE – 406BCE) and one writer of comedies, Aristophanes (446BCE – 388BCE).

This section will look at the works of two playwrights in this period, Sophocles' *Antigone* and Euripides' *Medea*.

### Antigone (442BCE)

**Plot**

**Further reading**

*Antigone* by Sophocles, translated by Don Taylor (Methuen 1986).

Creon is ruler of Thebes. Two brothers, Polynices and Eteocles, and sons of Oedipus, have died in the Theban civil war fighting against each other for the throne. Creon has decreed that Eteocles will receive a full ceremonial burial and the body of the disgraced Polynices will be thrown into the battlefield to rot. The two sisters Antigone and Ismene meet. Against Creon's will, Antigone plans to give her disgraced brother a full burial. Frightened, Ismeme refuses to help her but cannot dissuade Antigone.

Creon discovers that the body of Polynices has been buried and summons Antigone to him. She stands strong and does not deny anything. Ismene, eager to protect her younger sister, falsely confesses to the crime.

Haemon, Creon's son and Antigone's fiancée, pleads with his father to spare Antigone. Creon decides to spare Ismene but shut Antigone up in a living tomb. On a warning from the god's prophet Tiresias, Creon changes his mind and agrees to free Antigone and bury Polynices. A messenger enters – Haemon and Antigone have killed themselves. Eurydice, Creon's wife, runs in to the palace to do the same. Creon blames himself for everything – by acting against the gods he has lost his family. The Chorus speak of the learning that has taken place: 'We have seen an old man, through suffering, become wise.'

**Playwright**

Sophocles (495 BC – 406BC) was one of the most respected and celebrated poets and playwrights of his generation. He was born to a wealthy family and experienced a privileged upbringing. He was schooled in the arts and was a celebrated chorister as well as a playwright and poet. His output was prolific, writing 123 plays in his lifetime, of which only seven survive. When Sophocles was 28 he entered his first festival and won first prize. Over his life time he became the most awarded playwright of his generation. Aristotle, the great philosopher and thinker, writing in *The Poetics* (350 BC), cites *Oedipus Rex* as the archetypal model for the structure of tragedy.

From various sources we can gather that Sophocles led a moral and upstanding life. He was involved in politics, served as a priest and as a general in the Greek army. With this came an enormous love for his country, strong family and moral values and a belief in democratic rule. In all of his work one can find evidence of these themes being discussed.

Sophocles is also believed to have made advances in dramatic form by increasing the number of Chorus members from 12-15 and by increasing the number of actors from two to three. This served to increase the dramatic potential within the drama. He has been credited with being able to explore the complexities of human thought. Characters in his plays were thought to illustrate universal truths that audiences could recognise in themselves. His central characters have strong wills, passion and fight, and are confronted with great personal disaster.

## Original performance conditions

All of Sophocles' plays would have been performed at the festival of Dionysia in March on the Acropolis in Athens. Records show that *Antigone* won first prize. It is important to note that Greek drama had a huge impact on the society of the time, far removed from the way theatre is viewed in the western society of today. It was a central part of every individual's life and had great social and religious significance. The issues raised in the plays would have been topics of discussion, and in the complex dilemmas within the play of *Antigone,* the audiences of the time would have had a great deal to contemplate.

Today our focus would be on Antigone, the frail girl battling against the powerful machine of the state, as represented by the inflexible Creon; this was far removed from the focus of audiences in 442 BCE. We need to look at Creon as a tragic hero, having to make great personal and political decisions that lead to his own destruction. The key issue for audiences of the time was the consideration behind every political decision – the needs of the individual versus the needs of the state. Guiding principles behind the Greek way of life were a sense of order and justice, and this is exactly what Creon is attempting to achieve after a messy civil war. It would be a position that the Greek audience member respected.

The action of Antigone in burying her brother in defiance of Creon's decree is for modern audiences the moral thing to do. The gods in the play support Antigone's actions and punish Creon. This is a reading from a modern Christian viewpoint. For Greek audiences the debate was more clouded and it was deemed much more acceptable that a traitor to the country did not deserve the rights and respect of a holy burial.

Furthermore, Greek audiences would have seen an essential conflict in the play. This conflict is indeed timeless and the reason why 20th- and 21st-century theatre audiences have become so familiar with the *Antigone* story. The conflict is between the need for laws to avoid the eruption of chaos and the individual who must break those laws if they believe it is against their deeply held personal beliefs.

The role of the chorus is an important feature of the play in its original performance conditions. Throughout Greek tragedy they are a good mark by which to gauge the moral viewpoint of the playwright and the intended response of the audience. Although shaken by Creon's decision to abandon Polynices' body, the Chorus

**Further study**

For a more general background to Greek theatre performance and style, look to the *Edexcel AS Drama and Theatre Studies Study Guide* (Rhinegold 2008), pages 8–11.

**Theatre as culture**

**Individual versus state**

**The role of the chorus**

support it – 'we are all at your disposal … We know the law and the penalty for breaking it'. They try to advise him as the plot moves forward, based on their fear of the gods, but never condemn him as the villain of the play, a temptation in modern interpretations; instead he is presented as a man who has lost control of power and authority because he cannot be seen to lose face. We know that the final words of the Chorus would strike home to the audience of the time: 'We have seen an old man, through suffering, becoming wise'. This moral cathartic message is central to the learning experience of theatre at the time.

**The role of the gods**

The role of the Greek gods is a further important feature of the play in its original conditions. The gods in the times of ancient Greece were feared and revered. The whole competition of playwrights was indeed dedicated to the god of wine and entertainment, Dionysius. Greek gods, or prophets of them, figure heavily in Greek tragedy. The Greek gods held immense power; they controlled lives and determined the fate of every individual citizen of ancient Greece. To go against them was to risk damnation and punishment as was to assume a status that matched theirs. Creon is punished because he makes the wrong decisions. Even though the Greek gods do not figure heavily in *Antigone*, their power and presence is consistently alluded to by the Chorus and in the presence of their prophet Tiresias. Creon is punished because he makes the wrong decisions and is blind to the advice and warnings of those around him. The battle of words with Tiresias in which the prophet announces, 'The gods themselves are disgusted', is one that the Greek audiences would have thoroughly enjoyed. They would also have been entirely aware that in dismissing and insulting Tiresias, Creon was contributing to his own downfall. The Chorus confirm the audience's fears in their final speech:

> 'The proud man may pretend/
>
> In his arrogance to despise/
>
> Everything but himself. In the end/
>
> The gods will bring him to grief.'

**The role of women**

In the character of Antigone herself, we should be aware of the different attitudes that existed towards women in the society of the time. Whereas today we may interpret her as a heroine, a female asserting her right to choice and action in ancient Greece may have been interpreted differently by the audience. Women's status was low. Their choices and freedoms were extremely limited as they were passed between men in arranged marriages. Their role was to run the domestic household and many philosophers of the time held the belief that women were low on intellect and high on emotional reaction. Creon often refers to Antigone's gender as a reason for her irrationality and stubbornness. A main reason why he cannot change his mind is because he is being challenged by a woman and this would wreck his position both as a leader and as a man. Antigone's actions upset the natural social order that existed in ancient Greece and would have been seen as revolutionary by the audience. Ismene is present as the more appropriate role model for the audience, the passive girl, subservient and fearful. In the final reckoning, when Creon has lost everything, Sophocles is offering a challenge to the male-dominated hierarchy, warning that misogynistic actions are punished by the gods.

As referred to above the play, *Antigone* is open to many alternative interpretations. The tendency in modern times has been to see Antigone as a symbol of personal freedom, an individual making a statement against a tyrannical regime. There are so many reference points for this in the political landscape of the 20th- and 21st-century, which makes this play an ideal one to place it in a modern context. Two modern interpretations that have used Sophocles' play as a political vehicle are the French playwright Jean Anouilh's in 1944 and Bertolt Brecht's in 1947.

Anouilh wrote his play under the shadow of the Nazi occupation of France and presents a thinly veiled reference to the German dictatorship as represented by Creon, with hints that *Antigone* is closely associated with the French Resistance movement. The one significant change he made to the original text was to the Chorus. He did away with the numerous city elders who in the original are sympathetic towards Antigone's actions and replaced them with a solitary male character that was detached from the action of the play and provided commentary on the inevitability of tragedy. For the Nazi censors this interpretation was satisfactory. Antigone was seen as a stubborn little girl who was powerless to resist the enormous power of the state. Yes, she kept her deeply held beliefs, but had to die to do so. At her death, the machine of state continued to run.

The second significant adaptation was by Bertolt Brecht, the German theatre practitioner who was driven by political exploration within his work. He retained the elders of the Chorus, but instead interpreted them as the German middle classes who moaned but never rebelled against fascism. Brecht's approach centred on removing the emotional attachment an actor had with the audience. He felt that the emotions got in the way of the central political message of the piece and was keen to direct his actress playing Antigone not to look for sympathy for the audience, but instead to focus on the conflict between the individual and the state.

**Context**

From these two examples it is easy to see how a play can be interpreted to mean something new to a different audience. Every playwright or director should have something new to say. It is your job as active learners to find this message in the production that you will see and articulate it in your response.

### Key scenes

In order to give your answer weight and to justify your response you will need to refer to specific moments in the play. These moments need to be significant and represent the style of the production that the director has chosen. We will look at two key scenes from *Antigone* and draw out questions as to how they might be interpreted.

The **first key scene** is when Antigone has been brought to Creon by the guards. In this scene the two characters debate the central political concerns of the play – the rights of the individual versus the laws of the state. Both characters refuse to give way. Antigone quotes natural law as higher than the law of state, while Creon questions Antigone's duty and loyalty to her country in going against his edict not to bury her disgraced brother.

In a production of this scene you should firstly be looking out for the interpretation of the characters. What kind of leader is Creon? Has he been portrayed as a dark and menacing dictator or as an ageing man not up to the job of leadership who in attempting to assert his authority betrays his vulnerability? These are obviously two extremes of interpretation and there may be room for strands of both aspects in the portrayal of these charcters.

Similarly, in the interpretation of Antigone, is she seen as a young, passionate and irrational young girl or as a reasoned young woman with strong and justified deep beliefs? Select brief moments from this scene to illustrate your point.

You will need to consider how these interpretations are communicated to the audience, thinking in terms of voice, movement, character interaction, and status as well as any obvious design choices that have been made in this particular scene. Are there any other tensions in the scene based on age, gender, family loyalty?

The **second key scene** is the messenger speech at the end of the play. The messenger recounts the tragic events of the death of Antigone and her beloved fiancé Haemon. Every Greek tragedy has a messenger and the way that the director chooses to interpret the speech is significant. Firstly, the casting:

- Do the words come from one voice or several?

- Is the actor male, female, old or young, and how does this affect audience response? How is the speech delivered?

- Is it enhanced with any sound effects to further create mood or is a single raw voice used?

- Are any design elements used to enhance effect?

- How is the speech lit?

- Is there music or a soundtrack added?

- Are projections or mixed media used?

- Alternatively, has the director chosen to complement the language with live action, mime or movement?

You need to approach the live production being ready to analyse everything. Look for meaning and justify it.

## Past productions

In order to clarify the significance of directorial interpretation, it is worth looking at past productions of the play.

Included below are a range of extracts from reviews of productions of *Antigone* that give you an opportunity to see the huge range of styles and interpretations that can be employed. They can also give you the confidence to be able to constructively criticise what you have seen if you can justify your decisions.

The directorial notes and intentions in the programme are valuable resources to you. It gives you a reference point and in a position to make a judgement about whether their intentions were successfully communicated to you as an audience member. If not, why not? The political relevance of the play is evident in these comments.

Northern Broadside Production, 2003, translator Blake Morrison, director Barrie Rutter.

Reviewed by Paul Taylor in *The Independent* on 15 October 2003.

'We taught them shock and awe,' declares Barrie Rutter's sharp-suited Creon in this compelling, if unbalanced, revival by Northern Broadsides of Sophocles' *Antigone*. The unmistakable echo of George Bush – heard, too, in the Theban ruler's talk of wiping out terrorist cells – seems a touch excessive. Far from launching a pre-emptive strike of dubious morality against a foreign power, Thebes has just emerged victorious from waging a war of self-defence against an invading alliance... The best productions of this play, in the weight they give to both sides of the argument and in the temperamental similarities that they reveal in the heroine and her uncle, leave you feeling that the tragedy could as well have been called Creon. For all that he looms so vividly in Rutter's own staging, the new ruler is flattened into a two-dimensional figure who does not make you hanker for a rechristening.'

Greg Hersov's production at The Manchester Royal Exchange, 22 October 2008.

Reviewed in *The Stage* by Natalie Anglesey.

'Recently there's been an upsurge of interest in Sophocles' powerful play and director Greg Hersov's robust production of Don Taylor's vibrant translation is given a contemporary setting. This not only harnesses the conflicts embroiled in the aftermath of civil war, but makes the talk of protecting the state from terrorism even more relevant to today.

The stage of this theatre in-the-round is a faint echo of the kind of arena where this tragedy would originally have been performed and designer Laurie Dennett's cracked-earth flooring and wooden funeral pyre set the right atmosphere for the devastated, war-torn city.'

*Yup'ik Antigone* production, directed by the ensemble cast, June 1984.

Reviewed by Jennifer Dunning in the *New York Times*.

'*Yup'ik Antigone* combines Greek legend with Eskimo myth and ritual for theater of simple grandeur.

The bare-boned acting and storytelling evoke the long, cold nights, violent seas and ice floes, and danger of life ashore in Toksook Bay, the small, island fishing village that is the home of the production's four actors. The rituals and myths of Toksook Bay prove to be surprisingly similar to the Greek legend from which Sophocles drew his play.

*Yup'ik Antigone* unfolds in a handsome set designed by Bill C. Ray. Rearing tusks, painted with hieratic hunting figures, suggest a portal to the spirit world. Hanging on wires across the stage are traditional masks created by Patrick Fisher, themselves worth a trip to the theater. They are plucked unceremoniously and worn as the plot demands. Creon, King of Thebes, carries a harpoon, and the characters are dressed in parkas, fur-trimmed and beaded hats and boots.

**Extract one**

**Web link**

The whole review can be found at www.independent.co.uk/arts-entertainment/theatre-dance/reviews/antigone-theatre-royal-bury-st-edmunds-583443.html

Taylor's review warns us of the dangers of a completely modern interpretation without referring in some way to the original intentions of the playwright.

**Extract two**

**Web link**

Full review available at www.thestage.co.uk/reviews/review.php/22183/

The modern references are very clear here, bringing out the universal themes of the play. Elsewhere other reviews refer to police armed with riot shields, a clear and definite statement by the director.

**Extract three**

**Web link**

A full version of the review can be found at: theater2.nytimes.com/mem/theater/treview.html?res=9505E4DC1539F93AA15755C0A962948260

This review has been included as an off-the-wall interpretation of the play in which four actors decide that Antigone means something to their culture.

## Medea (431BCE)

**Plot**    The nurse begins by giving a context to the play. Jason of Iolchos has settled in Corinth with his bride princess, Medea, a prize from the victorious war in Colchis. He has had children with her but has soon seen greater prospects in an alliance with the daughter of Creon, king of Corinth, Glauce. He deserts Medea. She vows revenge. Creon, frightened by the mystical power of the princess, demands that she is banished. Medea cannot return to Colchis as she has murdered her own brother, and persuades Creon to allow her to stay for one more day. Jason offers her money and support in exile. She refuses and instead agrees to take refuge with Aegeus, King of Athens. She announces to the Chorus that she will get revenge by killing both Jason's new bride and her own children. She fakes conciliation and asks Jason if she can deliver a gift to his new bride. Alone with her children she questions her action, but resolves to carry them out. A messenger brings news that Glauce has died brutally, by wearing the poisoned laced dress and crown that Medea's children have delivered as a gift. Creon dies to in trying to save his daughter. Part one of her revenge complete, Medea goes in to the palace to kill her children. Jason enters, distraught. Medea enters in a chariot with the bodies of her children. She mocks Jason and refuses to give him the bodies. She escapes to Athens, leaving Jason to live in pain. The chorus offer a final comment on the nature of fate.

**Playwright**    Euripides has the reputation of being the most modern of the three great tragedians. His plays were not as popular in his own time due to the sometime disregard he had for the conventions of Greek tragedy, but modern criticism celebrates his approaches.

Euripides was born into a wealthy family and was schooled in both the arts and sport. He had a great interest in philosophical debate and was a friend of Socrates, one of the great philosophers of the day. Reports say that he was a private man who wrote much of his work in a cave in Salamis. He is said to have produced around 90 plays of which only 19 survive. He first entered the festival of Dionysia at the age of 24, but was in his 40s before he won his first prize. Medea came third. Euripides was married twice, both ending in his wives being adulterous and he spent his final years in quiet exile. It is only after his death that Euripides' genius has been recognised. Whereas Sophocles was praised for the perfection of his structure and form, Euripides is known for the skill he has in representing characters as real, human and fallible.

### Original performance conditions

**Reputation**    In the time of his writing, Euripides stood as the least popular of the tragedians. Although greatly respected by philosophers and thinkers, many felt that he brought the ugly and unfortunate to the stage. Aristophanes, the comic writer, regularly mocked Euripides for his too human heroes, his fondness for philosophy and weak verse. Euripides' strength was in the understanding he had for his characters. Unlike Sophocles, who was driven by the importance of plot and message, Euripides' concern was in the motivations and psychological internal debates within the character's mind. We see many occasions where

Medea questions her actions and justifies her decisions. It is possible that the audience of the time would have been close to the opinions of Aristophanes in the way Euripides was regarded.

**Role of women**

Within the play Creon is frightened by Medea. Her mystical powers, strength of character and resolve give him good reason to fear her. Greek audiences of the time, although familiar with the myth, would have shared Creon's suspicion of Medea. It is her emotions and decisions that govern the direction of the play. If you look at the portrayal of the male characters – Creon in his indecision and weakness of leadership and Jason in his arrogance – it becomes clear where Euripides' sympathies lie. This is not the image of women that Greek audiences would expect. The submissive, compliant female who bows at the feet of the male hierarchy was the accepted norm.

Furthermore, the most important duty of being a woman in the society was the priority of the family. The thought of the murderous heroine sacrificing her own children for revenge would have alienated many audience members. Jason's actions in choosing a more respectable bride in Creon's daughter would not have been seen as outrageous. This would have been to the society of the time a natural choice. The woman was daughter of a king. She had prospects and status and there was no other decision for him to make. A Greek woman would have accepted this fact purely as a reflection of her status in society and the lack of choice that she was afforded. Euripides was challenging the accepted order of society. He was writing in a democratic world that prided itself in the values of order and justice and yet he is prepared to expose the huge injustice of the treatment of an individual within that society. This play surely would have not sat comfortably with the political and social leaders of the state.

**Medea as foreigner**

In some ways Euripides gives the Athenian public a way out of this controversy. Medea does not belong to the world that she is so intent on destroying. She comes from an outlying part of Greece to the centre of learning, culture and reason, as Jason points out, 'You left a barbarous land to become a resident of Hellas.'

Medea has no respect for the expected behaviour of her gender. Her mysticism and strength of character would have been a source of fear and suspicion to the audience of Greece. Her irrational actions and behaviour worked against her role as both woman and citizen of the state.

**Chorus**

Euripides' portrayal of the Chorus is a further significant diversion from the expectations of the original audience. Traditionally, the Chorus represent the moral viewpoint. They guide the audience and provide perspective and wisdom, generally from a male point of view. Sophocles once again provides the model for the Chorus in tragedy. Euripides gives the choral role to the Corinthian women. They are not detached from the action but intimately linked with the central character, Medea. They act as a confidant, by hearing her plans for revenge and they sympathise with her feelings of rejection and loss, as indicated here in their remarks to Jason:

**Further study**

*Medea*, translated by Phillip Vellacott (Penguin 1963).

page 34, lines 576–578

'Jason, you have set your case forth very plausibly. But to my mind – though you may be surprised at this – you are acting wrongly in thus abandoning your wife.'

Although they ultimately condemn Medea for her actions, they never betray her. There is strange balance in their portrayal, half-way between horror and excitement. It is difficult to know how the original audience would have reacted to the Chorus, but once again we see Euripides challenging the very structure of both Greek tragic form and roles within the society.

The impact of Euripides' work must not be underestimated. We must remind ourselves that theatre in ancient Greece was an essential part of the spiritual and cultural experience of every citizen. Yet there is no sense of catharsis or moral learning delivered by the Chorus at the end of *Medea*, instead there is a comment on the unpredictability of fate and the lack of control that we as individuals have over our lives:

page 60, lines 1416–1419

'Many matters the gods bring to surprising ends;/

The things we thought would happen do not happen;/

The unexpected God makes possible;/

And such is the conclusion of this story.'

## Context

There is much in *Medea* to merit its exploration in a modern society. There are universal themes that it explores. Central is the theme of revenge and the study of how hatred can drive an individual to the most extreme actions. Gender roles in male and female behaviour figure heavily. A hierarchy dominated by men is challenged and dismissed by a woman. The role of the outsider and the relationship between the individual and the society in which they live are all key issues which should be considered when placing the play in a modern context. The decision Medea makes to kill her children to avenge the wrongs done to her is an action that any audience would be horrified by.

It is Euripides' focus in his tragedy that appeals to a modern audience. Criticised in his time for weaknesses in structure, verse and form, he is celebrated today almost as the father of psychological realism. His characters are undoubtedly modern. They are driven by emotions and struggle psychologically with the decisions that they make. In a time when characters were often drawn as heroic and noble, Euripides creates men and women with human weaknesses. Medea's anger and hatred, although extreme, can be identified with as can her isolation and treatment as a lower status character, Creon's lack of leadership, fear and indecisiveness has many parallels with modern leaders and Jason's extreme arrogance and misogyny, almost a parody of male behaviour, can be found in any sphere of any culture. The reaction of Euripides' Chorus can be seen as the silent voice of every woman who has been betrayed or dismissed.

Brendan Kennelly, the Irish poet, produced a rewriting of the Euripides text which gives it an immediate relevance. In the introduction, Kennelly describes writing the play while recovering from alcoholism in an intensive care unit. He heard a woman, who had been abused by her husband, talking to herself: 'After you hit me, beat me in the kitchen and the bedroom, I'll lie there, and I know that my moment of revenge is not far away. I'll be thinking of revenge when you're beating me tonight'. This powerful announcement was in the author's mind as he tackled the play.

A second rewriting of the play comes in novel form. The German writer Christa Wolf in *Medea – a modern retelling* (Dell Publishing 1996, translated by John Cullen 1998) focuses on the theme of Medea as an outsider, an individual who will never fit into to the corporate male-dominated world that is the setting of the novel.

Both adaptations are strong evidence that the themes and issues of Euripides' original text are still relevant.

## Key scenes

The most interesting areas of the play to explore are the relationship between Medea and Jason and the monologue she has before carrying out the murder of her children.

The **first key scene** that we will look at is the introduction of Jason to the play. He comes to offer Medea support in her exile, both in monetary terms and in contacts he might have. It is his attitude towards her in the scene that cements Medea's determination to seek revenge in the most horrific way.

In a production of this scene you should firstly be looking out for the interpretation of the characters. Medea is full of scorn, and hatred, her opening line being 'you filthy coward.' How has the production interpreted here? Is she a woman who we as an audience can like? What decisions have been made about her in the casting of the role, the make-up and costume to represent her foreignness, her passion and her mystical influences?

Similarly with Jason, how has the director influenced the audience response in terms of casting and interpretation of the key male role? He is supposed to represent the ideal male hero. How is his language delivered?

> 'If all's well with your sex life, you've everything you wish for; but when that goes wrong … If women didn't exist, human life would be rid of all its miseries.'

page 34, lines 570–575

Consider how the contrasting emotions of the two characters are practically portrayed on stage; Medea as a raging woman and Jason as the calm, superior man. Particularly relevant in this scene will be the use of the stage space and how the characters physically interact with each other.

The **second key scene** is the Medea monologue just before the messenger speech, delivered to her children in the moments before she kills them. How has the actor managed the intensity of emotion at this climactic moment in the play?

He was inspired by a female audience member's comments after his production of *Antigone* in 1986: '*You understand woman's rage. Do* Medea *next. Many people say the play is about jealousy. It's not, it's about rage. Do it.*'
(Kennelly in Preface to *Medea* in *When then is now – Three Greek tragedies*, Bloodaxe Books, 2006.)

### Further reading

The full text can be found in *When then is now – Three Greek Tragedies* by Brendan Kennelly (Bloodaxe Books 2006).

Within the speech there is an incredible emotional journey as Medea struggles with guilt, hatred, anger, resentment and remorse. All of this is delivered in front of both her children and the Chorus. How is this practically managed on stage? What are the most impacting moments within this scene that really drive home the complexity of the characters' emotions?

Once again you need to approach the live production being ready to analyse everything. Look for meaning and justify it.

## Past productions

In order to clarify the significance of directorial interpretation it is worth looking at past productions of the play.

Included below are a range of extracts from reviews of productions of *Medea* that give you an opportunity to see the huge range of styles and interpretations that can be employed. They can also give you the confidence to be able to constructively criticise what you have seen if you can justify your decisions.

**Extract one**

Medea, Boston Court production, 2005, translated by Paul Roach, directed by Stefan Novinski.

**A contemporary showing**

Reviewed by Ariana Mufson in *CurtainUp*, Los Angeles Review.

> The production has already begun when we enter the theatre – the chorus, made up of kitchen staff, furiously works in the background in a top of the line industrial kitchen of a grand hotel. Off stage, the wedding takes place. However, we stay behind the scenes, separate from the wedding party, just as Medea is excluded and must work in secret to take revenge. The chopping, dicing, and sizzling create an eerie atmosphere that hints at the violence to come. Just as wait staff often know the secrets of any royal family, this chorus enlightens us because they are privy to Medea's disclosures.'

An example of a thoroughly modern interpretation. The decisions that the director has made regarding setting can be justified by the text and just remain faithful to the original intentions of the playwright

**Extract two**

By the Bog of Cats, by Marina Carr, Wyndhams Theatre, London 2004.

**The role of Medea**

Reviewed by Paul Taylor in *The Independent*.

> 'What is disappointing is not Hunter's portrayal, but Carr's sentimentalised makeover of the Medea character. The great shaping event in the life of this heroine was, we learn, abandonment by her mother at the age of seven. So here, it's less the desire for revenge against her former lover than fear that her daughter will suffer the same pangs of loss when forcibly parted from her that pushes Hester to slit the poor child's throat.
>
> She even manages to have a conciliatory woman-to-woman chat with Carthage's new bride. Hunter communicates the plaintive undertow well, but the moral ambivalence and the savagery of the original are lachrymosely diluted.'

**Extract three**

Medea, directed by Deborah Warner, Queen's Theatre, London 2001.

Review by Paul Taylor in *The Independent*.

> 'The director's searching vision can be seen in her treatment of the ending … Warner evidently regards [Euripides'] conclusion as a cop-out, untrue to the play's own deepest and darkest intuitions. There are no gods to provide getaway vehicles in the bleak world created here on Tom Pye's stark killing-field of a set. Instead, the play ends hideously unresolved. Spent and blood-spattered, Fiona Shaw's superbly reckless and unsparing Medea slugs it out with Jonathan Cake's excellent public-school sporting-god of a Jason in the central pool where she has been washing the dead bodies. She snaps the sails off the children's toy boats, as if to say that she announces that she means to stay put and, still ignominiously desperate for his attention, flicks water at her husband's turned back.

This modern-dress production has made a decision to restage the Euripidean ending. Clearly in this case the director is in control of the interpretation and has made a clear statement about the emptiness of revenge through extreme violence in a very modern world.

## 1564–1720

The main playwright that dominates this era is William Shakespeare (1564–1616), other notable playwrights being Christopher Marlowe (1564–1593) and Molière (1622–1673).

In using Shakespeare's *Othello*, a great deal of the contextual information will be relevant to other Shakespearean tragedies and in Moliere we have a contrasting comedy of manners from France, written later in the period.

### Othello (1602)

**Plot**

The play opens with the news that Desdemona has married the black commander, Othello. We are introduced to Iago who serves Othello but hates him for being passed over for promotion by Cassio. Othello and Desdemona are about to leave for Cyprus to fight the Turks.

As they arrive news is brought that the Turkish fleet is sunk. Cassio greets Desdemona warmly; Iago sees this as a chance to revenge himself on Cassio. Iago manufactures a fight between Cassio and Roderigo. Othello strips Cassio of his rank. Iago advises Cassio that he can win Othello round by using his wife as an intermediary. Iago tells us he will frame the two lovers, making Othello jealous.

Iago puts the seeds of doubt in Othello's mind. Othello becomes increasingly distracted. Desdemona drops her handkerchief, a gift from Othello. Iago's wife, Emilia, takes it to Iago who plants it in Cassio's room. Othello demands proof of the affair. Iago arranges Othello to spy on a meeting that he has arranged with Cassio. Othello's fears are confirmed when he hears Cassio laughing about a woman who he has been led to believe is Desdemona. He sees Cassio's woman with his wife's handkerchief. This has all been stage managed by Iago. Othello accuses his wife of being a whore and tells her to wait for him in the bedroom. Iago kills Roderigo who knows too much and wounds Cassio. Othello kills Desdemona for her infidelity before finding out the truth from Emilia who betrays her husband. Othello kills himself and Iago's execution is ordered.

**Playwright**

Shakespeare is regarded as one of the most influential playwrights in English literature. He wrote 37 plays and 154 sonnets in his life time. Shakespeare was born into a middle-class family in Stratford-on-Avon before moving to London to work as an actor and a playwright. His writing covers four main periods; in the earlier stages of his career he produced mainly comedies influenced by classical stories of the time. His first play, however, is believed to be the history play *Richard III* (1591). In the second phase of his career he wrote both comedies and histories, although he did produce two of his most enduring tragedies *Romeo and Juliet* and *Julius Caesar*. The third phase of his career is known as the tragic period, during which *Othello* was written. In the final phase of his life, the pastoral or romance plays were produced, plays that were more reflective and conciliatory. Plays such as *The Tempest* (1611) were written in this period. Shakespeare's body of work was published after his death in the First Folio of 1623.

He was recognised during a lifetime that spanned two monarchs, Elizabeth I and James I, both of whom recognised his talent. James I gave Shakespeare the honour of allowing him to name his company, 'The Kings Men'. With increasing wealth, Shakespeare was able to part-own The Globe Theatre and retire to Stratford with his reputation as the greatest living playwright intact.

It's the body of work that Shakespeare produced and the broadness of his scope and subject material that ensures he has remained the most popular and critically acclaimed playwright of his generation throughout the centuries. His themes and issues are timeless and the fact that his plays are continually performed around the world is an indication of both his immense talent and his influence on Western culture.

## Original performance conditions

The Renaissance period in England was a time of immense change and development. Originating in Italy, the movement spread across Europe and was marked by a period of time when England began to question its own identity, to look beyond its shores to other worlds. There were great developments in exploration, the arts and science.

**Race**

There was a fascination with different cultures born out of a period of exploration. Sir John Hawkins, in his slaving voyages of the 1560s, was thought to have brought back African slaves to England. Queen Elizabeth herself grew concerned by their presence and issued deportation orders for these immigrants, on the grounds that they were using the resources of the country that should be saved for the English.

It was against this background of suspicion and ignorance in 1604 that *Othello* was first performed. There would have been no possibility of Othello being played by a black man. The art of theatre was illusion and just as boys played girls, so white actors would have blacked up. The first recorded performance was at the court of King James I on 1 November 1604. The first actor to play the title character was Richard Burbage, one of the greatest tragic actors of that time, who also played

---

**Further study**

You will need to have a broader understanding of life in England during this period. There are many websites that give you good general information www.elizabethan-era. org.uk/elizabethan-england.htm is a good starting point. Liza Picard's book *Elizabeth's London* (Phoenix 2003) is also good to dip into.

---

You can still here these arguments being raised today when discussing the UK's immigration policy and this shows the continued relevance of Shakespeare's work.

characters such as Hamlet, Lear, and Richard III. The part of Iago was actually given to a comic actor (although there is no record of his name) who was known for playing characters such as Falstaff. Iago was meant to make the audience laugh in several places in the play. Seeing a black character on stage was meant to be a thrilling and moving spectacle for the audience, and the actors who played Othello painted their bodies and even experimented with fake woolly hair and thick lips in order to make him seem more realistic.

When approaching *Othello* in its original conditions it is important not to impose our own sense of acceptable interpretation on the play. Othello would not have been played so much as a tragic hero, more as a figure of intrigue and fascination. Iago would have been seen as the central figure of the play – the white cunning superior villain manipulating the black emotional victim. There was a common held belief that the black man's mind was not as developed as the white man's and the element of control and logic was missing. Othello reacts the way he does because he cannot control his emotions and this leads ultimately to the murder of Desdemona. Not all Shakespeare's audiences were impressed by the presentation of this interracial love story, however. Thomas Rymer, an English historiographer writing in 1623, describes disbelief at what Shakespeare is attempting to do:

> 'With us a Black-amoor might rise to be a Trumpeter; but Shakespeare would not have him less than a Lieutenant-General. With us a Moor might marry some little drab, or small-coal Wench; Shakespeare, would provide him the Daughter and Heir of some great Lord, or Privy-Councellor: And all the Town should reckon it a very suitable match.'

He also shares his opinions on the characters of Brabantio, Desdemona's father, and Iago, in the presentation of the marriage:

> 'Which instead of moving pity… can produce nothing but horror and aversion, and what is odious and grievous to an Audience.'

This reflects Brabantio's views about the betrothal of his daughter, accusing Othello of witchcraft:

> 'She is abused, stol'n from me and corrupted by spells and medecines.'

> Act 1, scene 3, lines 60–61

**Source**

Shakespeare takes the plot of *Othello* from an Italian source, the playwright Cinthio. Many of the original audience might well have been familiar with the story, but what Shakespeare does is focus the play more on the behaviour of human nature and the psychological workings of a man on his way to a breakdown. The Iago figure develops significantly. In the original he turns to revenge because Desdemona rejects him. In Shakespeare's version Iago's motives are much more open to interpretation. One might even link Iago's character to archetypes found in the medieval morality plays, in which the personification of Vice takes great glee in tempting the hero. Iago shares this wicked enjoyment in his own cunning. Both characters end the plays with punishment by death, necessary in order to restore order to the world in which they exist.

Shakespeare had introduced black characters before in his work. In *Titus Andronicus* (1594) the character of Aaron is introduced. He plays a similar role to Iago in his scheming and manipulation of characters but is seen as no more than a devil villain with anger, lust and hatred as his motivations. Othello is written with far greater nobility and sensitivity and, despite how he may have been received by audiences of the time, Shakespeare's writing of the character, particularly the beauty of much of his language, does indicate a portrayal of a black character that is far ahead of its time.

**The role of women**

Shakespeare can be criticised for his portrayal of female characters in the play and it is difficult for a modern actress to tackle the submissive and innocent Desdemona who is unable to prevent her own death. She is a voiceless presence in the play, existing as an instrument of male power. No great consideration would have been given to the role of Desdemona in the original conditions. Originally a pre-pubescent boy would have taken on the role. It is the inevitability of her fate that is the most tragic aspect of the female character and reflects her status within the male-dominated society at the time of its first performance in 1604.

## Context

The theme of race is a universal one that crosses all historical periods since the first performance. The interpretation of the Othello character very much reflects the attitudes to race in the time that it was performed. The play can also expose the prejudices that exist within the theatrical world. As late as 1981, Jonathan Miller's production cast a blacked up Anthony Hopkins in the lead role. The first black actor to play Othello was not until 1833, when Ira Aldridge took on the role in a time when the anti-slavery debate was gathering pace. It seems that *Othello* is produced during times of rebellion, upheaval and change to represent a society questioning its own systems and attitudes.

Throughout its performance history the play has received great attention. Some have chosen to ignore Othello's colour and focus on the theme of jealousy. Samuel Coleridge, writing in 1809, is convinced Othello is white: 'it would be something monstrous to conceive this beautiful Venetian girl falling in love with a veritable negro'. Others have recommended that the play be read rather than performed because the sight of a black man embracing a white woman is too much to grasp. In 1869, a female critic, Mrs Mary Preston, continued to reflect the inability of society to confront its own racial prejudices:

> 'In studying the play of *Othello*, I have always imagined its hero a white man. It is true that the dramatist paints him black, but this shade does not suit the man. It is a stage decoration, which my taste discards; a fault of colour from an artistic point of view. I have, therefore, as I before stated in my readings of this play, dispensed with it. Shakespeare was too correct a delineator of human nature to have coloured Othello black, if he had personally acquainted himself with the idiosyncrasies of the African race.'

Approaching the 20th century, and a somewhat more enlightened world, Paul Robeson's performances in the 1930s and 1940s emphasised the nobility of the black man existing in a world of incredible racial oppression.

In 1997 Jude Kelly produced a bold experimental production of the play – casting Othello as a white actor, Patrick Stewart, living in a world of African-Americans. The production was heavily criticised at the time in making it even more difficult for black actors to secure lead roles.

In 2001, a BBC television production cast Eammon Walker as Othello. The play was set in the modern world of the British Metropolitan Police force. John Othello is promoted to commissioner while his former best friend, Ben Jago, sets about destroying him out of jealousy. The production not only explores the inherent racism that exists in the police, but also hints at ambition and greed behind Jago's action as well as a latent repressed homosexuality.

There is a huge amount to consider in this section, but what it does make clear is the incredible importance of theatre in mirroring the attitudes of the day. Any production that you see will be making a statement about the interpretation of *Othello* and the motivations of Iago, and you will need to carefully consider what the directorial intention is.

## Key scenes

It is necessary to look at the central relationships of the play in the study of any key scene. Iago's motivation and presentation is vital as is the central tragedy of the doomed relationship between Othello and Desdemona.

The first key scene is the interpretation of one of Iago's soliloquies at the end of Act 2 scene 1 (lines 265–292).

The convention of a character directly addressing the audience is one that would have been familiar to original audiences and is also part of our modern experience through genres such as pantomime. Shakespeare puts his audience in a privileged and yet very uncomfortable position in knowing what is going to happen to Othello. How are we supposed to feel towards Iago? Obviously we condemn him for his manipulation, but aren't all villains strangely attractive? He is open and honest with us and incredibly clever. Are there times in the production when you admire his work? Is he presented as an attractive character or as a man eaten up by jealousy and race? The interpretation of the role asks us serious questions about our own attitudes.

After the other characters leave the stage, how does Iago approach us? Is it with confident glee or is a darker and more suspicious relationship established? He confides in us during the speech that he suspects Othello of sleeping with his wife and this is what drives him to revenge. How much of Iago's hurt does the actor let us see at this point? Is the soliloquy delivered seated and still or does he move around the stage. What does this indicate to us about his mood and motivation?

Consider how our relationship with Iago grows throughout the play as he confides in us more and more. What decisions has the

> **Further viewing**
>
> The DVD of Trevor Nunn's production of *Othello* in 1990, which featured Willard White as Othello and Ian McKellen as Iago, stands as a very convincing interpretation of this central relationship.

director made about how we feel about him? Voice, movement and use of the stage space provide us with the answers.

The second key scene we will look at is the start of Act 5 scene 2, the death of Desdemona. The scene starts with Othello's entrance looking over his sleeping wife. Consider how this moment has been staged. What kind of mood do the positioning of the bed, the design of the set and the lighting create? What kind of mood is Othello in as he enters? Consider what he has gone through and what he is about to do. How does the actor communicate the character's state of mind to the audience?  As Othello begins to speak before she wakes how are the lines delivered? Is there still doubt in Othello's mind or is he resolved to carry out the murder. What emotions govern the delivery of the lines? As Desdemona awakes how does the actor's tone change? How is the relationship between Desdemona and Othello communicated moments before her death? Consider how as an audience member we are supposed to feel towards Othello and Desdemona at this point and what practical decisions the director and actors have made to govern our response.

Once again, in the analysis of key scenes, it is vital that you keep asking questions and that you always remain aware that a specific interpretation has been made. You are in a position as an informed audience member to make a judgement about the success or failure of that interpretation.

## Past productions

**Extract one**    Cheek by Jowl production directed by Declan Donnellan and Nick Ormerod.

**Characterisation**    Reviewed by Ben Brantley in *The New York Times*, 2004.

> 'The only scenery is five coffin-size trunks. And the production begins, in what has become a Cheek by Jowl signature, with the entire company assembled on-stage with the formal frozenness of chess pieces waiting to be moved into play.
>
> Characters are often summoned into being by mere description, gliding impassively before those who are talking about them, products of the mind's eye. (This means, for example, that we get to see Caroline Martin's Desdemona as a sort of Exhibit A before the script calls for her to appear on-stage.) And when people cite the words of others, whether accurately or not, Mr Donnellan usually has the characters being quoted speak those words.

> This review gives a clear indication of a particular company's style of performance. It uses self-conscious dramatic techniques to highlight the relevant issues of the play. Look out for specific techniques such as this in the productions that you go to see.

**Extract two**    Directed by Doug Hughes as part of New York Shakespeare Festival, 2001.

**Performing Iago**    Reviewed by Ben Brantley in *The New York Times*.

> 'Taking advantage of such handy camouflage, this Iago proceeds to write the script of the undoing of his charismatic boss, barely able to repress a murmur of delight when props, actors and scenery all conspire to fall into place. You'll often find him in an aisle of the theater, looking on like the archetypal nervous director, nibbling his fingers with a mixture of satisfaction and anxiety. He's like an evil urban twin of Prospero, the world-ordering wizard of *The Tempest*.'

> His production gives a very specific interpretation of the Iago character. Again the review refers to theatrical techniques that bring the interpretation of the character to life.

Directed by Gregory Doran at The Swan Theatre, Stratford 2004.

Reviewed by Pete Wood in *The British Theatre Guide*.

> 'The setting has been updated to the 1940s or 50s. The splendid set...
> all corrugated metal and chain-wire gate, allows the scene to switch
> effortlessly between Venice and Cyprus... The play opens amid storm.
> The set is black; the soldiers wear black, the politicians dark grey:
> Othello alone wears white. When the scene switches to Cyprus, the
> set is backlit by a fierce yellow which modulates finally into night and
> storm again. In the deathbed scene, a long-lit muslin mosquito net
> drapes from ceiling to floor in which Desdemona is trapped, like an
> insect in a flytrap, while Othello paces and circles outside.
>
> This production is notable for featuring two South African actors in
> the two leading male roles... This is a society riven by racism which
> has only allowed Othello, a black man, to enjoy respect because his
> skills, as a military leader, are sorely needed by the Venetians.'

**Extract three**

In casting two South African actors –
one white, one black – the racism is
overtly explored to reflect the horrors
of apartheid.

## Tartuffe (1664)

The family of a well-respected wealthy gentleman, Orgon, are
furious that he and his mother, Mme Pernelle, have fallen under
the spell of a religious fraud, Tartuffe, who they have invited to live
in their house. Orgon announces that his daughter Marianne, who
is already engaged to Valere, will marry Tartuffe, much against her
will. The family are determined to expose Tartuffe and plan to trap
him in confessing his lust for Orgon's wife Elmire. Tartuffe does
indeed lust after her but when Orgon is presented with the truth
by his son Damis, who has been spying on Tartuffe, Orgon throws
his son out of the house accusing him of being a liar. As a gift to
Tartuffe, Orgon signs all his worldly goods over to the fraud. Orgon
eventually catches Tartuffe with his wife by hiding under a table
and sends him from the house. Tartuffe returns and blackmails
Orgon, sending him from his own house. He sets about evicting
the family, but as he does so a police officer arrives, sent by the
king to arrest Tartuffe. He is finally exposed and the family return
to their house grateful to the king for their lucky escape.

**Plot**

Jean-Baptiste Poquelin (1622–1673) was an actor and playwright
who took up the pen name of Molière. He is credited for reshaping
French comedy using satire and complex plot devices. He was born
into a wealthy family and had access to the king's court through
his father's job as a fine upholsterer. His mother was a deeply
religious woman who died when Molière was 12. His exposure
to court at such a young age and his experiences of religion did
much to shape the nature of his future work. He worked in his
father's shop where he would often watch street theatre and farce,
again influences on his work. At the age of 21, Molière founded
a dramatic troupe and he soon experienced the frustrations of
making it in the theatrical world. It was when he started writing
that Molière began to receive recognition and he was invited to
perform at the court of Louis XIV. With the king's blessing, Molière
began to produce work that satirised the pretentious behaviour of
the hangers-on at court. The king was said to have loved his work,
but Molière was making influential enemies. His first theatre was

**Playwright**

closed down but again by royal approval he was granted the use of the Theatre du Palais Royal and the company become known as 'The Troupe of the King'. Molière continued to write, direct and perform until his death shortly after a performance in 1673. The priests refused to hear his confession, with Molière's work often heavily criticising the church, but once again, with the king's intervention, he was given a holy burial.

## Original performance conditions

The reputation of actors and the theatre in France during the 1600s was much the same as the theatre of Elizabeth in England. Acting was not seen as a reputable profession, hence the possible reason why Molière took on a new name. Public performances took place in converted tennis courts where a large cross section of society could attend. Unlike England, there was no restriction on female actors although the Catholic Church excommunicated all actors, seeing involvement in the theatre as sinful. Companies would also be invited to the royal court to perform for the king's amusement. This is the world in which Molière operated for the majority of his career where he experienced a completely new make up of audience which would inspire both the content and style of his work

*The Pretentious Young Ladies*, performed in 1659, was the turning point of Molière's career. Its subject matter was the ridiculous pretensions of courtiers and ladies whose appearance at the king's court appeared to have no particular point. Their attitudes, affected behaviour and manners were a perfect target for the satire that would shape the future work of the playwright. His style was to caricature these individuals only to hold a mirror up to them when they sat in the audience of his court performances. Molière was establishing a new genre, being prepared to mock any figures of high society who showed a tendency towards arrogance and pretension and needed their bubbles bursting – noblemen, priests, doctors and academics were all subjects of his satire. Of course this approach would have made Molière popular among the ordinary people, but it also made him many enemies.

**Controversy** *Tartuffe* is a thinly veiled attack on the hypocrisy and piousness of the church and the individuals who hide their sinful actions behind the screen of the institution. It is of little surprise that the Jansenists, a devout branch of the Catholic Church heavily influential in the court of Louis XIV, soon had the performance heavily censored. The king himself was said to be fond of Molière and it is likely that without his support, the playwright might well have been in far greater trouble. The Catholic Church did in fact issue an edict threatening anyone who read or saw the play with excommunication. This extreme behaviour reinforced Molière's original point in his portrayal of Tartuffe, but this was missed by an angry church. Eventually Molière offered to rewrite the play.

**Support from the king** The ending of *Tartuffe* illustrates Molière's awareness of the importance of his patrons. Although he was merciless in his attack on elements of the Catholic Church, the institution of the monarchy was free from criticism. It is in fact the unnamed king in *Tartuffe* who saves the reputation of the Orgon family in arresting Tartuffe and exposing him as the conman and criminal that he is. It is the all-seeing monarch who has viewed the events of the play from afar who steps in and saves the day. The role of the king as the knowledgeable saviour was one that Louis XIV would have relished. The ending of the play is somewhat abrupt from a modern perspective, but it was a necessary sacrifice that the playwright makes in order to keep favour with his most valued supporter.

Of all the characters in the play it is the role of the servants to the Orgon family that provides the original audience with a sense of perspective and reality. Dorine, the waiting maid to Orgon, not blinded by wealth or position and with nothing to prove, provides resistance to Tartuffe and encourages her mistress to act to save her honour. By creating the intelligent and resourceful maid, Molière is further subverting the accepted order of court and highlighting the stupidity of those in positions of power.

**The role of the servants**

Molière's theatrical style and content was in some ways ahead of its time. The devout Catholic Church found it very difficult to laugh at itself, even though Molière had argued that he was presenting extremes of sinful behaviour. Our culture today seems very much more appropriate to the political and religious satire that Molière was producing. A branch of comedy in the 21st century is very much political satire. Molière reminds us of the political cartoons of Gerald Scarfe, the contorted puppets of *Spitting Image*. As in *Have I Got News For You*, no one is safe from the sharp tongue of the comedian. If you are in the public eye then you are there to take shots at.

**Context**

Tartuffe also makes us think of the modern television evangelist who promises the saving of souls and miracle cures in return for cash donations towards his new found church. An adaptation by Freyda Thompson does exactly this, updating the language of the original text to a southern American setting whilst remaining faithful to the structure of the original. A review of the production can be seen below.

> **Further study**
>
> There is no doubt that in his approach to satire and caricature, Molière was heavily influenced by the **commedia dell'arte**, the Italian form of improvisational theatre popular at the time. Performances followed conventional plots based around love, jealousy and revenge. They featured many slapstick and physical comedy routines and were performed by character types, represented by costume, masks and props. One can see in the presentation of Tartuffe himself, as well as the conceited and conned Mme Pernelle, the influence of this theatrical form.

## Key scene

It seems appropriate to look at *Tartuffe* in full flight in Act 4 scene 5 as he is about to seduce Orgon's wife, Elmire. She has set him up to be discovered by her husband who is hiding under the table. What decisions have been made about the design of the set to show the privilege and wealth of the family? Is the piece kept in its time or have decisions been made to create modern relevance?

This is a highly comic and farcical scene, with the comedy brought about by the audience in full knowledge of the planned exposure of Tartuffe. We are aware that Orgon is hiding under the table. Consider how the director makes this comic set piece work as the scene progresses and Tartuffe gets closer to having his way.

How is the character of Tartuffe presented? Molière is as much making a comment about the stupidity of the society that lets characters like Tartuffe exist as he is sending up the religious artifice of the central character. How would you describe the acting style? Does the piece attempt a realistic portrayal of the key character or are we dealing in caricature?

You might look closely at the actress playing Elmire, trying to persuade Tartuffe to fall for her plan on one hand, on the other ensuring that he is discovered by her hiding husband. The non-verbal communication, the pauses and looks as well as the secret shared with the audience is likely to be exploited in this scene and is worthy of note. Her coughing to attract the attention of Orgon begins half-way through the scene and yet he does not respond. The coughing gets louder and more pronounced until an obvious striking of the table eventually brings him out. How is this comic set piece staged?

For the first time in the play we see Tartuffe's mask slipping. His words are full of self-justification and religious references. Make note of the vocal delivery. How is this complemented by his actions? His aim in the scene is to have his way with Elmire. Consider the way the stage space is used in this scene. As Tartuffe closes in on his prey, Elmire tries to escape. The movement of the two might be heavily choreographed ending up on the table under which Orgon is hiding.

## Past productions

**Extract one**

*Tartuffe: Born Again* by Molière; adapted by Freyda Thomas, directed by David Saint.

**The period of the play**

Reviewed by Ben Brantley, *New York Times* 1996.

This is an example of a bold interpretation that this reviewer feels does not work. An initially strong modern context idea appears to have been squeezed and shaped to fit the play without considering every necessary aspect of the production.

'Certain ideas are so obvious that they really should be shot down as soon as they come to mind. Directors with a penchant for French classics are unlikely to leave the Circle in the Square's clunky production of *Tartuffe: Born Again*, which turns Molière's religious mountebank into a televangelist, murmuring "Now why didn't I think of that?" The odds are they already had, and wisely resisted the temptation.

And because Ms Thomas adheres pretty closely to the structure and form of Molière's original, right down to its intricate scheme of rhymes, the show works overtime in trying to make specific parallels between past and present stick. The whole thing feels like an exercise in squeezing a size-12 foot into a size-8 slipper.

**Extract two**

*Tartuffe*, National Theatre, London, directed by Lindsay Posner 2002.

**The role of Tartuffe**

Reviewed by Paul Tayor in *The Independent*.

Oddly svelte and plummy-voiced, ridiculously Rasputin-like and built like a softly flabby sumo wrestler, Clunes performs miracles of laid- back, watchful acting. He is a revelation. In not trying too hard, he achieves wonders. Even when – stripped down to a wobbly loin cloth – he attempts to roger Orgon's wife (a beautifully spoken Clare Holman) with (unknown to him) her spouse secreted under the table, Clunes takes his time and is all the more amusing for it.

## 1828–1914

This period is probably the most diverse of the three stipulated by the exam board. At the beginning of the 19th century, theatre was a truly populist art; a form of escapism for the working classes during the industrial revolution. Melodrama, farce and opera were the dominant forms. However, during the latter half of the 19th century, as technology and design skills improved, the subject matter tended towards more historical, period dramas which were popular with the middle classes partly due to the accuracy of the material. The success which stemmed from the reality of the performance led to the evolution of new genres which included Naturalism and drawing-room comedies.

During this section we have chosen to focus on two contrasting texts which highlight the diverse nature of the drama within this period: *Miss Julie* by August Strindberg and *The Importance of Being Earnest* by Oscar Wilde.

### Miss Julie (1888)

**Plot**

The play is set on a midsummer's night in the kitchen of Miss Julie's father, the Count. On stage is the cook, Christine, quickly joined by the Count's valet, Jean, who describes Miss Julie's 'mad' behaviour. She has been ignoring her social class by dancing with the gamekeeper and insisting on waltzing with Jean. The servants suggest that the strange antics stem from her recent separation from her fiancé and a fear of spending time with her family. When Miss Julie enters, the class difference between the characters is initially established. She insists once again that Jean waltzes with her and the two depart. However, when they return, the complex status battle between them begins. Initially, Jean warns his master's daughter about her behaviour, but as their flirtatious discussion continues, the situation becomes more complex. They are forced to hide when the peasants enter and during this interlude, the text suggests the couple have sex.

The action within the play intensifies after this moment of lust. Initially, they are filled with panic, electing to run away. Miss Julie packs and steals some money from her father. However, when Christine enters on her way to church, she shows her disgust at their behaviour, insisting she will tell the groom not to allow any horses to leave before the Count returns, blocking their escape. Miss Julie is consumed with fear as she hears the two bells, which signify the return of her father. She picks up Jean's razor and lacking emotional strength, asks him to command her to use it. He does so and Miss Julie leaves the stage.

**Playwright**

August Strindberg was born in Sweden in 1849, the third of eight children. His father, Carl, had been born into a bourgeois family and had become a successful business man; his mother was a former servant. However, by the time of August's birth, his father had been declared bankrupt and was facing the frustrations of marrying beneath him. As a result, the family lived in poverty and the father ran the home like a tyrant and August developed into a sensitive and insecure boy. The death of his mother in 1862

### Web link

The theatre museum has an excellent website which gives information about different periods of drama history. For more information about the 19th century, visit www. peopleplayuk.org.uk/guided_tours/ drama_tour/19th_century only served to deepen his anxieties and when his father remarried shortly afterwards, his unhappy childhood was confirmed.

Unsuccessful at university, Strindberg was employed in a variety of jobs as he attempted pursue a career in theatre. However, an encounter with Siri von Essen, a member of the Swedish aristocracy, brought happiness and then turmoil to his world. He became her lover and after her separation from her husband, the couple married. Initially, their mutual theatrical interest provided Strindberg with some creative momentum but his wife's aspirations to be an actor put a strain on their relationship. He began to doubt her fidelity and her influence on their three children. He expressed a desire to control her and the disharmonious nature of their relationship is evident in many of his early plays.

> 66 Strindberg's literary work is one long autobiography... he was dipping his pen, quite literally into his own unconscious. 99
>
> Thomas and Taylor, introduction to *Miss Julie* (Methuen 2006).

He was heavily influenced by the rise of Naturalism and used the style of performance to serve the complex emotional conflict within his writing. His attempts to stage a performance of *Miss Julie*, with his wife in the title role, was fraught with difficulty as the day before its opening night, it was banned by censors. He managed a temporary reprieve by performing the play to an invited audience but it received mixed reviews. August and Siri divorced shortly afterwards.

This served as a catalyst for greater theatrical experimentation. He was at times consumed by guilt for abandoning his family, and his fragile mental state is reflected in the themes of his 70 plays, as well as his novels and paintings. He was never content with one style of performance and his works reflect an evolving practitioner who moves from Naturalism to Expressionism as he explored the theatrical experience. He died in 1912.

## Original performance conditions

**Naturalism**

Strindberg was writing at a time when he thought theatre was dying. Populist drama was leading to the death of the art of great writing. He insisted that the dialogue spoken by characters should be less mechanical and structured than that of his contemporaries and his solution was to focus on the psychology of the character.

He became interested in Darwinian theories. The premise of 'the survival of the fittest' dominated his thoughts as he explored the base animalistic behaviour of humans. His writing became a tool to examine behaviour under a microscope, presenting individuals in a truthful manner, exposing their various flaws. He was influenced by the rise of the Naturalist movement in France and forged links with the founders of Theatre Libre who themselves were reacting against the overtly romantic French drama. Strindberg used *Miss Julie* to demonstrate their theories.

At the core of the Naturalist movement is the influence of both heredity and the surrounding environment. Essentially, humans are animals responding to their inherent needs; Miss Julie and Jean are driven by their desire for sex rather than a relationship. However, this act is made more complex by the pressures of their surrounding environment. In many respects, the characters are lacking free will, circumstances appear to dictate how they should behave until they ultimately become trapped. As Miss Julie observes at the end of the play, 'I can't go! I can't stay!' Their conflict is intensified by Strindberg's original decision to remove any intervals, creating a play lasting 90 minutes in real time. The audience are forced to watch the intense drama unfold before them unable to escape until Miss Julie leaves to commit suicide.

Strindberg's difficulties in getting the play published and performed reflect the controversial content of his work. After an initial attempt to produce it at the Dagmar Theatre in Copenhagen was halted by the censors, he reverted to a more intimate performance to a select group at the Copenhagen student's union. The critics were not particularly enamoured with the acting but the set impressed:

> 'To our surprise, it resembles a real kitchen. A plate-rack, a kitchen table, a speaking tube to the floor above, a big stove with rows of copper pots above it – in short, everything is there, presenting the living image of a real kitchen.'

In staging the play, he made a deliberate attempt to create a location which both served his dramatic purpose and enabled him to move away from some of the unforgivable weaknesses in 19th-century theatrical staging. The play exists within a single location, ensuring that the set can be created in exquisite detail. He removed the need to enter and exit through doors, since unstable canvas scenery is often exposed through the slamming of a door. The kitchen table was positioned perpendicular to the back wall so when both actors were sat down, half of their faces could be seen. He abhorred the use of footlights to illuminate the stage since he believed it created a false atmosphere and led the actors to perform in a more affected manner.

Perhaps the greatest of the battles Strindberg faced was with the actors themselves, wanting them to perform to rather than with the audience. In order to do this successfully, he had to unravel the unrealistic tendencies of 19th-century performers, preventing them from slavishly facing front. He doubted his ability to make the actors turn away from the audience during major moments of dialogue, showing their backs to the audience as they might in real life. However, with his stage filled with furniture, he insisted on the notion of an imaginary fourth wall between actors and audience, encouraging performers to focus on the world of the play. As he observes, at the end of this preface:

> 'I have made an attempt! If it has failed, there will, I hope, be time enough to make another!'

In his preface to *Miss Julie*, Strindberg celebrates how he made his 'protagonists somewhat lacking in character.' He explains that the word 'character' appears to have lost any true meaning and has evolved into a term associated with lazy, formulaic writing. Roles which are taken from stock and are presented as archetypes of society lack reality. He argued that the most interesting portrayals are those based on 'the man who goes on developing, the skilful navigator of life's river'. True exponents of Naturalism, he suggests, should always present people in this way.

**Staging the production**

*Strindberg's Dramatic* by Gunnar Ollen (Sveriges Radio 1961), translated by Michael Meyer.

**The presentation of character**

He fully recognised that he was writing in a time of social change and as a consequence, Miss Julie and Jean are figures of the falling aristocracy and the rising underclass respectively. Their blurred status echoes that of Swedish society and as consequence, his controversial text would have had even greater power. However, his celebration of Miss Julie as a 'modern character' does not hide his inherent misogynism. He describes the role as a 'half-woman', a 'man-hater', 'synonymous with corruption' and details the many failings of her and females in general. Jean, however, is at times celebrated as a 'polished but coarse' individual who is able to dismiss the guilt that is experience by Miss Julie. Ultimately, this masculinity makes him stronger, physically and emotionally, providing him with the skills to 'seize the initiative'.

## Context

**The male/female divide**

In the original performance of the play, Miss Julie would have been perceived as behaving in a hysterical manner. From the beginning of the play she is out of control and this would effectively be presented as her feminine weakness whilst Jean attempts to offer some stability. A modern production should look at the relationship between the individuals in a more even way. Twenty-first century audiences may still question the notion of lust rather than love but may praise instinctive desire rather than simply condemning it.

**Class**

The challenge to the traditional class divide was successful as it reflected the social upheaval in the society of the time. A contemporary performance may struggle to communicate this in a modern version of the play. The period in which the play is set will clearly influence your understanding of the characters and the pressures they face. Look at how the notion of class is explored and whether it has meaning to you as an audience member.

**Actions and consequences**

Strindberg celebrates the fact that his characters are trapped by the circumstances of the play, being left with little freedom to control their own fate. Consider whether this is conveyed through the version you see. Do the characters choose their own destiny and if so how do they respond to the consequences of their choice?

## Key scenes

**The opening**

In a truly naturalistic performance, the opening of the play should create a slice of life. There should be a reality to the staging which transports the audience to the setting of the play. Many modern productions have chosen to use the set in a more symbolic manner, representing the environment rather than creating it. Others have chosen to relocate the action within a different time period. Use the opening action to gauge the nature of your modern production and compare it directly with Strindberg's staging. Make a note of how location is created and what further aspects of the set are revealed as the action progresses.

**The re-emergence of Miss Julie and Jean after the ballet**

The mere suggestion of an encounter fuelled by lust rather than love was deemed to be scandalous by to a 19th-century audience and worthy of censure. The fact that the act is not physically implied on stage is not only a mark of subtlety but an awareness of the controversial subject matter. A modern production may not feel as constrained by such values. The suggestion of offstage action during the ballet could be made more explicit by positioning the actors partially in view of the audience. Look at the decision made by the director and consider what it communicates to the audience.

The apparent hypnosis of Miss Julie by Jean at the end of the play emphasises the characters lack of control over their destiny. Strindberg concludes by alluding to Miss Julie's suicide, although this isn't presented on stage. The production you see will present the audience with clues about the protagonist's impending fate and the razor blade should be revealed in such a way as to communicate the tragedy of her suicide. However, there may be more brutal and depressing methods of portraying her suicide or indeed using their parting moment as a way of communicating more contemporary themes. Look at the direction of this scene closely and use it to draw comparisons with Strindberg's original intentions.

**The end of the play**

> **Further viewing**
>
> Mike Figgis' film version of the play creates a brutal, animalistic sexual encounter, driven by carnal lust rather than love. Look at how this is created by the actors and consider how this could be recreated in a theatrical version.

## Past productions

*Miss Julie*, The Peter Hall Company, Theatre Royal, Bath. Review by Pete Wood.

> 'Frank McGuiness ... relocates the play in rural Northern Ireland at the turn of the 19th century. The move makes sense if Jean's fear of and loathing for his Anglo-Irish employers and determination to get on and out, which is also combined with a sense of pride and being even a minor member of an important family. It also allows McGuinness to ratchet up the ferocity of the subsequent exchanges between Julie and Jean, with the former declaring furiously she'd like to drink wine out of his skull.'

**The period of the play**

Mercury Theatre Company, review by Mary Redman, www.thestage.co.uk/reviews/review.php/14398/miss-julie

> 'The main stage's enclosed space deliberately imposes intimacy. Cooking smells mingle with the scripted "scent of violets" as a real meal is prepared and eaten. The close-up reveals fascinating minutiae.'

**The staging of the play**

Mercury Theatre Company, review by Mary Redman, www.thestage.co.uk/reviews/review.php/14398/miss-julie

> 'Victor Gardener's Jack the Lad servant has an irresistibly sexy, wicked grin. This unapologetic, calculating chancer is utterly cocksure of himself. Even his working class accent varies in depth according to whether he is wooing or degrading Miss Julie.

**Characterisation**

> Directed by Patricia Benecke, Kate Copeland's Julie is a right little madam. Aware of her status, she flirts with danger regardless of consequences, or whether or not people slave for her comfort. Clearly not in the first flush of youth, she behaves like a spoilt child.

> **Further study**
>
> If you are interested in this style, look at: *The Cherry Orchard* by Anton Chekhov; *A Doll's House* by Henrik Ibsen.

# The Importance of Being Earnest (1895)

**Plot**

The relatively simple plot follows two young men, Jack Worthing and Algernon Moncrieff, who fall in love with two women, Gwendolen Fairfax and Cecily Cardew, while pretending to be someone else. The skill of Wilde's writing, however, is in the structuring of the play's action. The circumstances leading to the couples meeting each other is, unsurprisingly, far from straightforward. As the focus of the play moves from the city to the country, the men become embroiled in a complex web of deceit, which leads them both to separately approach the local priest in the hope that he will baptise them Earnest. The situation is made more complex by the arrival of Algernon's aunt, Lady Bracknell, who has concerns about the suitability of Cecilia as a suitable niece in law and doubts the credentials of Jack Worthing as an appropriate husband for her daughter. In the play's famous denouement, it transpires that Jack is adopted having been accidentally abandoned in a handbag in Victoria Station by his nurse-maid, 28 years earlier. The handbag belonged to Cecily's governess, Miss Prism, Jack is actually the long lost nephew of Lady Bracknell and his real name is Earnest.

**Oscar Wilde**

Oscar Wilde was born in 1854 in Dublin. His father, Sir William Wilde was a leading surgeon; his mother, Jane Wilde, was a successful writer poet and staunch Irish nationalist. Oscar was educated at home until he was nine before attending Portora Royal School and Trinity College, Dublin. His academic success earned him a scholarship to Magdalen College, Oxford where he quickly established himself as a wit. He also developed his passion for the aesthetic movement and became famed for his long hair, distinctive dress and the extreme décor of his student room. He graduated with a first in 1878 and returned briefly to Dublin before relocating to London. During his time in the capital he developed a reputation as a socialite and he formally began his literary career by paying for a collection of his own poems to be published.

In 1881, he embarked on a lecture tour of America where he successfully spoke on art and the human aesthetic. It was on his arrival in New York that he was reported to state he had nothing to declare except his genius. On his return in 1884 he married Constance Lloyd and they had two children. His wife's allowance of £250 enabled the family to live in relative comfort although their marriage was constantly undermined by Wilde's frequent homosexual relationships. During the next few years, he was involved in a range of projects with different publications which honed his skills as a writer.

In 1892 the first of his five plays, *Lady Windermere's Fan*, was successfully performed in the West End. It was during this time that he began an affair with Lord Alfred Douglas, the son of the Marquis of Queensbury. His new partner made huge demands on his time and made it increasingly difficult for him to write. However, in 1895, *The Importance of Being Earnest* opened at St James' Theatre to great critical acclaim and Wilde became the celebrated personality of which he had dreamed.

His world quickly collapsed around him a couple of weeks later. Queensbury left a card for Wilde addressed 'For Oscar Wilde, posing as a Somdomite'. Enraged by the slur against his name, Wilde attempted to sue for libel but was unsuccessful; his impulsive reaction led to charges being brought against him for his homosexual relationships. Eventually, he was convicted and served two years hard labour in Reading prison, which effectively destroyed his spirit and made him bankrupt. He spent his final years living in Paris and eventually died of cerebral meningitis in 1900.

## Original performance conditions

Wilde's plays were performed at St James' Theatre and the fashion-conscious audience were reflected in the upper middle-class characters. The theatre was managed by George Alexander, a man of strong artistic vision and considerable acting skill. He expected his productions to utilise truthful settings and the content often mirrored the values of the audience member. Reacting against the working-class spectacle of melodrama, Wilde's society dramas spoke to a different demographic and began to draw them back to the theatre.

> Wilde's original version of the play was written in four acts. Alexander reworked the play, cutting some of the material and reducing it to three.

The audience's evening out was one complete spectacle. From the moment they entered the space, they were greeted by a lavish space. Etchings by local artists and flowers helped to provide a more decadent fell to the event. Programmes were free (a successful gimmick by Alexander) and the stage was lit using electricity, one of the few theatres which could boast this at the time. Scenic artists, or set designers, were acknowledged in the programme along with the wig-makers. A pianist offered the musical accompaniment to the play. Wilde's play was originally combined with another one-act play of the time. This was often referred to as the curtain-raiser and set the tone for the events that followed.

The majority of his plays were based on a similar moral code, where the expectation was placed on male characters to solve the problems of society. Those that were successful earned the respect of the women, the self-appointed judge of male behaviour. Effectively, they are characters of folly but the audience enjoy their moments of confusion and their attempts to solve the problems they face.

Wilde's characters are well rounded and, despite their errors in judgement, contain within them a psychological complexity which is unusual for this period. He resists the temptation to have his male characters speak in upper middle-class slang. Similarly, the females have greater independence and self-awareness than other roles of the period. Wilde demonstrates with excellent skill how the convoluted action of melodrama can be adapted to create a new form which demonstrates greater control and subtlety.

In his writing, Wilde revels in this task. The complex scenario is revealed with apparent pleasure and the characters approach each new twist with an unnerving positivity. The traditional stock characters of melodrama are adapted to flatter and ridicule the behaviour of the audience in equal measure. Wilde even introduces himself in the role of the fop or dandy, Algernon, to parody his own behaviour.

## Context

**Love and marriage**

At the play's heart is a comment on relationships. In the opening scene, marriage is discussed and immediately ridiculed. Algernon and Lane present it as a 'demoralising' event, a thought which could also mirror Wilde's personal experience. A contemporary production should, through humour, question our own response to love. Do we recognise or ridicule the blind and superficial love of the protagonists and does it say something about the society in which we live?

**Class**

Fundamentally, the play ridicules the superficial behaviour of the upper middle classes. They are people who have limited awareness of the world as a whole, focusing instead on the microcosm of society which they inhabit. Algernon explains that he wishes to know very little about Lane's life and is thoroughly dismayed by his manservant's response to marriage: 'Really, if the lower orders don't set us a good example, what on earth is the use of them?' Look closely at how the class divide is presented in the play and whether the servants are equally as foolish as their employers.

**Morality**

Wilde appears to use his own failure to conform to the Victorian moral code as a catalyst for ridiculing the social etiquettes which dominated proceedings of the time. Through his wit and cutting observations, he deliberately sets about to ridicule all of the protagonists. In a play about being earnest, there are few examples of sincerity; apparently deep founded morals are undermined in an instant. The central premise focuses on the double lives of Jack and Algernon highlights the hypocritical behaviour inherent in the piece and society as a whole. How are the characters undermined in the production you see? Does any moral message survive?

## Key scenes

**Lady Bracknell's interview of Jack – Act 1**

66 The Truth is rarely pure and never simple. Modern life would be very tedious if it were either, and modern literature a complete impossibility. 99

Algernon, *The Importance of Being Earnest*

This scene wonderfully exposes the hypocrisy of the Victorian upper middle class. Lady Bracknell's vicious interviewing of Jack to see whether he is an appropriate young man for her daughter highlights her frivolous morals and the wit of Wilde as he cleverly arranges the language to undermine Jack's and the expectation of Jack and the audience. The skill of a contemporary production will be in making the exchange relevant to a modern audience. Is it simply a celebration of social humour which is meant to amuse or does it emphasise any of the pretensions of contemporary society?

**Gwendolen and Cecily – Act 2**

The complexity of deceit is revealed in the exchange between the two women as they attempt to make sense of the farcical events to date. Their explanation, combined with Wilde's humour, exposes their frailties and frivolities as they become increasingly curt with each other whilst maintaining the Victorian pretence of politeness. The arrival of Algernon and Jack undermines their interpretation of events leading them to feel outraged by the behaviour of the men and welcoming each other as sisters. This trivial presentation of love and emotion should enable you to focus closely on the performance skills of the actors. Stage space, pace and delivery and pause should all be used to heighten the impact of the exchange.

The denouement of the play, where the truth about Jack's abandonment is revealed, is a final celebration of the complexity of the piece. The notion of swapping a baby for a book is an absurd premise, fundamentally undermining any serious tone that exists. The increasing tension between the women, the noises off-stage of Jack frantically searching and the final revealing of the handbag should be greeted with a sense of celebration and relief. After the many twists within Wilde's structure, this revelation and the discovering of his rightful name Earnest, restore order to the chaos that has ensued. Does the performance you see build to a crescendo of complication? Is the reveal successfully conveyed and warmly received? How do the performers stage the comedy in this section and is it done successfully?

## Past productions: possible interpretations

Vaudeville Theatre, London, *The Guardian*. Reviewed by Michael Billington.

> 'Wilde's masterpiece is, of course, many things: an *Alice in Wonderland* fantasy, a running commentary on Victorian life, and even, conceivably, a coded gay comedy.'

Bristol Old Vic. Reviewed by Robin Markwell.

> 'And so, by staging *The Importance of Being Earnest* on an electric pink set under the shadow of an enormous handbag with an all-male cast, director/designer David Fielding has drawn a new, queer dimension out of this much-loved play.
>
> The subtext was always there, carefully concealed within the clever wording, but is often lost when the play is framed as a politer comedy of manners. Phallic cucumbers emblazoned across the walls, men in skirts and the medley of gay anthems that rings out during the two intervals leave little to the imagination.'

Oxford Playhouse. Reviewed by Natasha Tripney.

> 'As Lady Bracknell, Maggie Steed is suitably formidable, though she underplays "a handbag" to the point where it almost drifts by unheard. Steed is a strong stage actress; her snooty interrogation of Jack is fantastic yet her Lady Bracknell isn't a complete harridan, she shows a definite softer side when the play's final ironic revelations come to light.'

**Miss Prism's entrance in Act 3**

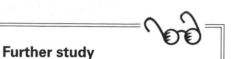

**Further study**

If you are interested in this style, look at: *Pygmalion* by George Bernard Shaw; *Murder in the Red Barn* by Peter Haining, an example of the melodramatic texts which Wilde reacted against.

**The meaning of the play**

**Web link**

www.guardian.co.uk/stage/2008/feb/01/theatre

**The interpretation of the play**

**Web link**

www.bbc.co.uk/bristol/content/articles/2005/05/06/earnest_reviewed_feature.shtml

**Characterisation of Lady Bracknell**

**Web link**

www.musicomh.com/theatre/importance_0805.htm

## Preparing for the Section C exam

You will be required to answer one question from Section C from a choice of two. This will be worth 30 marks. Approaches to Sections A and B have been covered earlier in the book alongside the specific texts.

**Choosing the play**

The play that will serve as you primary source text needs to be carefully considered by your teacher, and the period will obviously depend on what you have studied for Sections A and B of this Unit. The production will need to have made some attempt to interpret the play in order for it to have some modern relevance. Its subject matter needs also to be worthy enough for you to get your teeth into, particularly when contrasting with the original performance conditions – a good meaty Shakespearean tragedy is, for example, more easy to compare than one of the more plot-driven comedies. It is also asking your teacher to look out for theatre companies that are known for their cutting-edge work, their adventurous staging, or casting. It is difficult to draw comparisons with a 21st-century production that is completely faithful to the play's original conditions. Instead, imagine the material you can get from a two-man minimalist interpretation of a three-hour play that has been cut to forty minutes. Cheek by Jowl, Complicite, Kneehigh, DV8 and Northern Broadsides are some examples of companies who look to interpret classic stories in a modern and innovative way.

**Before the production**

Your teacher may wish you to read the play that you are going to see. Make notes on the key themes and relationships as you personally interpret them. Jot down some thoughts about your initial response to the play, what were your reactions to the central characters. Can you see any possible modern interpretations that would suit the play in its potential setting or location? What do you believe to be two or three pivotal scenes of the play, the scenes upon which the action hinges or the fate of the characters are determined?

It might be an idea for your group to allocate specific areas of the production to make notes on. This will hopefully ensure a greater level of detail. These notes can then be pulled together and shared once you return to your lessons.

If time allows you might experiment as a group with interpretation. Take one of the key scenes in the play and look to present it in different performance styles – as a piece of dance drama, non-verbally as mime, naturalistically or through abstract sounds. This will put you in the right frame of mind for the production and give you a more confident knowledge of both plot and theme.

### At the production

**Before the play begins**

Although it may be slightly embarrassing to take a notebook to the production with you, immediate thoughts and instinctive reactions are important. How do you feel as you enter the space? Your role as an audience member is vital. What decisions has the company made to make you feel comfortable or to alienate you. Is the foyer of the theatre decorated in a particular style? Are the actors engaging with you before the play begins? Does the space make you feel intimidated or comfortable? Look around at other audience members. What would you say is the majority 'type' of the audience and does this lead you to draw any conclusions? How might this compare to the audience make up of the original conditions?

As you sit down in your seat do two things:

1. Read the programme notes from the director. This will give you a clue as to the intended response that they are trying to elicit from you. What comments have been made about the style of the production or the company? What themes or issues have been highlighted? Some companies might also provide a useful performance history of the play that you are about to see, giving you useful contextual information.

2. Sketch a bird's-eye view of the set and properties. Annotate with colours, materials, levels, entrances and exits, size of performance space, and audience positioning. Are there further clues here about the style and period of the interpretation? Has the company tried to create real life on stage in Stanislavskian style or is the set more abstract and representational? Can you see the mechanics of the stage – the musicians and the lights – in a more Brechtian style of performance? Is there a key significant feature of the set – a staircase, a painting, or a statement of design?

**The opening**

The opening of any play makes a bold statement about the intentions of the director and the key features of interpretation. Does the play begin traditionally with the lights dimming and the curtain opening or is it a more organic opening with the audience being pulled in to the action? From the first entrance of the actors and their opening lines what becomes clear about costume, performance style and the role of the audience in the production? What role do you think music will play in the piece? Try and work out why the company have made these decisions and what direction they are trying to lead you in.

**Throughout the play**

Have your initial thoughts been confirmed or challenged? Does the interpretation work or are there contradictions within it? Consistently consider how the director is trying to manipulate your response to the central relationships. Focus on the key scenes that you identified before coming to see the play.

**The final moments**

The last images of the play will be the ones that have the most immediate impact on you when you leave the auditorium. What final statement is the director making? Make a note afterwards of how you feel as the piece ends. Is it what you expected to feel or have you been taken in a direction that you did not expect?

**Impact**

The play should have made an impression on you. It does not need to be entirely positive but you must be able to consistently justify your reasons either way. You should be able to consider both the overall directorial interpretation and the specific moments or scenes that reinforced this interpretation.

As in every play that you are asked to analyse, you need to ensure that you have covered every aspect of the production. Below is a checklist that you should consider:

---

**Directorial interpretation**

• Cultural context  • Themes  • Issues  • Period

---

**Acting style**

• Naturalistic  • Abstract  • Physical theatre
• Narrative driven  • Pantomime

---

**Audience**

• Actors' relationship with audience
• Intended audience response

---

**Creation of location**

• Set changes  • Scene changes

---

**Design elements**

• The performance space  • Costume
• Lighting (general and specific)  • Set  • Staging
• Audience positioning  • Props  • Make-up
• Sound (live and recorded, music and effects)

---

**Returning to lessons**

A short exercise to stimulate early discussion is for each member of your group to give the production a mark out of ten; give reasons for the mark awarded, one moment that impressed, and one moment that disappointed.

Now that you have seen the production and completed detailed research in to the original performance conditions of the play, you now need to start putting the information together in to your research notes.

**Research notes**

To help you in the examination, your notes and research will be compiled into a research notes document. These are notes complied in the best way that suits you and may include drawings, sketches and diagrams. This document should be no more than 1,000 words in length, approximately 4–6 sides of printed material in 12-point font. All the work in your document must be your own.

There are several different ways to consider compiling your research notes. It would be a good idea to head up a folder with the titles before the unit begins and use this folder as a working diary document in which sketches, notes and additions can be made at regular intervals as the process gets underway. Once all the work has been done, these can then be edited into a workable format that satisfies the examination-board criteria.

It is important to note that the essay will be a comparative question. Your primary source will be the live production that you have seen with the secondary comparison being to the original performance conditions of the play. Your notes should reflect this and it would be better to compile them comparatively rather than dealing with each performance period separately. Below is a suggested guide of how you might address the 1,000 words. There are suggested headings with word counts.

> **Tip**
>
> It might be an idea to use to different colours for easy reference during the pressure of writing to time: black font for live performance, red for original conditions, for example. You cannot afford to waste time in the examination searching for a piece of information, so careful consideration of the layout of your notes is essential. 1,000 words is not a great deal so you do have to be economical – note form and bullet points only.

| Acting | Performance style of period (100 words) | |
| | Original (O) | |
| | Live performance (LP) | |
| | Character one (e.g. Othello): voice, | |
| | movement, Interaction (100) | |
| | O | |
| | LP | |
| | Character two (e.g. Desdemona): voice, | |
| | Movement, Interaction (100) | |
| | O | |
| | LP | |
| **Design** | Set and staging | Costume/make up |
| | O | O |
| | LP | LP |
| | Lighting | Sound (100) |
| | O | O |
| | LP | LP |
| **Context** | Theatre culture (including audience, | |
| | popularity, status, attitudes) (100) | |
| | O | |
| | LP | |
| | Historical/political conditions (100): what | |
| | was happening to influence the production? | |
| | O | |
| | LP | |
| | Interpretation (100): practical application | |
| | of the above influences on the play itself. | |
| | These can include casting, use of chorus, | |
| | narration, puppetry, mask, cutting and editing | |
| | of text, structure, entrances and exits | |
| | LP | |
| **Key scenes** | Key scene one (e.g. Iago monologues) (100) | |
| | O | |
| | LP | |
| | Key scene two (e.g. death of Desdemona) (100) | |
| | O | |
| | LP | |

Below is an extract from an example set of notes written by a Year 13 student. She writes in note form with her observations providing a platform to kick off her thoughts and discussions when writing the essay. The performance she is writing about is The Little Touring Theatre Company's version of *Hamlet,* involving two actors, two musicians and two double basses. The piece was seen at the egg theatre in Bath in March 2008.

**Hamlet**

**Original**
- Always been popular
- Performed more than any other – continually in theatres since written
- Attraction Prince Hamlet, rapport with audience (given unmatched number soliloquies)
- Play always speaks to audience – relatable.

**Live production**
- Play aimed at young audience
- Problems of Shakespeare. Seen as old text – untouchable. Text in archaic English. Seen as holy text. Studied in schools – stale and in the past
- Text brutally cut. Only essence of story. Suits today's audiences
- I.e '2 b or not 2 b' distilled to essence from extremely long speech. Universal meaning
- Young people switched off from Shakespeare. Dead text
- Breaks down preconceptions for audience. Takes back to original conditions
- Breathes new life into Shakespeare
- Recapture audience. Must be praised
- Audience = children. Educational purpose. Looking for inventive way-bring play to life. Range of techniques
- Visual society (computer, TV, cinema) Visual entertainment expected – less importance on words/language.

- - - - - - - - - - - - - - - - - - - - - - - - - - - - - - - - - -

**Performance space**

**Original**
- Huge (seats 2–3,000), modern seats 1–200
- Pit/yard with no roof-poor people/groundlings diameter 100 ft. Three tiers of roofed galleries– higher class (more expensive). Extra money to sit on balcony
- Stage 4–6 ft above ground
- No set. Location was announced, no curtains, scene change shown through speech.

## Live production

➢ The Egg. Young person's Theatre. Promotes young people.
➢ Aimed at children. Vibrant, come alive. Performance must have relevance for children
➢ Small, intimate space. Stage comes right to audience. Small semi-circular balcony above. 80-100 audience members
➢ Studio performance – came alive end of 20th C. More connection/closer to audience. Thrust staging. Intimate/closed in. Engages audience – focused. Can see other audience faces
➢ Similar to Brecht. Theatre practitioner (1930s). Audience asked to accept theatricality (i.e. double bass onstage). Modern audience = willing suspension of belief. Used to seeing things. Not shocked by Ophelia's scarf etc.
➢ Artificiality always emphasised. Actors present themselves and play. Use narration to audience
➢ Breaking fourth wall.

- - - - - - - - - - - - - - - - - - - - - - - - - - - - - - - - -

## Interpretation

## Original

➢ Acting – pantomim- like (OTT). Loud, booming voice. Spectacle. Exaggerated gestures. About power of words, unrealistic performance
➢ Open air-poor acoustics, actors had to shout lines. Stress enunciation
➢ Audience enjoyed involvement-shouting etc (pantomime) – talked over acting. Sometimes drunk – hurled abuse, didn't respect Shakespeare – had to get attention with words.

## Live production

➢ Now – realistic performance, emotional interpretation
➢ Brave production. Cutting lots of text
➢ Reshaping role of Horatio – becomes major role.
➢ In Shakespeare, Horatio is only supporting role for Hamlet. In this he is storyteller/narrator. Plays on Hamlet's last words – asks Horatio 2 tell his story
➢ Horatio = Hamlet and our companion. Narrates cut scenes. Plays role in Hamlet's mind (tells us how he feels). Deals with themes of ISOLATION and LONELINESS. Hamlet given someone to talk/reflect. Makes play more accessible
➢ Hamlet's soliloquies (originally) become duologues between Hamlet and Horatio. Modern interpretation. Promotes idea of ensemble. More interesting and accessible.

- - - - - - - - - - - - - - - - - - - - - - - - - - - - - - - - -

## Design elements

### Original

- Costume/props – generic. Villain costume/hero costume/ heroine costume. Same every play. No message/ meaning in costume, no connection with specific play
- Restrictions due to time of day – performed in afternoon settings – otherwise too dark
- Play held together, flowing transactions, no stage/ set changes. Allowed rapid pace. Aided by stage conventions (e.g. soliloquies, asides) – clear, economical story telling. Showed the location through language
- No stage lighting – actors and audience shared afternoon sun – unity in performance – cannot be recreated
- No specific costumes – same king outfit for all kings etc. No design interpretations occurred
- Audience focus on words – language = important. No focus on visuals – more on speeches, delivery of lines. Shakespeare's power of words respected.

- - - - - - - - - - - - - - - - - - - - - - - - - - - - - - -

### Live production

- Two actors, multiple roles
- Now – costume has meaning – detailed – represents themes/character
- Now – night time atmosphere, glamorous, evening out, occasion, dress up etc
- Set/props – minimal/representational. Similar to 16/17th c (e.g. gym bench = battlements of castle, throne, bow of ship. Places upright, spun around to show passing of time. Goblet for poison wine. Props/ set has meaning – an interpretation, not generic
- Double bass – vital scenery, coffins, benches, the ghost (skull attached), dancers, doors. Echoey, unnerving. Suited mood. Create location and atmosphere
- Velvet red curtain – upstage hanging
- Characters – some represented by props, items of costume. Ophelia = orange wrap. Red clothes = blood spilt
- Final scene – two swords for battle
- Set = always fluid-vital part of style of production. Lovely moments of movement (e.g. bench & actors spin into scene, show fragmented/confused mind)
- Costume – no distractions. All cast = dark jeans, jackets, white trainers. Informal approach. When watched, thought they were staff (introducing play)
- Lighting – no change throughout play.

## Tackling the question

Finally we approach the actual examination question that focuses on a comparison of the two productions.

Below are three examples from each of the two styles that the examination board have used. The first three use a quotation that deliberately challenges you as an audience member and is intended to stimulate debate.

1. 'Theatre should be about the way we live now, not the way we used to live.' Discuss this statement, in the light of the production you have seen, to show your understanding of how you think the impact of the play has altered since its original performance.

2. 'Theatre is a product of time but its themes and issues are timeless.' Discuss the play you have seen in performance in the light of this statement and with reference to the original performance conditions.

3. 'Theatre in the 21st century is full of tricks and gimmicks.' Comment on the play you have seen in production in the light of the above statement and its comparison with the original performance conditions.

The next three questions ask you to focus on a particular area of the production and directly compare their execution across the two time periods.

4. Discuss the effectiveness of the performances in the production you have seen. How might the acting style in the original performance of the play have differed?

5. Discuss the way(s) ideas were communicated to the audience in the production you saw, comparing it to its original performance conditions.

6. Evaluate the influence of the director on the theatre of the 21st century by comparing the production you have seen with the original performance conditions.

Now that you have seen the questions, the importance of the notes becomes obvious. You should have written the notes under the headings outlined above, with the areas of performance covered section by section. The two productions should be covered side by side as in the example notes above, and this is exactly how you should approach the essay.

At the start of the essay you must make a strong statement that outlines where you are in terms of the quotation. You do not have to totally agree or disagree with what is suggested but make a reasoned argument that reflects how you feel about the production that you have seen. The example paragraph below, the answer to question 1 above, gives a very well-reasoned response that captures their understanding of both the original conditions and the live performance:

**Writing the essay**

> Society and, therefore, audiences change with time and so a modern, contemporary audience would react differently to a production from the original Elizabethan audience for which the play was intended to be performed. The statement 'Theatre should be about the way we live now, not the way we used to live' seems to imply that the play *Othello* has no reference to a modern-day audience. However, I would assert that many of the themes which are tackled or implied in *Othello* are still very much relevant to a modern-day audience.

The focus of the question, be it audience, context or staging, must be at the forefront of every paragraph that you write. Refer back to the key words in the question and go through the essay area by area with the two productions side by side.

The example below covers a production of *Much Ado about Nothing* seen at the Theatre Royal, Bath in 2004 by the German/British Bremer Shakespeare Company. The candidate is answering question five above and shows clearly how to get directly to the heart of the argument skilfully comparing both texts maintaining the live production as the focus.

> One of the main areas was the key relationships in the performance. In 1598, the key relationship in the play was that of Beatrice and Benedict, the reason being because of the witty banter and playful relationship. The two were so popular that sometimes the play would even be called 'Benedict and Beatrice'. However, in the 2004 production the key relationship was that of Don Pedro and Leonata. Don Pedro's and Leonata's relationship was based on sexual chemistry, lust and equal status. The way in which they moved around together was based on a conventional relationship of the 20th century. As Don Pedro entered the stage he was clearly a very proud man, he held his shoulders back, held his head high and walked upright. His eye contact was always heavy with Leonata and straightaway there was sexual chemistry between them.
>
> Don Pedro then sliced an orange in half, held it above Leonata's head and squeezed it in her mouth; this was very sexual as she giggled erotically after. This relationship would have probably not been successful in 1598 because people were not familiar with this kind of relationship and being this open would have been frowned on. This is why Beatrice and Benedict's relationship was liked so much because they made jokes, played and exchanged lots of witty banter. However, in the production I saw their relationship was not valued as much. They cut most of their lines and they had very little interaction. Maybe the point that is being made is that there is no place for sweet and innocent relationships in 2004. Those of lust and sex are far more interesting and dramatic.

The second point to be noted about this essay is the confidence with which the candidate handles their material. They balance the two periods well throughout and uses specific and well-chosen practical examples to illustrate the strong points that they are making.

Another thing that the Shakespeare Company did in order to communicate ideas to the audience was to switch gender roles. The different role reversals were a man playing Hero and a woman playing Claudio. The woman playing Hero was a humorous concept to us as normally we are used to women playing women and men playing men. However, to see a woman playing a man didn't work but seeing a man playing a woman was comical. Gender issues in 1598 were very controversial as all characters were played by men and women were not allowed to act in theatre. Clearly by doing this they were missing out on emotions from relationships as we did with the killing of Hero. Because Claudio was played by a woman she didn't have the physicality to act like a man therefore, we lost a lot of her anger as all she seemed to do was frantically pace across the stage muttering words. This was not a good effect and the company clearly did it in order to poke fun at old traditional gender roles where men played all the characters.

Another problem with this is that in 1598 not only were men played by women but a woman's character was very weak and pathetic. In 1598 women were supposed to be seen and not heard, which is why they were always played weakly and girly. However, in 2004 the idea of a strong female character was played by Leonata. Leonata appeared on stage wearing a long purple velvet dress with a hat that covered her hair; she walked out gracefully and looked as if she glided across the stage. She stood upright and stuck her chest out and her shoulders back. Her position in society was clearly stated by her costume and the bold gestures that she used. For example, when she spoke she would use her hands to sweep across the stage or to point out her finger or to embrace Hero or Don Pedro. Therefore, compared to 1598 women have become a lot more powerful in society, they are able to vote, get good jobs in powerful positions and are also as powerful as a man. Therefore, Leonata represents all women of 2004 as she is as powerful as Don Pedro.

Another way in which ideas were communicated to the audience was through an on-stage musician. The musician played music throughout the live production and also made sound effects such as washing, a duck, and splashing. She did this when Benedict was washing his feet in the 'pond'. He sat at the front of the stage and took his boots of, he then one by one washed his feet. Using her hands and a bucket of water the musicians splashed the water in order to create the correct sound. However, in 1598 again this would have been frowned on as the stage was very bare and very natural. The importance of a play was to listen to the words that were being said rather than have emphasised by sound, lighting or music. Therefore, there is an incredible difference in the 2004 production and its original performance conditions in order to try to communicate ideas.

It is impressive how the candidate is able to switch between time periods. Look at discourse markers such as 'whereas', and 'however' to link performances and contrast. As the essay develops they refer more and more to the question of communication of ideas, successfully illustrating with well-chosen examples.

The marking criteria for this essay states clearly that the live production must be the focus of the answer with the original performance used as a reference.

Answers at the lower level will be descriptive and simply retell the events on stage; there will also be little or no reference to the question.

Mid-range answers will demonstrate a clear link between the live performance and the original conditions but answers may be more text- than performance-based. Connections are being made, but not at a detailed level.

Top-band answers will show a clear understanding of the specific demands of the question with strong practical evidence. The focus will be on the performance of the play and not the text. There will be a strong balance between arguments and conclusions will be drawn about decisions made.

Clearly the secrets to answering this question are having a comprehensive set of notes that are structured in the right way, a general knowledge of the original performance conditions of the play, alongside specific information about the play's performance history, and finally a strong interpretative understanding of the play that you saw in performance. Underpinning this is a strong knowledge of the text itself.

# Appendix

## STAGING

How would you stage the play and to what effect? ☐

Should you use in-the-round, traverse, thrust or end-on/proscenium arch staging? Why? ☐

Would the audience be able to see one another? Is this important? ☐

Where is your piece set? Does it imply a specific period or do you want to make it universally applicable for any time or place? ☐

What flats are used? How are they painted? What do they represent? ☐

How do characters enter and exit the stage? How can you manage this to contribute to the theme of magic and surprise? Do any characters remain onstage throughout? ☐

How would the size of the performance space affect the production – grand set pieces or intimate and claustrophobic spaces? ☐

What props are used? What do they reveal about the characters and the play? Are they needed or can they be interpreted symbolically? ☐

Where will the Chorus be positioned? ☐

Have you considered use of levels in your design? Why are they significant? ☐

Consider the colours and materials that you might use to portray the contrasting moods in the piece. ☐

## LIGHTING

What lighting and special effects, if any, are needed or implied by the playtext? ☐

How is this interpreted? Can a moment sometimes be managed by the actors rather than the technical team? ☐

What coloured gels are used? Which lanterns are used when and why? ☐

How might fade times affect the mood of the piece? How can lighting be used to add to the impact of surprise appearances and revelations? ☐

Are there any difficulties in lighting your play? ☐

Are blackouts or cross-fades used? Does action ever take place in blackouts? If so why? ☐

Where should the lanterns be positioned in order to create your desired effect? ☐

Are shadows important to the mood of the piece? ☐

## SOUND

What sound effects, if any, are needed/ implied by the playtext? How could these be interpreted? (Live or recorded?) ☐

How is the action on stage affected by specific moments of sound? ☐

What music is used? Is it live or recorded? What cultural influences and periods affect your choice? (African drumbeat, Gregorian chants etc.) What mood would it create? ☐

How did the lighting and sound combine? ☐

## COSTUME

Describe each of your costumes in detail. Justify the decisions made in terms of how they relate to the character. ☐

How did the different characters' costumes relate? Is there a theme in the design? Why? ☐

Consider differences between the males and the females in costume. How would you dress the Chorus? ☐

Have you used mask in the performance? If so what designs and for what purpose? ☐

Will there be any alterations in the costume during the performance? How will this be handled? ☐

# Glossary

**Choreographed movement**. The skill of creating and arranging body movement and use of the stage space with as much detail as dance choreography.

**Chorus**. In simplest terms, words spoken simultaneously by a group of characters. In Greek tragedy, it refers to between 12 and 15 actors who provide a commentary on the main plot action as well as offering a moral viewpoint. They are traditionally seen as a link between the characters, the gods and the audience.

**Commedia dell'arte**. A dramatic form of the late-Italian Renaissance, which came to influence theatre throughout Europe. Actors used masks to represent their characters which led to an exaggerated, physical style of acting. Commedia plays were largely improvised in public places, and their plots involved a group of stock characters, which might include, for instance, the beautiful young woman Columbina or the greedy merchant Pantalone. Wit, topicality and physical humour were all important elements of the Commedia.

**Communion**. An element of Stanislavski's acting system with the aim of achieving a naturalistic performance. Before the actor can communicate meaning to his audience, he must first interpret his relationship with himself and the other actors. Once this is done, then meaning will be indirectly communicated to the audience.

**Conscience alley**. A rehearsal technique used to explore a dilemma that a character might be facing. An actor walks through two lines of other actors, who form an alleyway as they give advice or thoughts about a particular aspect of character or relationship. This will help the protagonist to gain a better understanding of character or help them to resolve the dilemma.

**Directorial concept**. The key vision or idea of the director that guides the interpretation of the piece of drama, be it improvised, devised or scripted. The most challenging task for the director is to translate his concept to the stage.

**Dislocating action**. Literally to put something out of its normal place. In drama, rather than two actors directly playing to each other, they turn out and play to the audience, whilst still creating the sense that they are playing to each other. This is a different way of interpreting a scene, which can challenge the expectations of the audience.

**Dramatic form**. The elements and techniques of drama that make up the structure of a piece of theatrical work – monologue and mime are examples of this form.

**Emotion memory**. A further element of the Stanislavski system with the aim of achieving a naturalistic performance. In order for an actor to better understand the emotional state of their character at a particular moment in the play, the actor looks into his/her own past for a moment in which he/she experienced a similar or identical emotion. He/she can then use this real moment and apply it convincingly to the piece being performed, thereby achieving a more believable emotional state.

**Farce**. A comic, theatrical style of performance that relies on unlikely situations, disguises, mistaken identities, humour, word play, sexual innuendo and fast paced plot development to entertain the audience. Farce is characterised by physical humour, chase scenes and a growing panic as the climax is reached. It generally finishes with a happy ending and all misunderstandings resolved.

**Flashback**. A scene is defined as a flashback if it presents action which took place before the events that are explored in the scene immediately preceding it. Flashforward – a method of presenting a scene in the future – is another frequently-used theatrical form.

**Melodrama**. A dominant form of theatre in the 19th century. Using stock characters and a musical underscore, it provided accessible entertainment for the working classes during the industrial revolution. Initially, it presented a world of absolutes, where good conquered evil. However, as this simplistic form was becoming a little tired, writers adapted their style to comment on real-life crimes or to question social injustice.

**Multiple narrative**. A method of complicating the audience's perception of onstage action. Rather than simply narrating through the eyes of one character, the techniques allows for several characters to comment on what has occurred.

**Naturalism**. A style heavily influenced by the work of naturalist Charles Darwin. Focusing on the concepts of heredity and the environment, playwrights such as Henrik Ibsen and Georg Büchner looked at how characters were affected by their parentage and the world in which they lived. See page 186.

**Physical images**. A useful rehearsal technique which makes performers condense the action into a single freeze or tableaux in order to communicate the central message at that moment.

**Prologue**. Originating in Greek theatre, it is a scene which takes place before the central action of the play begins. Traditionally, it was delivered by a god who introduced the protagonist and key themes.

**Proxemics**. A term originally used by anthropologist Edward T. Hall who looked at how the distance between people affected their emotional reaction. In theatrical terms, it focuses on the decisions an actor or director might make about where characters are positioned on stage.

**Satire**. A comic device, which presents human failings for ridicule to an audience. Often stemming from a playwright's frustrations at social injustice, the aim – in addition to humour – is to encourage people to modify their own behaviour.

**Total life of the character**. A term used by Stanislavski to encourage actors to use the given circumstances, or facts of the play, and their imaginations to create more rounded characters by considering what happened to the characters off-stage.

# Index

# Index